Crosscurrents / MODERN CRITIQUES

Harry T. Moore, *General Editor*

Hemingway's Craft

Sheldon Norman Grebstein

WITH A PREFACE BY

Harry T. Moore

SOUTHERN ILLINOIS UNIVERSITY PRESS
Carbondale and Edwardsville

FEFFER & SIMONS, INC.
London and Amsterdam

Library of Congress Cataloguing in Publication Data

Grebstein, Sheldon Norman.
    Hemingway's craft.

    (Crosscurrents: modern critiques)
    Bibliography: p.
    1. Hemingway, Ernest, 1899–1961—Style.
I. Title.
PS3515.E37Z597   813'.5'2   70–183304
ISBN 0–8093–0611–5

Once more, for my beloved parents

Contents

Preface

The title of Sheldon Norman Grebstein's Hemingway's Craft promises much. It is time we had a study devoted principally to Hemingway's art as such—his technique as well as his ideas. And this book amply fulfills its promise.

Literary criticism today is too often merely abstract. Too much of it deals entirely with the thematic aspects of written works, either giving scant attention to their organically artistic elements or paying them no heed whatsoever. The situation is extremely different in music and art criticism—yet the arrangement of sound in music and color and shape in art are no more important than the use of language, structure, and similar components of serious literature.

To say this is not to suggest that theme and idea are not an organic necessity in imaginative writing. Of course they are. As John Middleton Murry said in his usually impressive and sometimes annoying book The Problem of Style, attempts to separate ingredients in a written work are reminiscent of a statement in Swift's The Tale of a Tub: "Last week I saw a woman flayed, and you will hardly believe how much it altered her person for the worse."

Unlike those literary critics who abstract the thematic element as the only topic of discussion and so remain fixed at one extreme, Professor Grebstein doesn't isolate one aspect of Hemingway: true, he concentrates on the technical side of that author, but does so with meaning always in view.

We have from the first wanted a book on Hemingway in the Crosscurrents/Modern Critiques series, and now, after more than a hundred volumes, we have it. About ten years ago I rejected a manuscript discussing this author, politely turning it down because it was entirely thematic. It presented some interesting comments, but they existed in a void. Such novels as To Have and Have Not and Across the River and into the Trees were discussed as seriously as The Sun Also Rises, A Farewell to Arms, and the early short stories, with not even the vaguest suggestion that there might be qualitative differences among these items. The present book makes no such mistakes, in any direction.

Professor Grebstein says, at the opening of his first chapter, "We begin, as Hemingway began, with the short stories." And the reader begins an exciting volume of criticism. Sheldon Grebstein has read Hemingway since he was a boy, he has used his books in lecture courses and seminars, and he has written about him. Now he presents a full study, so closely packed that not a line is wasted.

He deals with narrative perspectives, structure, dialogue, and similar matters, always perceptively. You begin to wonder what else he can do, and you find that one of his later chapters has the title, "Further Observations on Style and Method." But some of the previous critics have dealt with these subjects; is there anything fresh to say about them?

Plenty.

There is, among other matters, Hemingway's relation to painting. Professor Grebstein quotes the passage from A Moveable Feast in which Hemingway mentions the influence of Cézanne on his prose. Dr. Grebstein also refers to Lillian Ross's account of a visit to the Metropolitan Museum with Hemingway and his son, when he spoke of Cézanne as "his" painter and pointed out the trees and rocks in one of the landscapes: "I learned how to make a landscape from Mr. Paul Cézanne."

With a good ear for prose cadences, Professor Grebstein shows by notation and diagram just how expert Hemingway's prose is in the visual as well as in the pictorial sense. Then he concludes his critical study with an informing discussion of Hemingway's humor.

The book is further enriched by an appendix examining the manuscripts of A Farewell to Arms and For Whom the Bell Tolls, with the inclusion of some new material.

It seems to me that this book ranks, with Philip Young's, at the top of all Hemingway criticism. And it will be useful to all serious readers of modern literature, particularly because it deals with an important figure whose achievement is brilliantly analyzed in the following pages.

HARRY T. MOORE

Southern Illinois University
June 14, 1972

Introduction

That erratic pendulum, critical taste, so recently in the downswing against Hemingway, now moves in an upward arc. Several books, all appreciative, have recently appeared to augment the already substantial body of Hemingway criticism and to counteract the prevailingly negative critical trend of the years just before and after the writer's death. With Carlos Baker's *Ernest Hemingway: A Life Story* we have the definitive biography, and every new year produces at least a score of essays and explications in the scholarly journals. Although Hemingway criticism falls far short of the bulk which has accumulated around such figures as Melville, Twain, and James, and even amounts to less than that dealing with Faulkner and Fitzgerald, there is certainly no scarcity of it. As is the case with many another American author, the writing about Hemingway considerably exceeds the writing by him.

Why, then, crowd another book into the ample shelf of Hemingway exegesis? There are reasons. The most urgent reason is personal: I *must*. Hemingway fascinates me. I have been reading him since I was a boy and I have been studying his work and teaching it for more than twenty years, beginning with my 1950 Columbia M.A. thesis. So, I am compelled to write by a congenial personal demon; and perhaps in writing I can exorcise it. Furthermore, although there are a number of keen, judicious, and comprehensive books, for example those by

Carlos Baker, Philip Young, Earl Rovit, and Jackson Benson, important and relatively neglected areas of Hemingway's fiction remain to be explored. As good as the best Hemingway criticism is, too much of it has been preoccupied with the writer's values, personality, worldview, the Hemingway Code, and so forth. Most critics praise Hemingway's artistry, yet surprisingly few of them have really investigated it intensively, that miracle of craft—or so I deem it—which creates so complex and durable an art from such seemingly scanty and simple materials. In fact, in my review of hundreds of pieces of Hemingway criticism, preparatory to writing this book, I found but a small minority which offered hard, detailed analyses of *technique*. In contrast, surely several thousand pages have been written about the Hemingway Hero and The Code.

Therefore, I will say relatively little about these familiar matters and presume that anyone who reads this book is also already acquainted with them. Instead, my special concern here will be with Hemingway's craftsmanship: those aspects of structure, language, and narrative technique which distinguish his writing from all other. To paraphrase Hemingway, I seek to bring to the surface some of the submerged part of the iceberg. Although my discussion may sometimes reiterate or echo what others have said, it is not usually because I have deliberately and consciously borrowed from them. In my first thoughts about this book I called it "The Neglected Hemingway," and although much Hemingway criticism has appeared during the time between my earliest conception of this study and the final execution of it, my original ambition still largely persists: to treat what others have minimized, slighted, ignored, or merely labeled. However, it could well be the case that I have so thoroughly absorbed the views of previous critics I can no longer separate what I discovered from what I inherited, the result of reading the critics on Hemingway almost as soon as I read Hemingway himself with any real seriousness. Too, in teaching Hemingway over the years, including several graduate seminars, I have learned a great deal from my students and in the natural course of academic life have gratefully appropriated it as my own. Where I am aware of specific indebtednesses, these are clearly indicated in the notes.

This study depends upon a few fundamental assumptions about Hemingway. First, I believe that despite the shortcomings in even his best work, the relatively narrow range of his material, and the embarrassing badness of his worst books, he is a major and enduring artist rather than a minor writer possessed of a few peculiar aesthetic virtues and scattered glimmerings of genius. Second, as I have already implied, pertinent and memorable as are Hemingway's themes and worldview to the readers of this tormented age, he will last primarily because of his art not his ideas. I repeat a cultural fact that his detractors must also concede: after him the writing of prose fiction was different. Third, his depiction of a vivid and tangible surface reality, of physical action and sensation—in short, his verisimilitude—often merges inextricably with a deep symbolic understructure. The water is so clear it seems shallow to some, but when one dives in, one can go down and down and often never touch bottom.

My ambition is to persuade the reader to share these convictions by calling attention to them in the text itself, although I fear that many are too thoroughly confirmed in their view of Hemingway as a figure of declining importance to be won over by what I have to say. If I convince others whose minds are not yet made up, especially students, I will count my work more than fulfilled. To this end I employ no special method other than that of close reading, nor any critical terminology not current among serious readers. My most severe demand upon the reader is that he know Hemingway's work well.

Although I had hoped, when I first committed myself to writing this book (longer ago than I care to admit), that the Hemingway papers would be open to scholars so that I might base my study on the "complete" Hemingway, we must still await the construction of the Kennedy Library, where Mrs. Hemingway will deposit her husband's *nachlass*, before such access is possible. However, we can infer from the comments of the two absolutely trustworthy men who have examined this material, Carlos Baker and Philip Young, that nothing will be forthcoming to substantially change or improve the Hemingway already in the public domain. *Islands in the Stream* makes a case in point. It is an interesting book and bears its author's mark, but it neither alters our understanding of Hemingway nor records new departures in technique. In quality it falls somewhere between his best and worst novels, well above *Across the River and into the Trees* but well below *The Sun Also Rises*, *A Farewell to Arms*, and *For Whom the Bell Tolls*. Consequently, I decided to delay my work no longer, although I surely would have found invaluable the opportunity to examine those documents which testify to the creative process itself. No doubt someone else will do it a few years hence.

I wish to acknowledge my debts for the various kinds of aid and courtesy I have received. To my colleague and chairman, Mario DiCesare, and to the Dean of Harpur College, Peter Vukasin, I owe thanks for the research semester during which this book was finished. Michael Albes, Joseph Lisowski, and Paul Butera gave assistance in collecting material. Miss Janet Brown of the SUNY Binghamton Library staff was again helpful to me in this project as she has been in others. I am grateful to Charles Scribner, Jr. for permission to quote from Hemingway's books, published by Charles Scribner's Sons. The Research Foundation of the State University of New York supported my work on Hemingway with two faculty summer fellowships and grants-in-aid.

Finally, I begin with the ambivalently happy and despairing knowledge that criticism can never wholly circumscribe the literary work and reduce its technique to a formula for precise explanation and objective analysis, for the condition of the artist who makes the work is, in Emily Dickinson's remarkable phrase, "a soul at the white heat;" and in the same poem she goes on to remind us that the art, once made, "repudiates the forge." Nevertheless, we must at least try to apprehend the artist's design and to uncover some of the processes of his craftsmanship. The critic who succeeds does not despoil or exhaust the work, but replenishes it, himself, and its readers.

SHELDON NORMAN GREBSTEIN

Binghamton, New York
May 1972

Hemingway's Craft

1

The Structure of Hemingway's Short Stories

We begin, as Hemingway began, with the short stories. Hemingway's stories are microcosms in which his craft achieves maximum effectiveness within the least space. Few critics would dispute their artistry. Yet a surprising number of these stories have received almost no attention, and even the perennial favorites of commentators (for example, "The Snows of Kilimanjaro," "The Short Happy Life of Francis Macomber," "A Clean, Well-Lighted Place") are usually treated from the standpoint of character, theme, or what they illustrate of the Code, rather than from the perspective of technique. I propose to demonstrate that Hemingway's stories are organized upon certain fundamental structural principles. Once we perceive these principles and know how to apply them, the stories themselves take on larger and richer dimensions. Furthermore, these principles provide a useful approach to stories which at first glance seem slight and anecdotal, unworthy of close study and incapable of sustaining it. In my analysis of the stories I will also advance a number of considerations about technique, to be developed at greater length later in this study.

The first major characteristic which we must note about Hemingway's stories is their heavy reliance upon the dramatic method. In this respect to read Hemingway's stories in the company of those by such immediate predecessors and contemporaries as D. H. Lawrence, Sherwood Anderson, and F. Scott Fitzgerald is to realize how different Hemingway's are. Unlike the work of the others, which often reminds the reader of the presence of an editorializing and intrusive narrator, Hemingway almost always avoids direct exposition of theme, didactic description or discussion of character, and authorial commentary upon action and motive. Thus, Hemingway's stories show rather than tell. In its dramatic quality his short fiction most suggests comparison with that of Chekhov and Joyce, whose lessons he thoroughly absorbed and then turned his own way. Like them Hemingway appears not to have invented the life he presents but merely to act as the medium through which it passes. Indeed, Hemingway's method can perhaps best be inferred from Chekhov's dictum that in both scene and character the selection of significant details, grouped so as to convey an image, is the vital thing. Above all, Chekhov warned against the depiction of mental states except through action.[1]

This is not only an apt summary of his own technique and Hemingway's, it is also virtually a synthesis of what makes the modern story modern. Moreover, both Joyce and Hemingway probably learned from Chekhov the effectiveness of using brief passages of nature description to set or to counterpoint tone, mood, or psychological action. Hemingway may also have been influenced by Chekhov's technique of the "zero ending," which is exactly the contrary to the traditional well-made endings of nineteenth-century fiction, or to the kind of ending O. Henry carried almost to parody: the surprise-resolution neatly knotting up separate strands of plot by an ingenious twist of plot or revelation of character. The whole point of the zero ending is *irresolution*—to leave the reader suspended among the apparently unconnected lines of character and action, consequently forcing him back upon his own resources of insight and imagination. Although Hemingway never explicitly accounted Joyce as one of his masters, despite his fondness for Joyce as a man and reverence for him as an artist, he doubtlessly profited from Joyce's examples in the writing of interior monologue and the use of the limited-omniscient narrator. Perhaps, as Frank O'Connor argues persuasively, Hemingway's technique of repeating words and phrases in such a manner that they become incantatory was also imitative of Joyce.[2]

All these methods are now so familiar to us, have so thoroughly permeated our literary culture, and have been practiced by so many other writers, that we seem to have always known them. It takes an act of historical recollection to remind ourselves of how original they were in the unique forms Hemingway gave them in his stories. In fact, when those stories first appeared in the early 1920s they appeared quite radical, at least to American readers. Even if we concede Hemingway's stylistic debts to Twain, Sherwood Anderson and Gertrude Stein, no real precedent for his stories can be found in American writing—at least insofar as their general method and structure are concerned.[3]

It was just this originality of technique that recommended Hemingway to the attention of established writers at the very start of his career, before he had completed any substantial quantity of work. How many other young writers, on the basis of a handful of poems and stories, have won the support of such figures as Stein, Anderson, Fitzgerald, Ford Madox Ford, and Ezra Pound? The editors of the American periodicals to which Hemingway submitted his stories were slower to catch on and more cautious in their response. Repelled by Hemingway's stark subject matter and puzzled by the apparent artlessness of method and bare simplicity of style, editors did not put his work before their general public until he had already established a reputation among the Parisian avant-garde with *Three Stories and Ten Poems* (1923) and *in our time* (1924), and then brought out *In Our Time* (1925) with a New York publisher.[4]

Fundamental to Hemingway's craft in the short story are the archetypal principles of antithesis and opposition, or, very simply, the conflict and contrast of antipodal forces and values. These principles shape the structure of the work by organizing its action and movement into certain basic patterns. In turn, the pattern of action determines the symbolism, so that around the opposing elements of the antithesis are gathered the appropriate images and associational clusters. As a result, once we perceive the underlying structural design and the particular antithesis or opposition it embodies, such seemingly random and spontaneous factors in the story as traits of behavior, details of setting, forms of speech, gestures—in short, all the necessary components of the work's credibility and verisimilitude—take their rightful place in the pattern and become deeply resonant with meaning.

What I am saying should be sufficiently obvious to serious students of literature as to require no documentation. It is what Kenneth Burke calls "symbolic action," and it is inherent to literary art. Although Hemingway's work happens to be unusually rich in kinaesthetic images, namely those associations evoked by bodily states and physical activity, it contains other levels of implication— the social and metaphysical. Furthermore, my approach borrows support from some of the basic perceptions of earlier Hemingway criticism, notably Carlos Baker's important insight into the contrast between mountain and plain, or "home" and "not-home," and Philip Young's provocative thesis that the compulsive return to the scene of the wound is Hemingway's *ur*-plot. Each of these expresses in its own way the principles of antithesis and opposition. Finally, we must remember that the pattern of action and its attendant symbolic associations develop additional complexity in that they are often ambivalent or ironic. As E. M. Halliday pointed out, in responding to Baker's mountain-plain theory, Hemingway's symbolism functions at its best as it engenders simultaneously different or even apparently contradictory meanings.[5]

I find two dominant and recurrent structural designs in Hemingway's stories, each sometimes operating separately, the two sometimes integrated within a single tale. First, there is the design based upon the movement from outside to inside, or, conversely, from inside to outside. At its simplest level this movement records a change in the story's locale of action, or setting. Second, there is the pattern which uses a movement toward and away from a place or destination. These patterns usually provide a schematic symmetry in that they divide or distribute the action into two or three distinct parts or scenes, for example: inside/outside/inside, toward/ "there"/away. Although the protagonist's bodily movement or shift in locale from out-of-doors to indoors (or the reverse) comprises the essential version of the first pattern, the structure can also be that of a psychological shift or a shift in narrative mode: from the protagonist's physical action to thought, or from dialogue to interior monologue. Likewise, the simplest form of the toward/ away design is a trip or journey, the actual spatial movement or approach to a place, the arrival there, and the subsequent departure. However, once more the ground covered may be an imaginary terrain, an inner distance.

But enough abstraction. These structures must be observed in the stories themselves. We will look closely at several stories and merely scan others, as appropriate, to establish these patterns and trace some of their ramifications. For the outside/inside design I will discuss "The Doctor and the Doctor's Wife," "Che Ti Dice La Patria?" and "A Day's Wait." For the toward/away pattern "Indian Camp," "A Way You'll Never Be," and *The Old Man and the Sea* will serve as my examples. This selection both includes stories popular with critics and students, and others less often treated. Although my emphasis will be on structure, I will comment on such related matters as symbolism and significant detail, as the case requires.

The structural design of "The Doctor and the Doctor's Wife" is that of the outside/inside/outside pattern, and in this instance the literal physical movements divides the story into three scenes: out-of-doors, indoors, out-of-doors again. Hemingway seemed to favor this method of framing an indoor scene with two outdoor scenes (or the converse, an outdoor scene framed by indoor scenes), for he uses it frequently. One or the other of these patterns appears in such stories as "The Three-Day Blow," "Cat in the Rain," "Out of Season," "Cross-Country Snow," "The Undefeated," and "The Killers." If frequent, the design never degenerates into formula because it is capable of an infinite number of variations in scene length, scope, proportion, and intensity. In "The Doctor and the Doctor's Wife," as elsewhere, the outside/inside/outside structure not only provides the pattern of action, it also embodies the story's values and furnishes a set of dramatic metaphors which define the characters.

In the story's outdoor opening scene, at the lakefront, the doctor-protagonist backs down from a fight with Dick Boulton, the Indian he has hired to cut some drifted timber. The encounter reveals the doctor to be dishonest as well as cowardly. He then retreats indoors to his cottage, where he is further frustrated and enraged by his wife's admonishments. Finally, he goes outside again, headed for the woods with his son Nick, who chooses to accompany him rather than obey his mother's request to come to her. The movement of the locale of the action is thus from lake to cottage to forest.

This pattern of action, which perfectly illustrates the basic principle of antithesis, articulates the characters' conflicting values and standards of behavior and places them in juxtaposition. Dick Boulton, the Indian laborer, drinker, and brawler, stands as the outdoor prototype who represents an unreflective and pragmatic masculine ethic: take what you want, fight when your manhood is challenged. Juxtaposed against these "lake and woods" values are those of the doctor's wife, who advocates the civilized (or "cottage") Christian virtues of charity and self-restraint, summarized in the passage from scripture with which she chides her husband: "he who ruleth his spirit is greater than he that taketh a city." Between

these two extremes of savagery and civilization there is
the tormented doctor, who rules neither others nor himself and who conquers neither through primitive male
force nor Christian meekness. He attempts the role of
dominant male at first in the lakefront encounter with
Boulton but must abandon it because he cannot steal
when exposed, or fight when dared. He finds himself
equally uncomfortable in his wife's cottage domain because he falls short of her standards and because she
challenges his version of the episode. So, he fails to assert himself as a man either outdoors or indoors. His
final act, the retreat to the cool woods with his son,
holds but faint solace. Although he wins the boy's al-
legiance, he must be guided by the boy to where the
game is; he does not know.

This pattern of outside/inside/outside, with all its implications, is reinforced by a significant and repeated gesture: the opening and closing of a gate or door. Each of
the story's scenes contains this action as part of the
natural flow of events. In the first scene Dick Boulton,
the savage and triumphant male, enters the doctor's land
through a gate but later stalks off, deliberately leaving it
open. His companion Billie Tabeshaw, a timid, civilized
Indian, returns and closes it to assuage the doctor's
wrath. When the doctor leaves the house at the conclusion of the cottage scene he lets the door slam as he
goes out—his counterpart of Boulton's action—but
quickly apologizes for it at a covert signal from his wife.
Then, on his way out to the woods, he passes through
the same gate the Indians had used. By their placement
at the story's beginning and end, the gate and door serve
as a means of framing or closure (no pun intended), a
function which raises them from "realistic" scenic props
to symbolic status. Gates and doors mark the boundaries
of civilization, the female domain. Man's world, the
forest, lies beyond the gates.

Hemingway employs other associational techniques
and symbolic objects to carry out the structural antithesis. The males in the story are characterized by axes

and guns. Boulton carries an axe; the doctor fondles his shotgun. But the doctor's impotency as a true male is suggested by his handling of the gun *indoors*, within range of his wife's hearing and voice. His atavistic impulse, so thoroughly repressed as perhaps not even to enter his conscious mind, would be to use the gun on Dick Boulton or his wife or at least on wild game. He does none of these but only manipulates it purposelessly. Unmanned (and the gun's phallic connotations are obvious), he does not take it with him into the woods.

The doctor's wife is likewise characterized by a number of subtle details which stress the central opposition hinted at even in the story's title. She is surrounded by her holy books, which are neatly disposed; she lies in the darkness; she is a Christian Scientist. All of these contribute to the portrayal of the conflict with her husband and to the story's pervasive male-female antithesis.[6] The doctor, Dick Boulton, and Nick are seen in daylight; his professional journals are heaped up, unopened; he is a physician. What could be a more intrinsically discordant match than between a Christian Scientist and a doctor? A further incongruity stems from the doctor's proneness to anger and his fondness for guns, neither quite typical of a physician's character. The depiction of the wife as one who advocates the light of the Word yet prefers an environment of darkness is equally ironic. Note, too, that books as emblems of civilization characterize Nick, a minor but important figure in the work. When the doctor finds him, Nick is sitting on the fringe of the forest reading a book, indicative of his divided loyalties to his parents and the incompatible modes of existence they represent. However, when Nick decides to accompany his father rather than obey his mother, he gives the book to his father (another significant gesture) and leads him into the woods.

"A Day's Wait," one of the last stories in the Nick Adams saga, manifests the same basic structural pattern as "The Doctor and the Doctor's Wife" but with salient variations in the technique of symbolic suggestion. At first glance this seems among the most rudimentary and anecdotal of Hemingway's stories, charming in the quietness and modesty of its manner but not very deep. The story's narrator, who is not named but whom we infer to be a much older Nick Adams, provides the story's focus and rationale for its structure. That is, the situation identifies the narrator as the father of a sick child who attends to the child as the story opens, then goes out to hunt but soon gives up because of the treacherous footing on icy ground, and returns inside to attend to the child again. Too, Hemingway plots the story around a wryly humorous complication involving the child's fear that he will die because he confuses Centigrade and Fahrenheit thermometer readings. Thus, the story's action follows an inside/outside/inside pattern which straightforwardly narrates a commonplace sequence of events yet is highly suggestive.

Symbolically, the father's movement from his sick child's room outdoors to hunt quail both relieves his own tension through the release of physical energy and, in the act of killing, responds to the latent fear of his son's death. The same fear, of course, serves to remind him of his own mortality, whether he recognizes it or not. In the act of hunting he asserts his power over other creatures and wins a temporary control of death, for in killing, as Hemingway said elsewhere, man takes unto himself a divine attribute.[7] In contrast to the father of "The Doctor and the Doctor's Wife," the father in this story *uses* his gun. Moreover, the icy condition of the terrain represents for the father what the illness is to the son; in falling on the ice, he enacts the truth of man's helplessness against the forces of nature. The spontaneous and credible action of slipping on the glazed earth becomes Hemingway's paradigm here for man's uncertain grasp on life. It is the outdoor equivalent to illness.

Although this is not strictly a matter of structure, Hemingway's treatment of emotion in this story demands comment. He handles a potentially sentimental situation without expressing feeling in overt terms and without

calling directly upon the reader's sense of pathos. We
surmise the father's love and concern for his sick son
not from any declaration of it in exposition or dialogue
but rather from a series of observations, gestures and
dramatic metaphors: the father's perception from the
boy's face and manner that he is ill; the father's use of
the German idiom of endearment "Schatz" as a nick-
name; the small details of attending to him — particularly
the attempt to read to him.[8] Again, as in the previous
story, books serve poorly to allay strong feeling. The boy,
preoccupied by his private fear that he will die because
his temperature has reached 102° F., when his French
schoolmates have told him 44° C. is fatal, cannot respond
to his favorite book. The child's love for his father, perhaps in imitation of his parent's restraint, is also stoically
held in but still finds voice in the term "Papa" and the
worry that his father will catch the same illness. The
repressed emotion is at last released by the revelation of
the reason behind the child's strange behavior, the comic
revelation of the Centigrade-Fahrenheit misunderstand-
ing. Just as the father has let his emotion out by hunting,
the child is unburdened by confession. By this release,
both characters approach a state of health, each in his
own way.

Finally, Hemingway strengthens the story's total effect
by matching structural design to narrative technique.
The tale's division into almost perfectly equal parts of
dramatic scene/narration/dramatic scene conforms exactly with the inside/outside/inside pattern, as does the
alternation of stasis, action, stasis. But this correlation
of design and method, together with the symmetry of
scenic arrangement, remains unobtrusive. Consequently,
the story illustrates perfectly what Hemingway meant
when he said that good prose was "architecture, not interior decoration." [9] As well-wrought an example of Hemingway's craft as is "A Day's Wait," it preserves a characteristic illusion of artless simplicity.

Another deceptive case is "Che Ti Dice La Patria?"
At first reading and in light of its original publication in

the *New Republic* under the title "Italy, 1927," we would assume the story to be merely another instance of Hemingway's felicitous journalism, reportage enlivened by sharp observation and sardonic humor. Perhaps for this reason it has been ignored by critics. But if the story is only a slice of life, Hemingway has carved it skillfully indeed. Beneath the formal division of the piece into parts, with captions, which correspond to the major phases of the events reported, there is the deeper structure of the outside/inside pattern. However, here it works on a different level of abstraction.

Actually, the outside/inside antithesis serves two purposes. First, it helps depict a specific social milieu, Italy under fascism; second, within the context of Italian fascism it also connotes a general perversion of character in the country and its people. The "outside" values in the story are not those of the out-of-doors, but those of the world outside Italy—what a nation can and should be, as suggested in the narrator's closing description of the French town of Mentone, just across the Italian border: "It seemed very cheerful and clean and sane and lovely." In contrast, the "inside" is Italy, which the story portrays as melancholy, soiled, ruined, ugly. The whole antithesis is founded upon the narrator's attitude at the beginning of the story, his unstated but nevertheless optimistic anticipation as he enters the country, as opposed to the conditions he actually experiences there. This optimism is implied in the opening paragraph, which exudes the hopefulness and zest of the out-of-doors: "The road of the pass was hard and smooth and not yet dusty in the early morning. Below were the hills with oak and chestnut trees, and far away below was the sea. On the other side were snowy mountains." But the initial good spirits elicited by the idyllic setting soon become dispelled as the story proceeds.

Within the basic contrast between diseased and healthy nations, there is a specific outside/inside/outside movement in the story's three scenes: from road to restaurant to road. Unfortunately, whatever the narrator's location, inside or out, the environment is grim. Unpleasant and disillusioning encounters occur both outdoors and indoors, and, simultaneously, the landscape is also darkened and besmirched. In each of the story's episodes the narrator and his friend suffer abuse and hostility from the country's inhabitants, especially its newly ascended Fascist elite. But Hemingway never preaches. All is dramatized.

Just as the story opened lightheartedly, in keeping with the pastoral vista, the first cue that things go badly with the land is communicated by details that we might easily overlook as part of the story's "real" setting. The travelers pass barren, vine-choked fields and white houses stained by insecticide spray applied to the fruit trees in order to save them—and we interpolate, as fascism was to save Italy. Then, when the travelers are coerced into carrying a Fascist hitchhiker, they are angered by his arrogance, just as his extra weight causes their car to labor and boil over—an objectification of their feelings. From that point on, until they leave the country, the entire trip is downhill both actually and metaphorically.

The indoor scene in the restaurant at Spezia continues the dramatization of theme by means of action and setting. The restaurant's dim light implies its moral condition, for although food is served there, the main business is prostitution. Details of characterization underline the motif of deception and duplicity: the waitress whose face is attractive on one side but disfigured on the other; the glossy young manager described as though he were an actor or theatrical producer; the shadowy character whom Hemingway names the "property sailor." Later in the story there is another unpleasant indoor scene consisting of a second dispiriting meal in a cold restaurant, taken with bad wine and in the presence of an unhappy and mismated couple. The restaurant has no lavatory, and the neighbors who grudgingly allow the travelers to use their toilet are surly and suspicious. All this thoroughly discredits the "inside" of Italy.

In the story's final and most distasteful episode, an

outdoor scene, the travelers are stopped and fined by a Fascist policeman. In this episode the country's polluted atmosphere and the policeman's corruption have their counterparts in the miserable weather and road conditions. There is turbulent wind, rain, and the mud that soils everything. The policeman's pretense at levying a fine for a supposed traffic violation, when the money is obviously for himself, parallels the narrator's earlier restaurant-whorehouse experience. Most tellingly, Hemingway makes repeated reference to and use of the word *dirt*, which appears seven times in the story's last page. This effectively overrides the earlier comedy of the restaurant scene in Spezia and the wit of the travelers' continuous stream of wisecracks, so that the final mood is somber. Although the story concludes with a facetious statement, "The whole trip had taken only ten days. Naturally, in such a short trip, we had no opportunity to see how things were with the country or the people," it comes after too much nastiness to induce a humorous effect. The comedy is that of edged irony. What began in sunlight becomes obscured and then begrimed. This is at once the literal and figurative pattern of the story, both outdoors and in.

I would need the space of a monograph to do a structural analysis of all Hemingway's short fiction, and I do intend to return to his stories again from other standpoints. However, the usefulness of the outside/inside structure to communicate contrasts in values or lifestyles may be illustrated elsewhere by a cursory survey of some of the main forms of this pattern. For example, "Cat in the Rain" follows the symmetrical three-part design, with two inside scenes framing an outdoor scene, as do also "The Three-Day Blow" and "Cross-Country Snow." Each of these stories dramatizes a version of the pervasive Hemingway male-female or marriage-single life opposition. "Ten Indians" and "An Alpine Idyll," which contrast "savage" and "civilized" behavior, have a two-scene outside/inside design. The intense violence and heroism of the outdoor bullring in "The Undefeated"

are emphasized by its frame: at the start two dismal indoor scenes in Retana's office and the café, at the end
the dire episode in the infirmary, as Manuel sinks into
unconsciousness. A variation of this pattern occurs in
such stories as "The Battler" and "Big Two-Hearted
River." Although the action of these latter stories takes
place entirely outdoors, in them man palliates his loneliness by recourse to such indoor, civilized comforts as a
campfire, shelter, hot food. "Big Two-Hearted River" integrates the pattern so well as to be nearly invisible, yet
the story is, in fact, organized around the three-part structure. The "indoor" scene, that of the campfire and the
tent, comes exactly at the story's midpoint, at the end
of part 1 and the beginning of part 2. If it is true of
Hemingway's stories that the connotations of "inside"
are often negative, allied with confinement, entrapment,
female domination and male weakness, it is equally true
that the inside scenes in "The Three-Day Blow," "Big
Two-Hearted River," "A Clean, Well-Lighted Place,"
and other stories communicate positive associations as
well: physical well-being, security, comradeship, safety,
cheer—all the associations we make with "home."

Other examples demonstrate how, as in "Che Ti Dice
La Patria?" Hemingway renders different social milieux
and their appropriate values or moral qualities by means
of a subtle contrast of locales. The Africa of "The Short
Happy Life of Francis Macomber" and "The Snows of
Kilimanjaro," the Europe of "Soldier's Home," embody
those associations attached to the outdoors: freedom,
courage, danger, joy, potency. Set over against them are
the decayed "indoor" values of America. In "Soldier's
Home" what Krebs experienced overseas in the war now
remains to him only in memory and a fading photo-
graph: the excitement of combat, the friendship of comrades, the uncomplicated affection and sexuality of European girls. All this conflicts with the stifling proprieties
of his midwestern hometown, where the ultimate realities are job, marriage, and predetermined sentiment.

The same antithesis between freedom and slavery,

health and sickness, informs "The Short Happy Life of
Francis Macomber," although Hemingway portrays it
by more complex characterization and intense action
than in "Soldier's Home." Macomber's cowardice at the
story's inception springs not only from some deep personal source but also from a corrupt way of life. His debased habits of conduct, his money, his bad marriage—
all reflect a whole culture gone rotten, an "indoor" civilization: America. But removed from these conditions
and placed in Africa, the outdoors, where a man like
Wilson is moulded by the atavistic essentials which still
prevail, Macomber can regain his lost masculinity. If,
according to Wilson, female bitchery is characteristic of
the decadent American way of life, a man can liberate
himself from it in primitive Africa by shooting well. The
story conveys a paradox: although bad behavior derives
from bad values, good behavior can produce good values.

Africa also bears something of the same significance in
"The Snows of Kilimanjaro," that is, as a country where
decadent man is compelled to admit his true condition.
Confined to his cot with a gangrened leg and facing imminent death, the protagonist Harry can no longer evade
the fact of his moral deterioration. Africa obliterates the
outside appearance, the façade of bluff masculinity, and
brings out the inner condition of disease, for which
Harry's infected leg is the objective representation. Here,
then, there is no sequence of tangible action and movement; the outside/inside pattern is psychological, with
Harry's memories of his lusty and intensely-lived past
counterpoised against his present decay, both physical
and spiritual. However, Hemingway deepens the pattern by adding an interesting ironic dimension to the
customary outside/inside associations. Although Africa,
the epitome of the outdoor life, serves as a mirror for
character and a metaphor for life's heroic possibilities
(especially in the central symbol of Kilimanjaro itself),
it is also the scene of Harry's final ruination, while the
supposedly decadent lands of America and Europe are
associated with the protagonist's youth, vigor, and in-

tegrity. Finally it is the man and his conduct which matter, not the locale for that conduct, although the locale can effect moral recognition. Hemingway further strengthens the outside/inside design by his narrative technique in the story, juxtaposing omniscient narration with interior monologue and the protagonist's flashbacks (marked off in italic type) with his consciousness of the present time and place. Consequently, we have two levels of the outside/inside structure at once, one thematic, one technical.

At the beginning of this discussion I spoke of a second basic structural pattern in Hemingway's short stories, the toward/away pattern typically manifested as a movement through space, an actual journey. As in the outside/inside structure, the toward/away design often appears as a three-part schema, toward/"there"/away. The design can also function metaphorically and thematically as well as structurally, or, at best, all at once. Furthermore, although I did not labor the point during my study of "Che Ti Dice La Patria?" it should have been clear that the journey structure may quite naturally be combined with the outside/inside pattern. That is, I find a close correspondence between the outside and both the "toward" and "away" phases of the journey, while the "there" or arrival-at-destination phase may be nearly identical to the inside. To be more explicit, in the journey pattern the "toward" phase is the protagonist's approach to a place or destination, the "there" phase is his actual arrival at the destination and the experience of it or engagement with it, and the "away" phase is the breaking-off or departure. Or to put this in yet another way, in terms of that psychological or dramatic action which we know to be the classic sequence of experience for the Hemingway protagonist, we have the pattern of innocence, suffering, and awareness. Note again that the journey structure lends itself well to the symmetrical organization of a story into a set of scenes, and that it can easily merge with the outside/inside design. These properties will be apparent in the explications to follow.

"Indian Camp" exemplifies the journey structure as it is integrated with the outside/inside pattern. The protagonist, Nick Adams as a boy, travels across a lake with his father and uncle to an Indian camp and then, after a nightmarish experience there, away from it by the same route. An Indian hut is the focal point of his experience; inside it he witnesses the birth of a baby and the simultaneous suicide of the infant's father. The movement from outdoors to indoors correlates with the phases of the journey in that just as Nick's innocence is tested by what happens at the destination, nature's seeming benevolence of lovely lake and sky is contrasted against the pain and horror contained in a human dwelling. Although the journey away from the hut occurs in an outdoor setting sufficiently idyllic to confer upon Nick the illusion of immortality, with the sun rising, fish jumping, and water warming, Nick has been forever changed by the experience at the center of the journey, indoors. By his attendance upon the mysteries of birth and death, presumably for the first time, he has become involved in mankind and has observed human frailty in several forms: a woman's agony in labor, a man's inability to endure suffering, another man's—his father's—pompous vanity. Yet the story's deepest irony pivots upon the recognition that the indoor events are as much a part of nature as placid lake and sky.

Hemingway foreshadows the grim action of the central episode by several subtle but portentous cues at the story's opening. The cadence of staccato sentences sets an ominous tone as the voyage begins and the boats travel across the lake in darkness and through mist. The air is cold and the Indian rower works strenuously. As Nick, his father, and his uncle reach the other shore and walk toward the settlement, their Indian guide puts out his lantern. When they enter the hut, the woman in labor screams. The hut stinks. All these details function on two levels: as essential components of action and setting and as dramatic metaphors. A voyage undertaken in darkness, fog, and cold, continued with light extinguished, and ended at a place where there is stench and the cry of agony, has little likelihood of a happy culmination.

Another Nick Adams story, "A Way You'll Never Be," also offers a valuable example of the journey structure. Nick, now a soldier, travels toward the front lines through country where there has been heavy fighting. He reaches his destination, a unit commanded by a friend and former comrade-in-arms, and pauses there only to be afflicted by an attack of war-induced hysteria. Then, recovered, he begins the trip back. The story's central action, Nick's temporary nervous collapse, is prefigured by what he sees in the approach to his destination. The journey away represents a disengagement, a falling-off, after the cathartic experience at the front. Within this schema there is a corollary movement, a variation of the outside/inside design, in that we go (as in "The Snows of Kilimanjaro") from outside the protagonist's mind to a revelation of its innermost secrets. Or, the movement could be described as that from sanity to lunacy to sanity, corresponding almost exactly to Nick's physical movement and route. In other words, two journeys are being made concurrently: one toward the geographic setting, the actual scene of the fighting that caused Nick's wound; the other an inward journey toward a confrontation with the crippled psychic self produced by the physical wound.

The realistic details of the landscape through which Nick travels accentuate this correspondence. Just as the dead lying along the road are somehow rendered absurd by their awkward postures and the papers scattered around them, so the torn pieces of Nick's sensibility will soon spill out over his self-control, expose his naked self, and humiliate him before those he is visiting. Moreover, the debris around the dead soldiers, the thick rubbish of their personal possessions, parallels the dense detail of Nick's hallucinations and incoherent babbling. The papers contain the records of these now-grotesque young men, their loves and illusions, all made futile by the fact of death; similarly, Nick's delirium juxtaposes garbled fragments of his past with the tormented present. Within his frenzied and seemingly random recollections there is a design, for the peculiar admixture of military allusions with Nick's dissertation on grasshoppers as fishing bait connects men and grasshoppers: both are pathetic creatures to be destroyed without significance. It is another expression of the "ants on a burning log" passage in *A Farewell to Arms*, which forms in turn Hemingway's version of the poetic statement of human helplessness in *King Lear*: "As flies to wanton boys are we to the gods; they kill us for their sport."

The toward/away structure may be perceived in a number of other Hemingway stories, sometimes conjoined with the outside/inside pattern, perhaps most notably in "Big Two-Hearted River," "A Canary for One," "The Light of the World," "Wine of Wyoming," and "Fathers and Sons." However, it rarely works in exactly the same way. For example, the pattern of action in "Big Two-Hearted River" emphasizes the movement toward the destination and the experience at it, with the departure only implied. In that story the central experience or engagement is affirmative, although not unequivocally so because Nick cannot penetrate to the deepest core, the swamp. In "A Canary for One," the destination suggests an ironic or bitter conclusion to the journey. As the traveler-protagonist approaches his geographical destination, Paris, he is drawing away from his emotional center, for it is revealed that he will separate from his wife when the trip ends. The arrival thus betokens not culmination or fulfillment but dissolution. In "Fathers and Sons," as in the stories just named but even more intensively, the movement through space which comprises the work's structural frame is subordinated to an inward journey, a passage back through time, memory, and emotion. In a sense, all of these journeys delve deeply into the sources of the protagonist's psyche, to places and events connected with basic human relationships, to experiences which molded the protagonist and generated his fundamental values.

Accordingly, in each story Hemingway poses parallels

between outer and inner reality and the protagonist's actual progress through some region, fusing setting, character, action, and structure into a unified whole. Thus in "Big Two-Hearted River" the burned-over land which Nick crosses on his way toward the river can be equated with his war-scorched nerves; the river itself connotes the life-giving properties of the natural elements. Nick's ability to function at the destination, to stand in the river and fish using grasshoppers as bait (a link with "A Way You'll Never Be"), signals his ascension toward health and peace. In contrast, the physical milieu of "A Canary for One," as viewed by the protagonist through the windows of his train, has a generally depressing effect because the details he records: heat, smoke, a burning farmhouse, and, at journey's end, wrecked train-cars, are all really counterparts to his inside condition. The burning farmhouse makes an especially effective emblem for the protagonist's ruined marriage. In "Fathers and Sons" the country he traverses reminds the protagonist, in turn, of quail-shooting, his troubled relationship with his father, and his sexual initiation by an Indian girl. As he drives toward his destination with his own son beside him, he also nears an inner resolution with the past. The story's conclusion predicts still another journey soon to be made: a visit to the father's grave, perhaps the final reconciliation.

Yet another variation of Hemingway's use of the journey as structural metaphor is that of the anticipated, unfinished, or imaginary journey. In those stories which depend upon this method the static condition of the protagonist, that is, his inability to undertake or complete the journey, his immobility, suggests a more anguished, despairing, or dangerous condition than that of the protagonists of the stories discussed above. In "Indian Camp" or "A Way You'll Never Be," whatever the pain involved in the movement itself or the intensity of the trauma at the destination, the character at least retains the capacity for further action, for escape. Even if the departure represents a defeat or an evasion, life and an element of hope remain. The trip in "A Canary for One" is melancholy, but some sort of resolution has been made. In "A Way You'll Never Be" Nick can remount his bicycle and pedal away from the front, his fit of madness over. If he cannot quite face the swamp in "Big Two-Hearted River," there is the promise he will return to fish it one day. In "Che Ti Dice La Patria?" one can abandon Italy and go to better places.

But in such stories as "Hills Like White Elephants," "The Killers," "A Pursuit Race," "Homage to Switzerland," and "The Snows of Kilimanjaro" the protagonists either have not begun their journeys or are unable to travel any further. The static position of the characters in "Hills Like White Elephants," with their seemingly interminable wait for the train, suggests that their emotional condition also remains suspended. Their hearts, like their bodies, have not yet traveled the necessary roads. Waiting to continue their journey, they are paralyzed, perhaps permanently, by antagonism.

Even more desolate is the condition of the paralyzed characters in "The Killers," "A Pursuit Race," and "The Snows of Kilimanjaro," all immobilized by dire wounds of body or spirit. Neither Ole Andreson nor William Campbell can outrun their pursuers any longer; they are exhausted. The characters who try to persuade them to move, Mr. Turner and Nick Adams, retain the will to travel ("I have to go," Turner says repeatedly; "I'm going to get out of this town," Nick declares) — but are a little naïve in the very possession of it. They have not endured as much as the others; their health also implies an ignorance of what it means to reach a dead end. And despite their vitality, they remain futile to alleviate the others' exhaustion and despair. In a sense they, too, are immobilized. As I implied earlier, Harry's disablement by his diseased leg in "The Snows of Kilimanjaro" signifies also his corrupt moral condition, that is, the rotting away of his artistic integrity and physical vitality through abuse and disuse. He cannot move except in his mind, which recalls a vigorous former life, one characterized by action, travel, involvement—intense even when unpleasant. The only voyage now possible for him, the hallucinated flight over Kilimanjaro, is the passage to the grave. His spirit flies out of him, leaving behind a putrifying corpse, a dismal conclusion to the journey indeed. The "away" movement here is perhaps the most starkly ironic in all Hemingway's stories, sharpened by the portrayal of the death-moment itself as soaring and ecstatic.

As my last illustration of the journey structure I choose *The Old Man and the Sea*. I find no occasion in Hemingway's fiction in which the design is more fully realized in the whole work. In this *nouvelle*, as economical as a short story yet with something of a novel's magnitude of action, we also have an exemplary case of the integration of the outside/inside structure with that of the journey. The sequence of scenes can be described as land/sea/land, imitating the movement of a voyage as it would be made in reality. However, by its place in this sequence each of the elements becomes suggestive of multiple meanings, as does the entire sequence itself.

All the associations evoked by the "inside" in Hemingway's stories, associations both affirmative and negative, here attach themselves to the land. Affirmatively, the land is the locale of Santiago's kinship with the boy, the old man's last and deepest human relationship. The boy tends to the old man's needs as a wife would, reveres him as a son reveres a father, and loves him as a brother or comrade. The land, then, can be equated with family or domesticity, a place of shelter, rest, food, affection, and security. Negatively, and here again are Hemingway's recurrent principles of antithesis and paradox, the land is also the scene of Santiago's disgrace. On land the other fishermen mock or pity Santiago and judge him a failure, with the result that the boy's father forbids him to accompany Santiago. There, too, the old man returns with his skeleton-fish, to be misunderstood by ignorant tourists. It may also be true, as Bickford Sylvester has suggested, that Santiago's return to the shore, exhausted by his struggle with the giant marlin, is the final action of his life—that he has come back to die.[10]

Within the same structural and symbolic pattern the sea also conveys ambivalent meanings, those associated with the outdoors. Affirmatively, it constitutes the scene and condition for man's ultimate experience and his most heroic and intense moment, the combat with great natural forces. Negatively, it is the setting wherein Santiago recognizes himself as erring, sinful, and finally helpless. In nature, outdoors, when Santiago kills the magnificent fish he briefly attains the divine power of taking life; but in nature he is himself overcome by his own mistakes and those ever-present agents of brutish malevolence, the sharks. The sea is beneficent and beautiful. It breeds the creatures man needs for food. It is as thrilling to behold as a lovely woman. It exalts man and calls him out to noble quests. But the sea also entraps man, luring him out only to ruin him.

The voyage structure is, of course, implicit in all of this, but it has further dimensions and analogues. The order of action in Santiago's trip out to sea, his struggle with the marlin, and the subsequent return home, repeats again the basic pattern of the movement toward and away from engagement which we have observed before in Hemingway's fiction. Just as Nick Adams and other Hemingway protagonists are impelled into conflict and retreat from it wounded and disenchanted, so the aged Santiago leaves the shore hopeful, conquers his adversary in mortal combat, then makes a disastrous retreat. The voyage structure also organizes the *nouvelle* into symmetrical parts. The trip out, to the moment of engagement with the fish, occupies the first quarter of the work; the return to land takes up the last quarter. But the destination or purpose of the voyage, the battle itself, appropriately comprises the work's center.

Two other subpatterns are interwoven with the land/sea/land structure and call our attention to its inherent antitheses of the known against the unknown and the human against the infinite. Furthermore, each of these subpatterns reduplicates the three-part structure. These patterns are: together/alone/together, darkness/light/darkness.

In the first of these Santiago leaves the shore, where his intimate comradeship with the boy has been portrayed, ventures out to sea and to the struggle alone, then returns to the renewed and intensified love of the boy. During the long agony of the combat and the voyage back, Santiago's reiterated plea "I wish I had the boy" assumes almost the significance of an incantation or leitmotif. By implication, human love and help become man's major resources in the struggle with nature. At the voyage's culmination Santiago's wish comes true: he will indeed have the boy, for as long as he lives. He has earned at least this much.

The darkness/light/darkness pattern contributes to both the affective quality of the action and its moral ambiguity. As fishermen do in life, Santiago sets out before dawn, captures his fish in daylight, and returns to port at night. But the darkness at beginning and end of the voyage foreshadows and confirms the work's tragic effect, its themes of failure, loss, and error. In darkness the sharks complete their savage destruction, as darkness connotes bestiality and evil. Moreover, the sea itself is always and only "dark," with the word itself (or "darkness") used so frequently as a subtle form of incremental repetition—some thirty times (like "dirt" in "Che Ti Dice La Patria?")—that it, too, becomes incantatory, underscoring the sea's inscrutability and archetypal mystery. However, the darkness need not be wholly tragic or sinister in its implications, as evidenced in Santiago's thought, "The dark water of the true gulf is the greatest healer there is." [11]

Indeed, Hemingway incorporates a strong element of paradox into the darkness/light pattern. That the marlin is first hooked and later killed in daylight, that the first shark attacks when the sun is high, that in daylight Santiago begins to question the ethics of his action, all suggest that killing and moral awareness occur simultaneously and that both can be forms of illumination. Santiago's reflections upon the joy, the pride, and the sin of killing, ideas stated in full consciousness—in broad daylight, as it were—rehearse a lifelong preoccupation of Hemingway's, perhaps his most profound and disturbing literary idea. The killing of the fish is another of Hemingway's deaths in the afternoon, and the old man's thoughts about it remind us of Hemingway's overt statement of that idea in the opening pages of the earlier book on bullfighting, that for him the most intense and truest art is engendered by the presence and with the inspiration of violent death: "I was trying to learn to write, commencing with the simplest things, and one of the simplest things of all and the most fundamental is violent death."

The narrative and symbolic pattern of light and darkness also performs important service in the story as external frame and as internal imagery. Although Santiago's voyage begins and ends in darkness, the narrative itself opens and concludes in daylight—from the late afternoon of Santiago's eighty-fourth unlucky day, to the afternoon three days later when the tourists comment foolishly on the fish's skeleton while Santiago sleeps exhausted, a scenic contrast that poses a blatant irony. Within the story there are repeated references to light, bright colors, or light-against-darkness. For example, the sun hurts Santiago's eyes, but it also warms him and assuages his crippled left hand. He dreams of white and gold beaches where lions play; he is fed by white turtle eggs and silver-sided fish. He regards the luminescent moon and stars as his friends, and he associates the great fish with the celestial bodies. He knows the glow of lights from shore will guide him home from the sea, another aspect of the land/sea symbolism. However, and this is Hemingway's omnipresent ambivalence, silver is also the color of extinction, as the marlin changes from the regal and vibrant blue-purple of life to the pale hue of death, "the color of the silver backing of a mirror." Man sees himself most clearly in this mirror of mortality.

Although *The Old Man and the Sea* provides a singularly happy instance of Hemingway's method, a stirring tale of action which also achieves the resonance of parable, it is hardly unique in his work either in the strength of its architecture or the profundity of its meaning. On the contrary, it communicates what I believe to be the larger truth about Hemingway, a truth perhaps best observed in his short stories. It is this: if we approach Hemingway's fiction primarily by way of its craft, we will discover that the work offers its own reply to the major and persistent complaint that it is narrow in range and intellectually thin. In sum, the very structure or pattern of Hemingway's stories comprises a form of thought, perhaps for an artist the most cogent kind: form *as* thought. As more than one critic has pointed out, Hemingway's fiction at its best attains to the concreteness, compactness, and sensuousness of lyric poetry, embodying and demonstrating in the genre of narrative the fundamental literary method T. S. Eliot called the "objective correlative"—the technique by which the artist refuses to *name* emotion in his work, but rather recreates it in his audience by discovering and reproducing its sources.[12] If we can also understand "emotion" to mean experience, we have grasped a vital secret of Hemingway's art: that the structural design, the pattern of action, the antitheses and oppositions are intrinsic to human experience. Hemingway's craft both depends upon this experience and so orders it that the revelation seems to arise from within the reader, without his consciousness that the writer has bestowed a great gift upon him.

2

The Structure of the Novels

Many critics have learned to their dismay that the novel is too protean a form to permit hard and fast classification or absolutely final definition. We no sooner think we have it fixed than it changes under our eyes and becomes something else and something new. Perhaps no other species of art has given rise to so many mutations and hybrids. And if the novelist be a serious and resourceful craftsman, his work especially resists rigidly formulaic interpretation. Nevertheless, it is the critic's task, in his ambition to deeply comprehend the artist's work, to locate the controlling principles in it and describe them in some sort of meaningful order or pattern. This is not to suggest that the process of locating and describing these patterns constitutes a formula which will completely explain the work's magic and potency. One hopes only to learn where and how to look.

Although Hemingway's novels are not expansions or collections of his stories and thus intrinsically different from them, I see in the novels some of the same basic structural designs. The protagonists' movements from place to place, or, essentially, the journey structure, are central to the organization of *The Sun Also Rises* and *A Farewell to Arms.* Journeys also contribute, although less significantly, to the design of *To Have and Have Not*, *For Whom the Bell Tolls*, *Across the River and into the Trees*, and *Islands in the Stream*. In all of these novels we can observe the pattern of the movement toward a destination, the experience or engagement at the focal point, and then the departure or disengagement.

Another important structural design, one not really germane to the short stories although it could be said to have slight affinity with the outside/inside pattern, is the formal division of four of Hemingway's novels into "books," or sections: *The Sun Also Rises, A Farewell to Arms, To Have and Have Not, Islands in the Stream.* Hemingway so arranges these sections and so controls the focus on character, situation, and event that the parts represent thematic groupings, oppositions or antimonies. As in the cases of *A Farewell to Arms* and *To Have and Have Not* the divisions may clearly embody and emphasize the now-familiar principle of antithesis. Or, as in *The Sun Also Rises* and *Islands in the Stream*, they may mark off crucial phases of the protagonists' experience, phases which subsume contrasting or conflicting values. All these matters will be considered as I proceed.

Furthermore, we must pay special attention to a structural technique of prime importance to Hemingway's novels, the technique of alternation or counterpoint. By this I mean Hemingway's consistent practice of controlling the movement, mood, and intensity of his novels by alternating a sequence of action or scenes of one kind with action or scenes of another kind, or playing off one mode of narration against a different mode, or setting one character type or situation side by side with a contrasting or dissimilar character or situation, and so on. When the technique functions at its best, as in *The Sun Also Rises, A Farewell to Arms,* and *For Whom the Bell Tolls* —all books of goodly length—it results in a keen effect of variety, dynamism, verve, swiftness of pace. It operates particularly well in *For Whom the Bell Tolls*, a long and thickly detailed novel, and gives it a more concentrated impact than is usual in a book of its size and kind. This technique of alternation and counterpoint, although visible and efficacious to some degree in the short stories as a by-product of both the outside/inside and journey structures, is not truly fundamental to them. After all,

Hemingway's short stories *are* short, and there is little
need for alternation and variety in a work of brief span.
Where Hemingway does employ this design in the stories, it is not so much in the individual tales but in the
arrangement of the tales in a collection, notably *In Our
Time*. There, as some critics have remarked, one can discern a loose pattern of arrangement in the alternation
of the interchapters with various phases of the Nick
Adams saga. However, the effect is much more diffuse
than in the novels named above.[1] Now, to a demonstration of the various structural designs of the novels. I
will treat the journey pattern relatively cursorily since the
concept has already been introduced.

In adapting the journey design to his novels Hemingway augmented it, as appropriate to the longer form, by
sometimes incorporating small or side journeys within
the overall structure of toward/there/away. These function to parallel or reiterate the main journey, or to provide an ironic counterpart to it.

Hemingway's first novel *The Sun Also Rises* contains
a symmetrical form of the journey design, inasmuch as
the various phases of the action are organized around the
characters' travels: from Paris to Pamplona (including
the side trip to Burguete) to San Sebastian to Madrid. The Paris and Burguete trips comprise the "toward" phase, Pamplona and the fiesta the "there," or
destination-culmination, San Sebastian the "away." The
concluding Madrid episode both completes one whole
cycle of the journey and begins another, conveying the
novel's basic motif of the futile yet repeated and cyclical
nature of human experience.[2]

The structure gains symmetry because the novel's
marked sectional divisions coincide with the stages of
the several journeys, major and minor. Indeed, there is
an exact correlation. Book 1 consists entirely of the
"home" or Paris phase, which sets forward the plans for
the journey, introduces the travelers, and hints at future
complications. At the end of book 1 we learn that Brett
is leaving for San Sebastian, although it is not revealed

until later in the novel that she has gone there with Cohn. At the beginning of book 2 Jake and Bill depart for Pamplona. After arriving in Pamplona they take the fishing trip to Burguete. At almost the precise midpoint of book 2, which also approximates the novel's center, the entire group collects in Pamplona—the destination. Then, at the end of that section with the action at the destination completed, they begin to disperse, as Cohn, Brett, and Romero depart. At the beginning of book 3, the dénouement, the others leave, and the remainder of that brief section is devoted to Jake's excursion to San Sebastian, until, at the very end, he travels to Madrid for Brett. The final scene of the novel in the moving-then-stopping taxi highlights the symmetry of its design by repeating the crucial taxi scene in book 1, while both scenes together emphasize the anguish of Jake and Brett's relationship and the pointlessness of all their wanderings. Just as neither taxi has a specific destination, the passion of the protagonists, aroused by the proximity of their bodies, can find no satisfying outlet.

The general structure of A Farewell to Arms is almost equally symmetrical. It comprises three principal phases: Frederic Henry's movement toward the war, his intense involvement with it, and then a subsequent breaking-off. Actually, the larger design embodies two separate sequences or phases of action, each of them following the same pattern: an approach to battle, the crippling by it, the retreat from it. Thus one important aspect of the novel's title and theme are reduplicated in its structure. In the first engagement with the war the hero is physically injured and is carried away to recover; in the second his morale is shattered and he takes himself away from the conflict. There is a further parallel of the toward/away pattern in Frederick's relationship with Catherine, which resembles the sequence of movements in the war, although the correspondence is not identical.

To emphasize this basic structure the novel utilizes a number of journeys in miniature, a series of arrivals and departures which act as a major technique of closure.

Book 1 begins with troops on the road to battle; it ends with the wounded Frederic Henry en route by train to a hospital in Milan. Book 2 opens with the hero's arrival in Milan and concludes with him recovered from his wounds and aboard another train on his way back to the front. At the beginning of book 3 Frederic returns to his outfit by camion; at its end he rides another train away from the front, a deserter. He arrives in Milan at the start of book 4; at the end of that section he escapes Italy with Catherine into Switzerland. As the novel concludes he makes his desolate departure from the hospital where Catherine lies dead, his retreat from the arms of both love and war final and irrevocable.[3]

Something of the same structure, in looser form, may be remarked in *To Have and Have Not*, charting Harry Morgan's movement toward and away from Key West. Here the spatial movement toward home also ironically records the hero's decline, for each time he returns to Key West he comes back in worse condition. In the first return he is bereft of money and some of his equipment. In the second he is crippled. In the third he is mortally wounded. *For Whom the Bell Tolls* also contains a toward/away design, with the bridge as the focal point of the journey and the "away" phase, or aftermath, assuming what we now recognize as the inevitably tragic outcome. Although the journey design is perhaps not the primary structural pattern of *For Whom the Bell Tolls*, it nevertheless appears in a few of the novel's subpatterns, especially the trips from the cave to El Sordo's hideout, El Sordo's own retreat to his mountaintop, and Andrés's attempt to get through to General Golz and stop the attack. The latter journey is especially significant, in that Andrés's futile mission parallels Jordan's futile mission to the bridge, which parallels the futile attack by the Loyalists on Segovia, which suggests the entire futility of the Loyalist cause. *Across the River and into the Trees* also employs a variation of the journey design, with Venice as the destination or culmination of Colonel Cantwell's experience, and again the tragic departure. Indeed, the voyage both physical and mental back to a crucial place and the attempt to recall and surmount a traumatic time is the foundation for the entire novel.[4]

Finally, each of the parts of *Islands in the Stream* contains a journey of greater or lesser significance. In "Bimini," the arrival and departure of Thomas Hudson's sons frame the central episode of that section, the fishing trip and struggle with the huge marlin. The departure of the boys from Hudson's house at the end of the section presages the deaths of two of the three. The important journey in part 2, "Cuba," is not spatial but imaginary, as one of Hudson's wives, whom he had loved best, momentarily returns to his bed both to assuage and renew old traumas. In contrast part 3, "At Sea," is structured entirely around a journey, Hudson's hunt for the German U-boat crew. Indeed, the concluding episodes use the journey-within-a-journey technique when Hudson tracks the enemy through intricate island channels, as he himself is tracked and finally ambushed. It is obvious, then, that the journey design holds considerable value as a way of looking at the organization of Hemingway's novels, and that it remained one of his indispensable methods.

The two most conspicuous examples of structure by means of formal divisions which incorporate thematic units and oppositions are *A Farewell to Arms* and *To Have and Have Not*. I will deal with each in turn.

Readers commonly recognize that the dominant themes of *A Farewell to Arms* are love and war, and understand that the tension between them constitutes the novel's major action and shapes the protagonist's moral experience. However, this is not quite so simple as it seems. Closer inspection reveals not only that the dominant themes are proportioned and interwoven in a rather complex pattern, but also that underneath the two major themes is another, subsidiary theme, which nevertheless performs a distinct and necessary function. This subsidiary theme might be called "manners," that is, the depiction of social behavior, places, national character, life-styles—matters of persistent interest to Hemingway throughout his career yet generally overlooked in critical commentary. These three thematic lines, love, war, and manners, are apportioned among the novel's five books with effectively symmetrical results.

Book 1 is largely concerned with war, although it records the beginnings of love and makes passing comment on manners. The war emphasis is self-evident, culminating in Frederic Henry's wounding. Meanwhile, he has had four brief encounters with Catherine, including their initial meeting. In one of these the word "love" appears for the first time, although it is undercut by Catherine's sense that they play a "rotten game" necessitated by the exigencies of war. However, her gift of the St. Anthony's medal to Frederic, as he leaves for the front, portends something more than a sex fling. The commentary on manners, which brings out the protagonist's acuteness of observation and irreverence for established values—as well as his difference from his Italian comrades—is exemplified in several passages: the anti-clerical attitudes of the officers in the mess, the representation of the good life in the Abruzzi, Frederic's opinions on marble sculptures and frescoes, and a series of judgments on such various matters as Italian class-consciousness and Caruso's vocal abilities. We should also note that in the officers' cruel and ribald teasing of the priest, Frederic is an indirect target. He is a foreigner, and they know he is friendly to the priest. Yet, his own sympathies divided, he cannot wholly identify with the priest, either to defend him against abuse or to accept the pure and ascetic life-style the priest has offered.

Book 2, with the protagonist in the hospital in Milan, emphasizes love and manners, while the war recedes temporarily into the background. Deprived of his bravado and stoical manner by his wound, Frederic's vulnerability to emotion now exalts his attraction to Catherine into love, and she responds in kind. The genuineness of their feeling during this interlude in the war is counterpointed against the "manners" material, which connotes deception, treachery, and corruption: the pompous Italian doctors, incompetent under their officiousness; the Americans singing in Italy under Italian pseudonyms; a shady couple, the Meyers; the crooked horse races. In this book, also, Hemingway links the motifs of war and love and expands the concept of war from the military conflict to a universal condition with the first mention of the "biological trap," although the connection does not attain full significance until much later.

Book 3 reverses the emphasis of the previous section. It is almost entirely about war, with minimal attention to love and manners. Indeed, after the opening pages of the section Hemingway makes only two overt references to Catherine, strategically placing these to strengthen the dreariness of Frederic's mood: one in chapter 28, during the retreat, one in the concluding pages of the section, after he has deserted. Manners are also subordinated to the war, and enter only as bitter political commentary by Frederic's enlisted men.

Book 4 repeats the stress on love and manners in about the same proportions as book 2. In Stresa, as in Milan, there is a romantic interlude of deep intimacy lyrically portrayed. The manners material comes into two episodes: the delightful billiard game with Count Greffi, and the seriocomic encounter with the Swiss border officials and the subsequent byplay about painters and winter sports.

Book 5 combines the three basic themes, but with important differences. The manners treatment drops the satirical and jocular tone earlier characteristic of it and becomes a straightforward depiction of the daily life of Frederic and Catherine as they await the birth of their child. The war, which has seemingly been reduced for them to reports read in the newspaper, actually hovers over their existence in the form of the biological trap which finally annihilates love when it closes upon Catherine in the novel's last pages. Frederic's agonized recognition of the trap and his bitter response to it synthesizes the motifs of war and love and translates them into cosmic terms: nature makes constant war on man and inevitably destroys love.

Thus, the novel's formal structure reiterates its themes and underscores the characters' salient relationships. What we have in the five books is essentially this progression: war, love, war, love, love extinguished by war; with the recurrent element of manners as a modifying and mediating influence. Another way of describing this structure would be to compare it to the sonata or symphonic form, with war and love as the leitmotifs, and manners as the embellishment or minor motif. The books of the novel would comprise its "movements," each characterized by a dominant motif interrupted and interspersed with the other leitmotif, and the major motifs at last combined and transformed in the work's tragic coda.[5]

The same structural intention, the embodiment of thematic oppositions in the novel's formal divisions, may be discerned in *To Have and Have Not*, although the scheme fails in the execution. Quite aside from the problems inherent in Hemingway's ideological position, the intrinsic worth of his material, and his ambivalent attitude toward his characters, the circumstances of the book's composition affected its structure and contributed to its general weakness. Although the novel was originally conceived as an expansion and unification of stories Hemingway had published separately, a plan still apparent in that the three sections of the novel are titled with the hero's name and subtitled to indicate his decline during a span of time, i.e., Spring, Fall, Winter, Hemingway later adopted a more ambitious scheme. He wanted to enlarge the novel's significance by including material which he thought relevant both to the social condition of America in the mid-1930s and to the larger class conflict at issue in the civil war which had just erupted in Spain. We see this latter intention in the novel's shift of focus from Harry Morgan, the "have-not" protagonist who dominates parts 1 and 2, to the idle and depraved rich who command our attention throughout much of part 3. However, this shift of focus, carried out successfully in Hemingway's earlier novels, breaks down here. Although by part 3 we have already met some of these "have" figures, they lack the substance to contrast effectively with a protagonist who has been depicted at length and in detail. The quantitative weakness in characterization is compounded by a qualitative weakness. Vivid though they are, the characters themselves tend toward distortion and caricature. Even if Hemingway clearly dislikes the people he's describing, his distaste alone does not justify or explain the failure in characterization. After all, Robert Cohn is hardly a lovable character, yet he is brilliantly rendered. We cannot ignore the structural factor, the fact of disproportionate emphasis and imbalance, of too little too late.

Certain pieces of evidence may account for Hemingway's lapse in an aspect of craft that is usually among his greatest strengths. According to Arnold Gingrich, the founder and publisher of *Esquire*, who knew Hemingway well during the period when *To Have and Have Not* was written, a late version of the novel which Hemingway submitted to Gingrich for his opinion was considerably longer. It included full-scale and acidulous portraits of a number of upper-crust characters, but some of them were easily identifiable as real people. And worse, of real people supposedly Hemingway's friends. Gingrich then warned the writer that much of his material was libelous. Consequently, when Hemingway sent the book to press he excised major portions of it, but, already preoccupied with the Spanish conflict and his own activities on the Loyalists' behalf, neglected to make adequate revisions which would compensate for the deleted material.[6] The result is an atypically ill-structured novel, in which the thematic opposition explicit in the book's title and in some of its episodes draws small support from the general pattern of action. Furthermore, *To Have and Have Not* and another inferior work, *Across the River and into the Trees*, illustrate the unhappy result when Hemingway failed to maintain the proper distance from his material.

The Sun Also Rises and *Islands in the Stream* are also marked off into formal divisions; however, in these works the divisions represent not so much antimonies or antitheses as phases or progressions. By that I mean that the protagonists are not greatly altered from beginning to end and do not learn new values, as Frederic Henry learns love and Harry Morgan learns (incompletely and too late) the lesson of collaboration with others. As I implied in the discussion of the journey structure in *The Sun Also Rises*, the thematic movement is circular and at the end of the novel the protagonists are headed back to where they started. What the progression from Paris to Pamplona does accomplish is to contrast the effete and artificial values of the Paris expatriates and littera-teurs with the vital and integral values of primitive Spain and the bullfight, although ultimately the contrast merely reinforces what Jake and Brett knew before they began and are helpless to change. The entire episode therefore serves as a stage in the characters' experience rather than as a revolution in it. Their sensibilities are heightened, sharpened, or exacerbated by what they undergo; they are not transformed. I do not mean to suggest that this lack of profound change in the characters is a flaw in *The Sun Also Rises*. Quite the contrary. The basic and irreversible fact which determines the protagonists' behavior, the impaired sexuality of both Jake and Brett, coincides with the circular configuration of their fruitless quest for fulfillment, as they try to find meaning through changes in locale and participation in new, exciting activities. The essential tragedy of Jake and Brett, summarized in Jake's poignantly cynical "Isn't it pretty to think so?" is that they are as much themselves in Pamplona or Madrid as they were in Paris. The character who may have been taught the most by the experience in Pamplona, Robert Cohn, vanishes from the novel at just the point when those changes would become visible. The novel's pattern of circularity and cyclicality is, of course, also manifest in its title and the epigraph from Ecclesiastes.

Likewise, Thomas Hudson, the central figure of *Islands in the Stream*, remains basically the same from beginning to end, except to become slightly more desperate as his stake in life steadily diminishes after the loss of his children and his capacity to work. The individual sections of the novel measure off portions of the protagonist's life, but these seem only tenuously related in that they possess little thematic unity or structural symmetry. Perhaps, as the title implies, Hemingway meant each episode to be self-contained. In any case, each section represents a different facet of Hudson's character and depicts him in a different situation. In the first, "Bimini," he is portrayed as good craftsman, good father, and good companion. In the second, "Cuba," he performs as good talker, good drinker, and good lover. In the last, "At Sea," he behaves as the good warrior. However, although the novel provides some continuity in the recurrent allusions to Hudson's career as a painter, and to his wives and children, it does not make an especially strong case that Hudson's later behavior derives from his earlier motivations. We meet him fully formed and so he remains. Granted, Hemingway invests the narrative with some foreshadowing in that the deaths of the sons prefigure that of the father, all killed violently, and this in turn augments the novel's consistent mood of somberness, but these are as much products of the book's exposition and situations as of its structural organization. Of Hemingway's long works *Islands in the Stream* most resembles a story-cycle, perhaps a significant cue to Hemingway's reluctance to publish it during his lifetime. As we know from the case of the very inferior penultimate ending to *A Farewell to Arms*, the writer's final revisions—although perhaps not quantitatively large—can materially affect the aesthetic impact of the work.[7]

Before proceeding to a discussion of the structural technique of alternation and counterpoint, I should speak briefly of *Green Hills of Africa*. Although it is not a novel, it exhibits a careful and symmetrical design on the basis of formal divisions. In fact, Hemingway's skill in design helps compensate for his outbursts of surliness and braggadocio. Once we look behind the accounts of the slaughter of various kinds of animals and the writer's disquisitions on matters literary and social, we perceive quite a strong and consistent organization. The structure by division into distinct narrative phases implements the intention announced in the foreword: "The writer has attempted to write an absolutely true book to see whether the shape of a country and the pattern of a month's action can, if truly presented, compete with a work of the imagination." Although my own answer to this query is *No*, the structure is worth considering.

One pattern is evident in the titles and proportions of the sections. Part 1, "Pursuit and Conversation," and part 2, "Pursuit and Failure," have about the same length, are written largely in dialogue, and stress matters other than present action directly observed. Part 2, "Pursuit Remembered," and part 4, "Pursuit as Happiness," are longer, emphasize action scenes, and advance the book's subplot, the competition between the narrator and the character named Karl as to who will kill the best trophies. Another pattern involves a rather complicated time-scheme, interspersing retrospective with present narration. Parts 1 and 3 are set in the immediate past, that of a few hours ago; part 2 is in the retrospective sense of days and weeks which have gone before the present moment; part 4 begins with the immediate action, then recedes into the recent past of parts 1 and 3. The time shifts add a level of suspense and density not intrinsic to the material itself. Hemingway also unifies *Green Hills of Africa* by inculcating a journey or quest design, the hunt for the great kudu, within which are subordinated other journey-quests for other sorts of animals. The book's faults, then, cannot be attributed to structure. There's little wrong with Hemingway's craft here; rather, the defect lies in his values and tastes, which are displayed to their worst advantage.[8]

The foregoing remarks about Hemingway's practices of organizing his long narratives on the basis of the journey design, or that of formal divisions and thematic units, have already introduced, indirectly, the last of the structural techniques I will treat in this chapter, alternation and counterpoint. Obviously, when the locale of a novel's action changes from place to place, as in both *The Sun Also Rises* and *A Farewell to Arms*, or when the thematic emphasis is shifted from one body of experience to another or one group of characters to another group, as in *A Farewell to Arms*, *To Have and Have Not*, and *Islands in the Stream*, the work's mood and tempo are modulated, different kinds of actions and situations will be juxtaposed, and the total effect will be one of variety. However, this is not entirely what I have in mind. I believe that this generalized effect, germane to writers very unlike Hemingway and to many kinds of novels, can be demonstrated as operating in Hemingway's work with peculiar deliberateness and precision—enough to constitute a major structural method. Let us consider just a few specific examples of this technique in *The Sun Also Rises* and *A Farewell to Arms*, before examining *For Whom the Bell Tolls*, where it is the paramount structural principle.

In *The Sun Also Rises* the intense emotionality of Jake's relationship with Brett and the rapid, almost feverish pace of the Pamplona-festival scenes, are counterpointed by relatively static and tranquil episodes either focusing on Jake by himself or in the undemanding company of other males. So, for example, the series of encounters with Brett in book 1 and the beginning of book 2, and other encounters with Cohn during the same span, all of them irritating or unsettling, are diffused by their juxtaposition against other, more relaxing experiences: companionable meetings with Bill, the train ride to Bayonne, and especially the happy fishing trip to Burguete. The novel's turbulent climax in chapters 15 through 18 is modulated by tranquil passages at the end of chapter 14 and the San Sebastian interlude of chapter 19, before the novel again returns to the futile passion of Jake and Brett. This technique may also be observed in miniature, in single paragraphs or pages, as when Jake's misery at the end of chapter 4, produced by Brett, is offset by the opening paragraph of chapter

5, which describes his pleasure in the weather and sights of Paris and his comfort in doing his work well.[9]

Likewise, in *A Farewell to Arms* Frederic's several conversations with Rinaldi, most of them including humorous banter, temporarily relax the tension both of the war and of the hero's involvement with Catherine. Even Rinaldi's irreverent remarks about the sexual side of the relationship, comments annoying to Frederic, function as modulation. Significantly, Frederic's first visitor at the field hospital just after he has been wounded, is Rinaldi, and Rinaldi, as almost always in the early section, brightens the protagonist's mood. In the opening pages of book 2, a description of Frederic's arrival at the hospital in Milan, the little confusions about his unexpected presence and identity, and the observed detail of place, people, and behavior, lend the whole passage the desultory quality of an interlude. That is, the static quality of the passage allows it to create the very atmosphere appropriate to the situation, the more leisurely and less intense atmosphere now possible for a man removed from the war and the immediate possibility of death.

Throughout book 2 the serious and moving references to the love and intimate nights of Frederic and Catherine, all of them vaguely portentous and disturbing despite the lovers' rapture, are alleviated by the portrayal of their random and predominantly cheerful daytime activities. To focus more sharply, Catherine's premonition of her death in the rain at the end of chapter 19 is quickly followed by the vivid and high-spirited account of their day at the races. The pleasant and static scene with Count Greffi in chapter 35 immediately precedes the protagonists' danger-fraught nighttime escape to Switzerland. The idyllic narration of chapters 39 and 40 provides the last interval of happiness for the lovers before Catherine's torment and death in the final chapter, although Hemingway undercuts the seeming tranquility of these two chapters by their brevity and sequence. That is, two short structural units placed in succession produce an ominously heavy and emphatic effect, a staccato, which works against the flowing line of the narrative. The beat contradicts the lyric, so to speak.

This technique of alternation and counterpoint, which somewhat resembles the musical technique and which may be indebted to Hemingway's boyhood practice on the cello and participation in church choir (under the demanding aegis of his mother, who took music seriously and insisted upon it as an important part of her children's lives), functions nowhere better or more significantly than in For Whom the Bell Tolls. There it provides not only contrast and variety, it also comprises the novel's basic structural method.[10] Critics have often analyzed the book's thematic pattern with illuminating results. Carlos Baker's description of it as an epic tragedy unfolding in a series of concentric circles of ever-widening implication, with the bridge at the center, is especially insightful. But to the best of my knowledge no one other than Baker has speculated on the particular pattern or order of the book's organization or has written about it in depth.[11]

We note at once that the fundamental structural principle of For Whom the Bell Tolls is the same principle which serves Hemingway so well in the short stories: antithesis and opposition. However, the bulk of the novel about equals the total length of all Hemingway's short fiction, and it follows that a work of such scope and size requires a more complex and versatile method. Indeed, For Whom the Bell Tolls employs not one or two kinds of antitheses, but several operating concurrently. I see at least six distinct patterns of opposition integrated into the novel's structure, so alternated and interwoven that it attains a total effect of contrapuntal variety and complexity unsurpassed elsewhere in Hemingway's work. I will list these patterns in the order of their importance.

First, reminiscent of the love-death antithesis in A Farewell to Arms (the classic opposition in Hemingway), there is the juxtaposition of scenes and episodes depicting the temporary but passionate love of Jordan and Maria, or related scenes of vibrant and joyous life, against scenes portraying suffering, war, and death. However, in *For Whom the Bell Tolls* the love-death opposition is not embodied in or emphasized by formal structural units; thus it is less conspicuous as a principle of design, although hardly less important thematically. Second, scenes of a static or tranquil nature, usually scenes of dialogue or reflection, alternate with those presenting intense or violent action. Third, scenes constructed around a single character or opening upon the character's private thoughts are paired with scenes portraying that character with others or as part of a group. That is, Hemingway contrasts the private and the public self. It should also be observed that while the single or private character is most often Jordan, this method of contrast extends to such others as Pablo, Anselmo, El Sordo, Maria, and Andrés. Next, serious, portentous, or somber scenes are set over against comic passages or episodes. Fifth, Hemingway diversifies the dimensions of time and space, placing scenes occurring in the foreground of the narrative, its "here and now," between other scenes depicting memory, past action, background, and the elsewhere. Finally, Hemingway modulates the novel by constantly varying his narrative modes, shifting from scenes constructed dramatically, by dialogue and character interaction, to passages of exposition, the narrative rendition of action, or interior monologue.

But this list of structural patterns would be incomplete without a few important qualifications. We must be reminded that just as Hemingway's other fiction often integrates two different designs, as the outside/inside pattern merges naturally with the journey structure in *The Old Man and the Sea*, and the journey structure combines harmoniously with the thematic and formal units of *A Farewell to Arms*, so any one of these pairs of opposites may work together with any other pair or pairs, either concurrently or consecutively. For example, a scene of vibrant and pleasureful life recalled from the past and rendered dramatically in the presence of other characters may be counterpointed against a description of something disastrous in the present, constructed as narrative or as the interior consciousness of a single character. This exactly describes the design of chapter 8, wherein Jordan is first depicted by the omniscient narrator as he watches the overflight of Fascist planes and makes some gloomy private conclusions about them, then later joins the group in the cave and listens to Pilar tell of the marvelous eating, drinking, and loving of the good old days in Valencia. To enter another qualification: each element in a pair of opposites need not occupy the same space as the other element, nor is the structural unit necessarily the chapter. A single chapter may contain more than one juxtaposition, or an entire chapter may comprise only one half of an antithesis. In other words, the contrasts function qualitatively rather than quantitatively. Nor does this exhaust the list. However, we are now more than ready to look at the novel closely.

Perhaps the most apparent and certainly the most frequent contrapuntal pattern in *For Whom the Bell Tolls* is the alternation of life-enforcing scenes (usually, but not always, love scenes between Jordan and Maria) with passages communicating danger, disaster, or brutality. Thus the novel lends itself to a kind of outline-summary as follows, deliberately simplified to exhibit the antithesis of life and death. I include only the most salient instances.

Life: Jordan sees Maria for the first time (chap. 2).

Death: Pilar perceives something disastrous in Jordan's palm (chap. 2).

Life: Jordan and Maria make love in the sleeping bag (chap. 7).

Death: The Fascist planes fly over (chap. 8.)

Life: Pilar recalls the good life in Valencia (chap. 8).

Death: Pilar recalls the killing of the Fascists in the village (chap. 10).

Life: Maria and Jordan make love in the meadow and the earth moves. (chap. 13).

Death: It snows (chap. 14).

Death: Jordan confronts Pablo in the cave; Jordan ponders his disillusionment in the Loyalist cause, learned at the Hotel Gaylord; Pilar describes the smell of death (chaps. 16 through 19).

Life: Jordan and Maria again make love in the sleeping bag (chap. 20).

Death: Jordan kills the Fascist cavalryman; the Fascist unit tracks El Sordo and achieves his destruction; Jordan reflects on his father's suicide (chaps. 21, 23, 27).

Life: Jordan and Maria spend their last night together and speak of their life after the war; Maria tells Jordan of her rape by the Fascists and he comforts and reassures her (chap. 31).

Death: Jordan learns that Pablo has stolen the detonators (chap. 33).

Life: Later that same night Jordan and Maria make love for the last time, and the earth moves for them again (chap. 37).

At this advanced stage in the narrative the life-death antithesis blends into the climactic sequence of action, the attack on the bridge, although it reappears in a few vital episodes, when Maria prays for Jordan during the fighting, and he gives her his final benediction as he sends her away with the others. Note also that the opposition between life and death is almost equally balanced and symmetrical during the earlier portions of the novel, but that the death emphasis predominates as the work nears its tragic finale—an entirely appropriate transition.

The structural antithesis and alternation of life and death episodes are reiterated in the novel's major symbols. Their ambivalence reduplicates the primary structural pattern, in that each symbol advances both an affirmative and negative meaning. The bridge, an object that for Jordan culminates his whole participation in the Loyalist cause, the pivot on which the democratic future of mankind can turn (as bridges always link men with other men), also provides the place and circumstance of his death. The guerrilla cave, Jordan's temporary "home," locus of shelter, food, and for a time the best friends he has ever known, is also the setting for a bitter conflict of wills with Pablo. The mountains are beautiful, inspiring, and temporarily safe, the terrain where Jordan enjoys his most intense experience of life, but they are a trap in which he and other men die. In his sleeping bag Jordan enjoys rest and ecstatic love, yet it also prefigures his final destination, the grave. The Fascist aircraft are lovely to behold, but they signify Fascist power and "mechanized doom" to the Loyalists. Horses are valuable and noble animals, to be appreciated by any male, but they corrupt Pablo and inspire his cowardice and greed, the same greed for property he supposedly combats in the Fascists. Snow evokes man's sense of innocence and purity, but the unseasonal snow that falls in the mountains results in the discovery and annihilation of El Sordo and impedes Jordan's mission. The moving of the earth, significant of the good luck and rarity of Jordan and Maria's love, means destruction as well. The earth moves also for El Sordo when he dies, again when Jordan blows the bridge, and again, fatally, when a Fascist shell explodes under his horse.

The earth-moving episodes, really a kind of extended metaphor, relate to those scenes at the beginning and end of the novel and others interspersed throughout it which describe Jordan lying prone on the ground. This "to-earthward" metaphor is another instance of Hemingway's technique of incorporating recurrent actions into his structural designs, thereby investing them with symbolic power. We are reminded of the taxi rides in *The Sun Also Rises* and the rain in *A Farewell to Arms*. Too, by combining in the symbolism of *For Whom the Bell Tolls* both natural phenomena and man-made objects, i.e., cave, mountain, snow, bridge, sleeping bag, aircraft, Hemingway reinforces the novel's persistent suggestion of the conjunction between the human and the non-human, logic and superstition, the tangible and the metaphysical.

Despite the novel's emphatic treatment of the life-death antithesis both in structural pattern and symbolism, the result is anything but monotonous or mechanical. Hemingway achieves great diversity in mood and tempo by interweaving the life-death pattern with others. Consider some of them.

Because *For Whom the Bell Tolls* depends on certain specific and complicated historical developments for its frame of reference and is thus in one sense a "political novel," we might expect it to fall naturally into the modes of discursive narration and exposition. To the contrary, the novel's prevailing narrative mode is dramatic in the basic sense of the word, that is, the characters talk and interact directly before the reader as though he were observing them in life (or on a stage). Even passages that might have been rendered descriptively or discursively, for example, the story of Pablo's capture of the village and the killing of its gentry, take the dramatic mode by being told—as Pilar relates this particular episode to Jordan and Maria. Furthermore, her long monologue really achieves the effect of dialogue because Jordan and Maria frequently interrupt her with questions and comments. Similarly, the book's abundant political and ideological material (comparable to the "manners" dimension of *A Farewell to Arms*), especially as it conveys Jordan's—and Hemingway's—attitudes, avoids the dulling format of lecture or polemic by means of two stratagems. First, Hemingway usually limits the ideological passages to one or two paragraphs at a time; second, on the few occasions when such material runs consecutively for several pages, Hemingway casts these sequences into monologue form, either interior or dramatic. Thus, he retains the immediacy of the character's speaking voice. Moreover, in every case where the novel contains a statement of ideas, long or short, it is juxtaposed against an actual conversation, usually one discussing something basic, physical, earthy. For example, chapter 18, the extended statement of Jordan's political education by Karkov and written as exposition and interior monologue, is set between two vivid conversations with Pilar and Agustín about the smell and premonition of death, with hearty comic sidelights provided by Fernando. In the same way all of the novel's exposition and narration, whether of locale, character, or action, is balanced by an equal or greater amount of dialogue. For example, chapter 34, which consists entirely of a conjunction of narrative and interior monologue pertaining to Andrés as he makes his way toward the Loyalist lines, is placed between two chapters employing other narrative modes.

Because there are so many kinds of counterpoint and patterns of alternation in *For Whom the Bell Tolls*, a demonstration of all would be both superfluous and tedious. One of these, Hemingway's use of comic passages to relieve the tension of portentous and violent scenes, is a major technique in itself deserving of thorough analysis, and I will deal with it separately in the chapter on Hemingway's humor. Another, the alternation of static scenes or interludes with dynamic or violent episodes, has already been illustrated in *The Sun Also Rises* and *A Farewell to Arms* and need not be examined here in any length. For the moment I will treat some of the remaining structural patterns in the novel only in enough detail to verify their existence.

The alternation between past and present, often conjoined with a shift in locale, may be observed very early in the book and persistently throughout. Chapter 1 opens in the time-dimension of the story's "now," its narrative foreground, with Jordan looking down at the bridge, then flows into retrospective narration which replays Jordan's discussion with Golz in Madrid two days before, then returns in the remainder of the chapter to the immediate "here and now" of the ongoing action. In chapter 2 the past is revived by references to Jordan's predecessor, Kashkin, and Rafael's recollection of the guerrilla band's assault on the train and the rescue of Maria. Chapter 4 contrasts Jordan's presence in the cave with his memories, evoked by absinthe, of the happy life in peacetime in Paris. In the same chapter Jordan's interior passage back through time is paralleled by Pilar's account of episodes from her colorful past as consort of unsuccessful matadors. And so the technique recurs, if not in every chapter, frequently enough to expand the time-sense of the novel far beyond the moment of its present action. As Earl Rovit has observed, Hemingway's treatment of time in *For Whom the Bell Tolls* must be counted among the book's major triumphs and credited as a vital factor in its achievement of epic scope.[12] Once more, the constant movement between past and present, together with the repeated hints of the future conveyed through a series of signs and portents, produce a density and richness of texture which convince us, in our direct experience of the work itself, of the truth of Jordan's conclusion that a man can live as full a life in seventy hours as in seventy years. Note also that this interplay of past and present is accompanied by alternations in narrative perspective, the shifts from omniscient to interior narration.

The gathering excitement and concentration of the last half of the novel can be attributed to a structural technique which correlates with the accelerating intensity of the action and augments it. In contrast with the more leisurely first half of the novel, where we remain at some distance from the assault on the bridge and the general attack it signals, the pace of the second half is rapid. Of the first nineteen chapters, comprising slightly more than half the novel, fourteen are of moderate or substantial length. This naturally results in a more measured and deliberate rhythm, an *andante*, occasionally quickened by a short chapter or group of chapters (e.g., 5, 6, 7) to forestall monotony. Then, as the narrative approaches the crucial events which will settle the characters' fates, the chapters become much shorter, producing the faster tempo appropriate to the heightened quality of the action. From *andante* we go to *presto* and even *prestissimo*, in a driving series of very brief units. Of the chapters from 20 to 41, none exceed ten pages and most run considerably shorter, with an average length of about five. Only the last two chapters are of substantial length, and this is required by their function as culmination and resolution, a function which does not permit them to be fragmentary.

The acceleration of the tempo in the latter half of *For Whom the Bell Tolls* is accentuated by a contrapuntal technique of plot, as Hemingway intersperses the central action of the guerrillas' engagement with the bridge with two related but subsidiary lines of action which both enlarge the novel's scope and add to its suspense. In the first of these Hemingway temporarily switches the focus away from Jordan to El Sordo; in the second he divides the focus between Jordan's group and Andrés, as he attempts to reach Golz in time to stop the attack. The Andrés plot is especially significant to the novel's epic dimension, for through it we gain revealing glimpses into various segments of the Loyalist command and an understanding of the malfeasance which will waste the sacrifice of Jordan's life. Yet, Hemingway must maintain sufficient control of the focus to keep it from becoming diffuse, as he must also restrain the tempo to prevent it from breaking into frenzy. In my judgment, he succeeds on all counts.

For example (the last I will offer in this connection) in chapters 30 through 37, which switch back and forth between Jordan and Andrés, Hemingway holds the action in a kind of dynamic equilibrium. He allows the excitement to build in the Andrés plot, as Andrés moves through space and quickening time, encountering various obstacles and frustrations in his dash toward Golz; but he suppresses the overt action in the Jordan plot by slowing the passage of time and constantly returning us to the same spot, Jordan's sleeping bag. Thus Jordan's microcosm remains relatively static while Andrés' whirls in rapid motion, both existing in the same chronological time but in completely different psychological time. Then, in chapter 38, with Jordan's night over and the attack on the bridge about to begin, Hemingway unleashes the Jordan plot and lets it run headlong to the end, concurrently with the Andrés plot which continues until it, too, is played out. But as it must be, the final focus is on the Jordan plot, and the final stasis that of the crippled hero as he lies waiting to die.

Throughout this discussion of the structure of Hemingway's novels, which I will now conclude, and to some degree in the chapter on the short stories, I have been arguing against what I believe an outdated view of Hemingway's fiction, but one still common in Hemingway criticism. Here is a clear statement of it by a brilliant and deservedly respected scholar-critic who falls into the error of assessing Hemingway's craft as almost completely the expression of the writer's subjective attitudes:

> Hemingway is less concerned with human relations than with his own relationship to the universe—a concern which might have spontaneously flowered into poetry. His talents come out most fully in the texture of his work, whereas the structure tends to be episodic and uncontrived to the point of formlessness. *For Whom the Bell Tolls*, the only one of his six novels that has been carefully constructed, is in some respects an over-expanded short story. Editors rejected his earliest stories on the grounds that they were nothing but sketches and anecdotes, thereby paying incidental tribute to his sense of reality. Fragments of truth, after all, are the best that a writer can offer; and, as Hemingway has said, ". . . Any part you make will represent the whole if it's made truly." In periods as confusing as the present, when broader and maturer representations are likely to falsify, we are fortunate if we can find authenticity in the lyric cry, the adolescent mood, the tangible feeling, the trigger response.[13]

Hemingway's world view and sensibility, the *man* in the work, fascinate me as much as they do anyone, but they are considerations which have inspired and will continue to inspire vast amounts of biographical and psychological criticism. In the present context, therefore, I will take issue only with the statements about structure, and in reply reiterate the proposition these chapters have sought to demonstrate: if I am at all correct, at least four of Hemingway's novels, not merely one, exhibit a commendable strength, symmetry, and wholeness of construction. Furthermore, when Hemingway designed a work of fiction, long or short, he usually knew exactly what he was doing and he did it well. We can no longer accept the all-too-influential dictum that "the structure tends to be episodic and uncontrived to the point of formlessness."

3

Narrative Perspectives and Narrators' Voices

Whatever its uniqueness and originality in other respects, Hemingway's work makes only a small claim to a place in literary history for its innovations in narrative perspective. The great developments in the control of point of view which occurred in the last half of the nineteenth century and the first decades of the twentieth had been largely accomplished before Hemingway began to write. Flaubert, De Maupassant, Twain, Chekhov, James, Conrad, and Joyce were the artists who achieved the revolution in technique which banished the obtrusive and editorializing storyteller and replaced him with narrators whose visions and voices more subtly conveyed the characters' states of consciousness and posed the teller at a less easily measurable distance from the tale. These innovations and the general trends in method they inspired, for example, the tendency toward dramatic rather than pictorial presentation, the movement inward to register thought and sensation in the very instant of their birth, are now a matter of cultural record. We still ponder the significance of it all, but whether we view the development with implicit approbation, as do Robert Scholes and Robert Kellogg, or challenge it, as does Wayne Booth, the contemporary reader retains little doubt of the *fact* of the change in method.[1] Melville, Dickens, Thackeray, and Flaubert were all more or less contemporaries, but we are compelled to recognize that Flaubert is "modern" in a fundamental way that the others are not. By date a child of the nineteenth century, Flaubert belonged as much to the twentieth because he fathered a new generation of novelists, that which gave rise to Hemingway.

Hemingway's position, then, in this transition from traditional to modern methods of narration, should properly be located among those writers who consolidated and perfected what had been originated by others. His special distinction in this aspect of the art of fiction —narrative perspective or point of view—is as practitioner, not pioneer.

A survey of the range of Hemingway's fiction discloses that he wrote in both omniscient and subjective modes with apparently equal facility, though not equal frequency. Two novels, *The Sun Also Rises* and *A Farewell to Arms*, and twenty-nine short stories (including some of the interchapters of *In Our Time*) are in the first person, either the I-protagonist as in the novels and such stories as "My Old Man," "In Another Country," and "After the Storm," or the I-witness involved to some degree in the action as in "Old Man at the Bridge," "Fifty Grand," or "God Rest You Merry, Gentlemen." The bulk of the work, five novels (*The Torrents of Spring, For Whom the Bell Tolls, Across the River and into the Trees, The Old Man and the Sea,* and *Islands in the Stream*) and thirty-six stories (including the *In Our Time* interchapters), takes the third person narrator. One Novel, *To Have and Have Not*, and two stories, "A Canary for One" and "A Natural History of the Dead," are in a mixed mode, that is, a combination of first and third person. A few other stories, for example, "Today Is Friday," which is constructed as a miniature play, almost eschew narrative voice altogether. They can literally and accurately be called "dramatic." Although this tabulation does not lead at once to profound conclusions, it marks where we must begin. Critics hostile to Hemingway might seek to connect Hemingway's later preference for the third-person narrator with what they regard as the deterioration of his work after the 1920s.

However, such a deduction fails to explain why Hemingway's short stories, including such universally acclaimed masterpieces as "The Snows of Kilimanjaro" and "The Short Happy Life of Francis Macomber," both written in the omniscient mode, do not exhibit the same deterioration. Nor is there any consistent pattern of equivalence, as some might surmise, between a work's autobiographical content and its narrative perspective. True, *The Sun Also Rises* and *A Farewell to Arms* both extrapolate from Hemingway's own experience, and their first-person narrator would seem to speak for the writer himself. Yet *For Whom the Bell Tolls, Across the River and into the Trees*, and especially *Islands in the Stream*, also contain considerable autobiography and employ the omniscient viewpoint. Similarly, in the later stories the first-person speaker of "A Day's Wait" and "Wine of Wyoming" can be identified closely with the writer, yet "The Gambler, The Nun, and The Radio" and "Fathers and Sons" —particularly the latter—adopt the third-person mode, even though they draw directly on Hemingway's life. In fact, most of the Nick Adams stories, early or late, use an omniscient narrator. The last stories published in Hemingway's lifetime, "Two Tales of Darkness," likewise resist quick classification. The I-witness account of "A Man of the World" is obviously further removed from Hemingway's experience than the objective rendition of "Get Yourself a Seeing-Eyed Dog." [2] Consequently, we must beware the tendency to make simplistic correspondences between the writer and his material.

The single qualitative conclusion I would put forward with any assurance is that Hemingway is neither intrinsically different nor better in one or another narrative perspective, but that the success and credibility of his work do depend heavily upon the consistency of his command over the method chosen. Conversely, many of the flaws of his bad work can be attributed at least in part to lapses in the control of point of view. Such consistency need not be an inflexible canon of literary quality nor one applicable to all writers, as E. M. Forster argued decades ago and Wayne Booth has recently re-iterated, but it does pertain to Hemingway. However, my major intention in this chapter is not so much to judge Hemingway's fiction against a rigid standard of narrative propriety, but rather to investigate its varied perspectives and voices. Judgments, where they appear, will flow out of inquiry. My procedure will be to begin with the works which use the first-person narrator and to explore their ramifications as determined by narrative mode, then briefly consider the small body of fiction in the mixed mode, and conclude with an analysis of the various types of omniscient narration.

In regard to Hemingway's craft, the salient question about those stories which employ the I-witness or I-protagonist mode is how the narrative voice in a particular work shapes its characterizations and communicates its meanings. We must once more be warned against approaching Hemingway's I-narratives with the comfortable supposition that the first-person narrator invariably functions as a reliable spokesman for the writer's ethic or as his thinly disguised persona. Even in those cases where the I-narrator's attitude or values (or, to use the classic Hemingway word, *code*) can be equated with the writer's, we notice certain ambiguities. A few representative stories will illustrate the varying distances at which Hemingway stands from his first-person speakers.

Two examples of I-narrator accounts in which the writer impersonates a character very unlike himself are "Fifty Grand" and "Mother of a Queen." In the first the speaker is Jerry Doyle, a trainer for the story's prize-fighter-protagonist, Jack Brennan. In "Mother of a Queen," the narrator is one Roger, ex-business manager and former friend of a Mexican matador named Paco. In both stories the narrator's proximity to the protagonist and his familiarity with the milieu, prize ring and bull-ring, produce the appropriate idiom and atmosphere of authenticity. This alone lures the reader into accepting the narrative at face value. However, since in both cases the speaker's version of action and character is the only account we have, his reliability becomes a crucial consideration. It is precisely this question of reliability which lends complexity to all I-narratives, yet, surprisingly, the question has not been sufficiently stressed in readings of "Fifty Grand," among Hemingway's most popular stories, and has been totally ignored in "Mother of a Queen." These stories require a closer look.

On the surface, a surface so convincing no critic has ever peeked behind it, "Mother of a Queen" professes to be the portrait of an utterly contemptible matador who betrays virtually every commandment in the Hemingway code. Not only is the man immediately identified by the speaker as a "queen"—and Hemingway's scorn for homosexuals resounds throughout his work—he is accused of other serious breaches of conduct: miserliness, dishonesty, treachery to friends, incompetence, disregard of obligations to filial duty and family honor, total absence of pride as a man and as a Spaniard. All this we learn from a witness who was once the matador's intimate associate but has broken with so repulsive a creature and now publicly vilifies him. Just there lies the problem. Not only should the narrator's vehement hostility and contempt (as well as his readiness to tell the story to any who will listen) arouse our suspicions about his reliability, Hemingway also provides us with an important clue to the narrator's bias. Toward the end of his monologue he says: "I got the car out to go to town. It was his car but he knew I drove it better than he did. Everything he did I could do better. He knew it. He couldn't even read and write." [3]

Once we remark this element of competition and jealousy, "Everything he did I could do better," we must discount at least some of the speaker's testimony and perhaps most of it. Several intriguing possibilities emerge. For one thing, the shape of the story changes. It is no longer a simple I-witness account, with the matador as protagonist, but as much about the narrator himself. Indeed, a rereading of the story with that in mind reveals that in almost every episode the narrator himself is the hero: he is punctual and efficient where the matador is negligent; he fulfills his duties where the matador evades his; he upholds the standards of honor which Paco disgraces, and so on. Too, all the charges laid by Roger against Paco become suspect. If the matador is truly a homosexual, why does he consort with women or want to impress them? If it is Paco's custom to have a liaison with his manager, why has he not made a pass at Roger? If the narrator keeps possession of the cashbox, why not help himself to what he claims is owed him? Why does he call the matador a "bitch"?—a strange epithet for a man to use, even to a homosexual. It seems more typically what one homosexual would call another. Furthermore, despite his boast, the narrator omits one important field of competition from his claim of superiority: he offers no evidence that he himself has ever faced the horns of a bull. If all these conjectures do not amount to overwhelming proof that Roger is a thoroughly unreliable narrator, I do suggest that once we take Hemingway's cue and query the speaker's honesty, the story becomes much more interesting and substantial than anyone had thought.

"Fifty Grand" has been studied recently by such able critics as Earl Rovit and Sheridan Baker, among others. Baker notes with amusement the narrator's peculiar and narrow sophistication in the tough world of his métier, while Rovit stresses the absurdity of the story's central situation wherein the protagonist can only win by losing.[4] However, neither Baker nor Rovit (who characterizes the narrator as uncommitted and somewhat naïve) treats the story in enough detail to fully explain the narrator's role or settle the issue of his reliability.

The technique itself supports the speaker's credibility. Unlike "Mother of a Queen," which is entirely a monologue, "Fifty Grand" is much more objective. That is, although the only speaking voice we hear is necessarily that of the narrator, this narrator does not constantly interpose himself between reader and protagonist. Roger reports only *his* encounters with Paco; Jerry Doyle reports a series of encounters between Brennan and a variety of characters. Furthermore, the quality of the narrator's perception, wary of making judgments and usually limited to what was actually done and said, commends his truthfulness to the reader. Nor do I wish to impugn it. Doyle is reliable, insofar as he sees. But what and how does he see?

One significant aspect of his vision has been little emphasized: his affection and loyalty to the protagonist, the reverse of the prevailing situation in "Mother of a Queen." This need not contradict the narrator's testimony nor invalidate it, but it does impinge on the story's rendition of character and add overtones to Doyle's seemingly flat and laconic voice. Hemingway sets down a number of cues which document the speaker's bias in favor of the protagonist: "He liked me and we got along fine together," Doyle tells us early in the story; "He's a good fellow," Doyle assures another character who attacks Brennan; "Well, he's always been fine to me," Doyle says to another critical acquaintance; "You're the only friend I got," Brennan confesses to Doyle in an unguarded moment. Also, we notice Doyle's immunity to Brennan's edged tongue, his truthful responses to Brennan's worried queries about his shape for the fight, his attempt to placate the protagonist's fears with commonsense advice, and especially his solicitous attempt to keep Brennan from getting sick-drunk. What this brings to the story, despite the narrator's attempt to efface himself, is a more complex view of the protagonist's character. Because Doyle observes Brennan through eyes that seem wholly clear yet are slightly misted over with loyal affection, we, too, remark those human traits in the hero, the admixture of good and evil, which dignify "Fifty Grand" as more than a mere sports story and constitute its superiority to the hundreds of hard-boiled imitations. Only to such a narrator as Doyle could Brennan uncover his loneliness for his family, an emotion Doyle can recognize and record but, as a bachelor, not really share.

What the narrator, a horseplayer, does fully understand and covertly communicate is the gaming principle and the gamester's desperation, a vital part of Brennan's motivation in the crucial moment. Too, by advancing subtle hints Doyle's narration prepares us for Brennan's ability to keep his feet after a smash to his groin, when almost anyone else would fall. Throughout the story this ability—not so much courage, as readers usually interpret it, but sheer instinct to survive—is foreshadowed; at the very start Brennan says to the narrator, "He ain't going to last like you and me, Jerry." [5] Brennan's survival instinct goes beyond the money-lust so evident in the story's literal dimension. Money is symptom, not cause. In short, the I-witness of "Fifty Grand" can be named an "almost-reliable" narrator, dependable enough for the reader to accept his account as substantially true, thus assuring the story of its basically "realistic" and "objective" quality, yet biased to the extent that we must read between the lines. In this Hemingway achieves an imitation of life: we can agree on what happens; we cannot agree on the precise meaning of what happens.

Two other worthy stories, "Wine of Wyoming" and "The Denunciation," again almost without annotation in Hemingway criticism except for fleeting references to their biographical sources, embody first-person narrators who function significantly in the action and who convey an ethical norm which reflects the writer's own values.[6] Although the stories seem different in almost every way —locale, mood, situation—similarities can be descried. In both, the narrator-protagonist's social relationships have a moral context; in both he is thrust into the role of arbiter and adviser, which he carries out by giving verbal advice; yet in both the narrator falls short of his own standards of conduct and cannot fully redeem himself. In these stories the ironic effect and complexity arise not only from the disparity between the reader's clear view and the narrator's clouded sight but also from the narrator's own recognition of the discrepancy between his ideals and his actions.

"The Denunciation," first published in *Esquire* in 1938 and lately collected with a body of Hemingway's other work about the Spanish Civil War, revolves around a figure who has nearly the same relationship to the writer as Robert Jordan in *For Whom the Bell Tolls*; he is an American committed to the Loyalist cause yet involved in acts repugnant to his personal creed. That is, both Jordan and this protagonist are projections of Hemingway's own experience in Spain and his somewhat ambivalent identification with the Loyalists. In this case the narrator must decide whether or not to betray an old acquaintance, Luis Delgado, now on the Fascist side, whom he sees masquerading in Loyalist uniform in the Madrid café they both patronized before the war. The café is not just a place; it is a way of life, a tradition. At first the narrator attempts to serve both creeds by allowing a waiter, who has also recognized the daring Fascist, to report him to counterespionage. Thus he keeps faith with the cause which demands destruction of its enemies, yet he evades the direct responsibility of betrayal. Then, at the conclusion, in a paradoxical reversal provoked by his personal ethic, the narrator asks that the arrested Fascist be told that he, not the waiter, had reported him; thus Delgado can go to his death still believing in the splendid tradition of the café's eternal loyalty to its patrons.

By creating a narrator who demonstrates at each stage of his behavior a high degree of moral consciousness, Hemingway appears to sacrifice one of the prime advantages of the I-narrator mode, the reader's superior perception of the consequences of the narrator's actions. If the speaker sees as much as the reader, what remains for the reader to do except to listen? However, closer inspection divulges two deeper layers of meaning, one moral, one aesthetic. The narrator's vision, acute as it is, turns out to be only the eyepiece of the telescope.

First, despite the narrator's keen sensibility, he does not fully comprehend that his own tortuous moral decision is not unique to him but collects and intensifies the decisions made by all the other major characters. The precipitating decision had been Delgado's, to risk recognition in a public place behind enemy lines. From the narrator's standpoint this proves him an "utter bloody fool," but also characteristically sporting, "cheerful" and "brave." Moreover, we can infer that although the Fascist carries out a useful mission, Delgado's real motivation is his gambling impulse and his belief, announced to the narrator in the good old days when the stakes were only money, that one made the game interesting by betting more than one could afford to lose. In turn, the waiter's decision balances between his own set of personal and political ideals, whether to betray a Fascist and so uphold the cause to which he has given his sons, or to preserve the cherished name of the café and the honor of his profession as a waiter. By supplying the waiter with the number of the secret police, the narrator helps the waiter resolve his dilemma, for this can be construed as an indirect order from a preferred customer. However, by this act the narrator complicates his own problem. The waiter's dilemma would be almost comic, were not a man's life at stake.

The story's aesthetic level also attains something of the irony of the split perspective in that a number of actions unfold and are related or recalled by the narrator, but they are actions whose purport he only partially apprehends. What the narrator does not quite realize is the similarity between this episode in the café, which costs Delgado his life because his luck runs bad, and the other, years before, when the narrator had won all Delgado's money. In both episodes the narrator, a lesser but luckier man, prevails—yet without full awareness that Delgado has engaged him in a second contest. This recognition whets the reader's appreciation of the story's conclusion, for we discern that the narrator's underlying motivation is not to save the waiter's and café's good name but to repeat his earlier triumph over Delgado and ensure that the loser know the identity of the winner. In this sense the story completes the central metaphor of life as a game of chance.

The ironies of theme and character are further enhanced by our perception of certain elements ostensibly part of the story's objective scene and so routinely reported by the narrator, but without his overt recognition of their appropriateness. The narrator's conversation with the Greek comrade, which seems to be a digression, really serves a double function: as comic relief for the narrator's strained dialogue with the waiter and as corollary for the major action. The Greek's jocular accounts of his burial by a bomb and his encounter with huge octopi in deep water are paradigms for the story's motifs of the narrow margin of luck between life and death, and the wisdom of keeping away from dangerous places. Similarly, we perceive that the narrator's package of freshly butchered meat which he brings into the café and is reminded to take with him when he leaves—just after Delgado has been betrayed—objectifies his conscious self-characterization as Pontius Pilate.

So far we have observed three different uses of the first-person narrator: an unreliable I-witness in "Mother of a Queen," a relatively reliable I-witness in "Fifty Grand," and an I-protagonist in "The Denunciation." The last example of the I-narrator to be considered in the short stories before turning to the novels might be described as an I-witness-protagonist, the narrator of "Wine of Wyoming." Although these samples hardly exhaust the range of possibilities of Hemingway's first-person narrators in the short fiction, they serve quite well as models or types. For example, "God Rest You Merry, Gentlemen," "The Revolutionist," and "Old Man at the Bridge," could be grouped with "Fifty Grand"; such others as "On the Quai at Smyrna" and "My Old Man" resemble "Mother of a Queen"; and "In Another Country" and "Now I Lay Me" use an I-narrator like that in "The Denunciation." I have chosen to deal with "Wine of Wyoming" both because of its interesting technique and because it offers an opportunity for critical analysis not previously exploited by others.

I have called the narrator of "Wine of Wyoming" an I-witness-protagonist because he begins as one and becomes the other, thus combining the functions of both. As witness he speaks, or seems to speak, directly for the writer, effacing himself for much of the story and concentrating primarily on the words and actions of other characters. For three-fourths of the story's length, marked off exactly in the text by formal divisions, our attention focuses on the Fontan family, an elderly French couple and their teen-aged son. We learn only enough about the narrator to justify his presence on the scene and delineate the relationship with the Fontans which comprises the story's situation. Then, in the story's concluding section the narrator's role changes because one of his actions—his failure to keep an engagement with the Fontans to taste their newly vinted wine—precipitates the story's crisis and provides the means by which character is illuminated and values conveyed. In other words, for most of the story the narrator is needed only to tell it; in the end he is needed to make it happen. The story's irony, apprehended simultaneously by the narrator and the reader, is that a seemingly trivial decision (breaking a promise in a small social occasion) can cause irreparable damage to a fragile relationship and produce strong moral consequences.

The narrator is aligned with the Fontans in two ways. By the very nature of the story's narrative mode, his sight and hearing become the reader's. Accordingly, the narrator's affection for these people, communicated not by direct assertion but by his report of the cleanliness and order of their household, the excellence of their food and drink, and the delightfully candid and unaffected quality of their speech, converts the reader to the same attitude. Nor is our participation in the narrator's viewpoint impaired by any discrepancy or hint of unreliability in the speaker's account. His report is also authenticated in that he speaks their native language and converses with them in a mixture of French, English, and a hilarious "Franglaise" patois.

Secondly, before the story has proceeded very far, we recognize that although the narrator is American, youngish, and a writer, and the Fontans French, elderly, and barely educated, he shares their values—including their distaste for boorish Americans and the corruptions of American life. He "speaks their language" in this sense, as well. Indeed, by means of the narrator's (and the reader's) identification with the Fontans and against the "others," Hemingway poses a much more effective indictment against his homeland than those delivered as broadsides in *Green Hills of Africa*. The narrator and the Fontans represent European values: the appreciation of good food and drink, friendship based on a shared ethos; individual freedom and responsibility; self-respect as evidenced by cleanliness, order, and pride in one's work; an awareness of the greater worth of things because of their scarcity. Against these values are contrasted American behavior and standards: hypocritical and restrictive laws (Prohibition) which deny individual freedom and responsibility, and stimulate rather than suppress misconduct; people who drink to get drunk and then vomit on the table; wives who feed their husbands canned beans because they are too lazy to cook; over-abundance; prejudice; a popular culture built on the aggrandizement of sex and violence.

The story's crisis pivots on this very contrast, for in the end the narrator and the Fontans also behave like "Americans"; that is, each betrays the relationship and its common values. By not keeping his appointment with the Fontans because it was inconvenient, the narrator proves himself no better than the other customers who use the Fontans merely as a source of food and alcoholic drink. And Fontan, by drinking all the new wine he had promised to share with the narrator, demonstrates that he is prey to the same animal appetites he despises in those American *"cochons"* whom he bars from his table. Together, the narrator and Fontan suggest to us the story's theme that even the kindest and best-intentioned men are victims to their weaknesses and impulses. They, themselves, voice this recognition in their last conversation:

"Good-by," I said. "Don't think about the wine. Drink some for us when we're gone." Fontan shook his head. He did not smile. He knew when he was ruined.

"That son of a bitch," Fontan said to himself.

"Last night he had three bottles," Madame Fontan said to comfort him. He shook his head.

"Good-by," he said.

Madame Fontan had tears in her eyes.

"Good-by," she said. She felt badly for Fontan.

"Good-by," we said. We all felt very badly. They stood in the doorway and we got in, and I started the motor. We waved. They stood together sadly on the porch. Fontan looked very old, and Madame Fontan looked sad. She waved to us and Fontan went in the house. We turned up the road.

"They felt so badly. Fontan felt terribly."

"We ought to have gone last night."

"Yes, we ought to have." (*The Short Stories*, p. 466)

As in "The Denunciation" the narrator's awareness of the nuances of the human relationship and the consequences of his behavior is underscored by objective factors in the story's action and setting, some of them within the speaker's range of perception, others not. He does perceive, as the title implies, that wine amounts to more than a drink; it is an essence. The whole contrast between Europe and America (also suggested by the title's incongruous juxtaposition), and the basis for the affection between Fontan and the narrator, depends upon their mutual response to wine, which they regard not as an alcoholic beverage but as a distillation of the good things in life—taste, in the fullest meaning. Likewise, the narrator associates the Fontans with the Wyoming they inhabit, still relatively open and free but already falling into ruin. What the narrator's perception misses, but we see, is that his very description of the story's setting, the opening view of sun-baked country, parched and dusty against distant, cool, snow-capped mountains, embodies the story's conflict and foreshadows its melancholy conclusion. The Fontans' house, with its shade tree and drink, is an oasis in this desert, but not for all. The ill-behaved are turned away. When, at the end the narrator passes through the desert, with the mountains still distant, and despite his remark about the transience of good people and good land, he does not totally admit his own part in the deterioration. The oasis has been despoiled both by those who kept it and those who came to it. The sadness of the concluding episode, and the emphasis of the story's framing scenes upon the distance between the desolate here and now and the remote ideal, also quell the often exuberant humor of the work's earlier sections. Our final impression of "Wine of Wyoming" is serious rather than comic.

Both of Hemingway's masterpieces of the 1920s, *The Sun Also Rises* and *A Farewell to Arms*, are, of course, I-narratives, with the narrator as protagonist. Although neither represents a new departure in the I-narrator mode, they are exemplary of it and have so entered the literary record. For example, Scholes and Kellogg cite *The Sun Also Rises* to refute what they believe to be Joyce's artificial distinctions of literary art as lyric, epic, and dramatic, with lyric as the least estimable form because the most personal. They say, "In reality it is possible for a narrative work to be lyric art. In *The Sun Also Rises*, for example, the artist, the narrator, and the protagonist are almost united and certainly share the same viewpoint on the action and the same attitude toward it." [7] While I am not entirely easy with the characterization of *The Sun Also Rises* as "lyric," if that term tends to exclude "realistic," certainly the remarkable technical feature of the novel is the consistency and control of its narrative perspective and narrative voice.

We can discover no instance in which what Jake Barnes says to us exceeds what his vantage point in time, place, and experience allows him to know. In this Hemingway had to exercise special caution, for in his proximity to the real people and events which form the prototypes for the novel's characters and action, and in his employment of a persona only once-removed from himself, there were powerful temptations to confess too much. (According to Baker's biography, he even attempted a revision of the book into third-person narration, but abandoned it.) Consequently, the success of *The Sun Also Rises* is heavily contingent on the control of narrative perspective, a consideration not always true of I-narratives in which the writer closely identifies himself with the narrator. *Moby-Dick* is perhaps the most famous case in point. Although Ishmael, surely Melville's surrogate and spokesman, passes in and out of the tale at whim and reports many scenes he could not possibly have overheard, the consistency of the narrative voice becomes ultimately only a minor factor in the novel's totality. However, the major challenge for Hemingway, with his novel's setting in a real world and his action dependent upon specific patterns of behavior in a particular social milieu, is to preserve the illusion of immediacy, of "nowness," of the story's unfolding in the moment of its telling, despite the reader's full cognizance that the tale is already past.

Of course, there is the convention we accept automatically which requires us to suspend our disbelief when we open a book, and the I-narrative partakes of the benefits of this convention. Yet convention cannot exist in the abstract; it must be enacted in form. Accordingly, Hemingway brings into play certain effective techniques which close the juncture between the narrator's speaking voice in the "now" dimension and the action's "then." "Now" and "then" must be conjoined into a single entity; the narrator's voice must become indissolubly and indistinguishably integrated with the story it relates, if the effect of truth or realism is to be attained. Nevertheless, the freedom must be preserved for the narrator to detach himself from the action when necessary and even make comments about it. How does Hemingway accomplish this?

For one thing, he deliberately avoids identifying the narrator at a precise point in time and space and thus minimizes the artificiality that sometimes attaches to the

I-narratives of James and Conrad. Next, he has Jake step out of the narrative and speak directly to the reader almost at once. The second sentence of the novel begins, "Do not think that I am very much impressed . . ." The reminder of a separable narrator and his direct utterance ("now") is strengthened by a similar cue at the opening of the second paragraph, "I mistrust all frank and simple people . . ." Thereafter in the next several pages Hemingway continues to distinguish between the background of the action and the foreground of Jake's utterance, but always so subtly and in so firm a context of the recent past that the speaking voice soon begins to fade into the events themselves. This simple sentence indicates how Hemingway conjoins past and present tenses and alludes to the larger context in order to produce the double effect I am describing in Jake's asides to the reader: "During two years and a half I do not believe that Robert Cohn looked at another woman." [8]

However, although there continue to be frequent moments of direct discourse, Jake to the reader, throughout book 1, (e.g., pp. 9, 13, 15, 20, 22, 27, 31, 34, 39, 42, 45, 49) by the end of that section Jake has been wholly assimilated into the action he describes. We hear his asides from time to time, as in his sardonic comparison of French and Spanish waiters (p. 233), but we no longer distinguish the voice from the action because we have become habituated to their confluence. Before he vanishes into the narrative, Jake also hints at future developments without actually divulging them. A passage on page 45 is important in this respect, to provide the transition to later events and arouse the reader's curiosity yet not give anything away prematurely:

Somehow I feel I have not shown Robert Cohn clearly. The reason is that until he fell in love with Brett, I never heard him make one remark that would, in any way, detach him from other people. He was nice to watch on the tennis-court, he had a good body, and he kept it in shape; he handled his cards well at bridge, and he had a funny sort of undergraduate quality about him. . . . He had a nice, boyish sort of cheerfulness that had never been trained out of him, and I probably have not brought it out. He loved to win at tennis. . . . On the other hand, he was not angry at being beaten. When he fell in love with Brett his tennis game went all to pieces. People beat him who had never had a chance with him. He was very nice about it.

This passage also contains a number of cues, as do most of Jake's other remarks about Cohn throughout book 1, that he is not a wholly reliable narrator—at least not in his response to Cohn.

As E. M. Halliday has trenchantly written in an essay which must be the starting place for any critic who studies point of view in Hemingway's work, the writer's use of the first-person singular mode to depict Jake Barnes, a protagonist who searches for a way to live without relying too much on others, constitutes a brilliant instance of organic form: the perfect integration of theme, character, and method. Halliday says: "All of Jake's protective reserve, his individualism, and his bitter honesty, are explored and reinforced by a technical perspective which in effect is itself necessarily exclusive, individual, limited (confined to Jake's point of view), and authentic (having the tone of an eye-witness report)." [9] Furthermore, as he goes on to argue, and as I have demonstrated in the short stories, Hemingway intensifies the force of his I-narrative and deepens its resonance by correlating and counterpointing it with gestures, actions, and components of setting. Halliday calls this the "objective epitome." Since I will later treat this technique in detail, I will refrain from extensive discussion of it now. However, we can note in passing some of the recurrent patterns of objective epitome in *The Sun Also Rises*. Drinking and bathing, for example, two activities Jake reports with unusual frequency and fidelity, form a kind of ritualistic counterpoint to the characters' moral and psychological desperation, an attempt to assuage a yearning that seems physical but actually is not. Other objective epitomes of great import are the characters' travels (already mentioned as basic to structure), dancing, and especially the bullfight, which synthesizes the whole conflict between secular and ideal values, between the effete civilized life and vital primitivism.

Another issue to be summarized but not argued here since there is already an exhaustive body of criticism about it, is Jake's relationship with the "villain" of the story, Robert Cohn. As I read the story, Jake's contradictory remarks about Cohn in book 1, and his emphasis on Cohn's misbehavior thereafter, display his ambivalent feelings toward Cohn. Some of these he recognizes and confesses, others he does not; but altogether they add up to a whole conglomeration of conflicting responses: tolerance, envy, contempt, amusement, irritation, jealousy. Thus, even when Jake strives mightily to be dispassionate about Cohn ("Somehow I feel I have not shown Robert Cohn clearly"), his account communicates subliminal tones which undercut the literal message. The very fervor of Jake's indictment against Cohn's chivalric attitude toward Brett, and his anger at Cohn for refusing to give Brett up gracefully after he has fallen in love with her, amount to an unconscious identification with him. In the literal dimension of the narrative Jake overtly satirizes Cohn and finally rejects him, but, I think, covertly admires him for the same qualities he mocks. In a sense, Cohn is Jake's double, and only behaves toward Brett as Jake himself does—in his own way. The real difference is in their style: Cohn's sentimentality and loss of control in public contrast sharply with Jake's stoicism and restraint, but what they feel is really much the same.[10]

One aspect of narrative perspective which has not been much detailed, although Halliday considers it briefly and cogently, is the method by which Hemingway expands the limits of his first-person account by melding into it interludes of interior monologue without sacrificing the convention or immediacy of the speaking voice. For example, in the long passage (chap. 4) when Jake looks at his damaged body in the mirror and thinks about his wound, Hemingway conjoins several levels of narrative voice simultaneously. There is the leading voice of the narrator speaking within the convention: "I lit the lamp beside the bed, turned off the gas, and opened the wide windows." There is the "now" sense of Jake's asides to the reader: "I try and play along and not make trouble for people." There is Jake's thought to himself, silent interior monologue: "That was a typically French way to furnish a room. Practical, too, I suppose." And then there is Jake's interior monologue structured as though spoken aloud, direct discourse to himself: "To hell with you, Lady Ashley." In fact, such moments as the last one neutralize the reader's awareness of the artificiality of the "aside," because after only a few such cases we neither can nor want to differentiate between Jake's comments to himself and his asides to us.

The pivotal distinction between the perspectives of the first-person narrators of *The Sun Also Rises* and *A Farewell to Arms*, a distinction which has sometimes escaped even watchful critics, is that of the time-dimensions each narrator occupies. Jake Barnes's point of view, as we have seen, evolves out of a sense of the continuous present, of the narrator's close proximity in time to the events he recounts. To recapitulate: although we begin the novel with the awareness that Jake speaks to us about events already transpired, the action is so recently completed and the narrator so quickly steps down from his vantage place and into the action that the total effect of the novel is that of "now," or "just yesterday." By simple deduction, one of the prominent reasons why Jake generally refrains from subjective interpretations of character and action, and why, when he does so with Cohn, his opinions are inconsistent, is that he lacks sufficient time to distance from the events narrated and explain them fully. This situation squares with the chronology of the novel's composition. Hemingway started a draft of the novel in July 1925, only a few days after the experience of the trip to Pamplona in the company of Harold Loeb, Duff Twysden, Donald Ogden Stewart, Bill Smith, and Pat Guthrie, prototypes of the book's main characters; he finished the draft in less than two months. Even with some delay for revisions the novel appeared in October 1926, only fifteen months after the real-life events which inspired it.[11]

In contrast, the first-person narrator of *A Farewell to Arms*, like Jake Hemingway's persona, speaks from a position several years remote from the occurrence of the action he describes. Unlike *The Sun Also Rises* there is a considerable span between the telling of the tale and the living of it—just as the novel itself was written some ten years after Hemingway's wounding at Fossalta and his romance with Agnes Von Kurowsky. I cannot stress this factor too emphatically because it offers a direct answer to the criticism that the novel is flawed by editorial intrusions (and thus inferior to *The Sun Also Rises*), and it explains why Frederic Henry can appear so calm while he recounts his tragic losses, a calm many interpreters confuse with incapacity for feeling.[12] This situation challenges the artist in the opposite way from the problem raised by *The Sun Also Rises*: to insist too blatantly upon the narrator's distant removal from the action is to reduce its immediacy and reality, as well as the narrator's credibility. Yet, to merge him with it as thoroughly as Jake Barnes is finally integrated would be to risk the reflective quality, the poignancy, the overview requisite to a tale in which the hero abandons his duty as a soldier to have the woman he loves, only to lose her as well. The problem, then, is to place the narrator at exactly the right distance from the narrative, far enough to see it whole, not too far to see it clear. Hemingway relies upon three methods to attain his ends.

First, he tends to avoid the urgent nowness of the narrator's direct utterances and asides to the reader, especially in the early portions of the novel. Where Jake slips easily into direct discourse in the opening chapters to explain more fully about Cohn or tell us what Pernod is, Frederic Henry remains much more consistently within the strict convention of the narrative past. In those salient later instances where he does temporarily abandon the past tense or seems to speak to us man-to-man—as in the cases Halliday calls subjective intrusions: the famous rejection of the abstract terms "sacred," "glorious," and so forth (chap. 27, p. 191), or the bitter statement about how the world kills the best people first (chap. 34, p. 258–59), I would argue that these are precisely the evidence of the narrator's sufficient removal from his experience to be able to draw profound conclusions about its meaning.[13] In retelling what he once had lived, he naturally and spontaneously joins his musings and reflections with the real events that produced them. In the first instance, the "sacred" passage, Hemingway keeps his narrator's opinions rigidly within the convention of the past tense; in the second case he breaks him out of it momentarily to convey the effect not so much of an aside to the reader but of the interior monologue so painful it forces itself to be spoken aloud. The other such "subjective" passages in the novel are likewise controlled in this manner, either the retrospective conclusion or the brief, intense dramatic monologue—both extrapolations from the action.

The second and more significant method by which Hemingway maintains the proper distance between teller and tale is the establishment of a historic sense, an atmosphere proper to action completed long ago. Hemingway attains this sense by strategically placing a series of cues which emphasize the lapse of years and the narrator's present removal from what he had once experienced. These cues tend to melt into the text (like Jake's asides) once the reader is caught up in the narrative momentum, but if we search for them we find them without great difficulty. "In the late summer of that year," the novel begins, while chapter 2 begins "The next year there were many victories." Here are other such cues, which I merely list:

"We knew it was all over for that year" (chap. 2, p. 6).

"He had always known what I did not know and what, when I learned it, I was always able to forget. But I did not know that then, although I learned it later" (chap. 3, p. 14).

"I did not know until later" (chap. 10, p. 65).

"I never learned anything about her" (chap. 17, p. 112).

"We had a lovely time that summer" (chap. 18, p. 116).

"The summer went that way. I do not remember much about the days" (chap. 19, p. 122).

Another less evident method Hemingway uses to suggest action completed in the past is to vary verb tenses, juxtaposing the conventional narrative past, the perfect tense, which conveys action circumscribed within a particular span of time, with the imperfect tense connoting a continuous stream of action over an indefinite period. He brings this technique to bear especially in describing the relationship of Frederic and Catherine. Consider this sample, noting especially the use of the imperfect form "would":

> I loved to take her hair down and she sat on the bed and kept very still, except suddenly she would dip down to kiss me while I was doing it, and I would take out the pins and lay them on the sheet and it would be loose and I would watch her while she kept very still and then take out the last two pins and it would all come down and she would drop her head and we would both be inside of it, and it was the feeling of inside a tent or behind a falls.
>
> She had wonderfully beautiful hair and I would lie sometimes and watch her twisting it up in the light that came in the open door and it shone even in the night as water shines sometimes just before it is really daylight. She had a lovely face and body and lovely smooth skin too. (Chap. 17, p. 118)

By such a conjunction of tenses, augmented by the repetitions and the syntactical parallelism and balance, Hemingway instills the narrative with multiple levels of appeal. The long sentences, given flow and continuity by the "and," suggest that through the agency of memory Frederic's account has been transformed from report to lyric evocation. In the memory every attribute of the loved one becomes exalted and rendered more precious than in life. What were tender moments are recalled as sheer and unbroken rapture. Memory confers upon physical actions the quality of metaphor: "the feeling of inside a tent or behind a falls," "as water shines sometimes just before it is really daylight." Yet, simultaneously, there is the portentous and disquieting finality of the simple past tense: "she had," "she had"—innocuous within the narrative convention but in retrospect the sound of doom. What was is gone and can never be regained. I find no instance of a passage of like effect or construction in *The Sun Also Rises*.

All these techniques, the conflation of retrospection with action, the view of the past as a historic entity, and the employment of a rhetoric of nostalgia, come together in three passages in the novel's last chapter which record and seal the protagonist's anguish: the first, a dramatic monologue, voices the fear that Catherine may die; the second, a combination of interior and dramatic monologue, relates the imminent threat of death to nature's biological trap; the third, a frenzied dramatic monologue, prays against Catherine's impending death. The remaining pages return to a completely objective account, cast in the conventional narrative past and devoid of overt feeling. The protagonist has spent it all and Hemingway must exercise caution that the closing paragraphs of the novel do not lapse into melodrama. They must reduplicate the hollow tones of the narrator, come to the end of his tale a decade after it happened and now drained of feeling, numbed by the reliving of the story in its retelling. Thus the reader's emotion must be evoked, not manufactured.

The consistency of Hemingway's control over the first-person narrative mode in his best work sets the standard against which we judge his less successful writing. By this standard I find several instances in which the mixture of first person with other voices appears to have no justification or effective purpose. In all these cases Hemingway's personal or polemical impulses overruled his discrimination with more or less serious consequences. The default is not disastrous in "A Canary for One," wherein the first-person speaker follows a lady into her train compartment and into her psyche, when he has no business in either place. Once the major action begins, the story hews to its proper perspective. The only reason we can surmise for any lapse is the narrator's dislike for the character and his need to stress her private weaknesses so as to later discredit her public opinion. Otherwise, it is a well-crafted story, especially in its use of objective detail to epitomize the narrator's mood and condition. In "A Natural History of the Dead" the lapse is more serious and reflects a general disorder in form. In fact, the work cannot properly be called a story at all; some such term as *sketch* would be better. Actually it is a personal essay, with a tacked-on fictional episode as conclusion, whose narrative voice can be equated with Hemingway's own, heard all too frequently during the 1930s in *Green Hills of Africa, Death in the Afternoon,* and a series of contributions to *Esquire.* As one critic has demonstrated, the work has some interesting features and there are vivid flashes of writing in it; but judged by the canons of craft we are applying here, it is very defective indeed.[14] Students of Hemingway's career will find it mainly intriguing for its revelation of the writer with his craft unbuttoned.

The worst, because extended, example of Hemingway's malfeasance in handling the first-person mode is *To Have and Have Not,* where it signifies the fundamental problem of Hemingway's relationship with his material. I will not heap much more abuse on the already large amount which has been provoked by this novel. On this occasion errors in narrative perspective are as much symptom as cause of the novel's defects. When Hemingway breaks into the narrative as an editorializing omniscient speaker to praise, blame, or advertise elements of the action he should have dramatized or objectified, we can see that the writer's broader perspectives, not only those of the method, have gone out of focus. Conversely, when the novel does remain consistent, with the writer totally absorbed into his first-person narrator—as is the case in all of part 1—the aesthetic result is at least tolerable.

Finally, there is Hemingway's frequent and accomplished use of the perspective of limited omniscience, that point of view in which the third-person narrator so systematically confines himself to the focus on a single character the effect closely resembles the I-narrative. The great difference—a prime advantage of limited omniscience—is that the narrator retains the freedom to go outside the character's perspective and supply information beyond his scope. This information may consist of the depiction of action in another time and place, the thoughts and emotions of other characters within the protagonist's sphere, or the protagonist's own affective states rendered as interior monologue or stream of consciousness. What distinguishes limited omniscience (or "selective omniscience" as it has been variously called) from traditional, full, or editorial omniscience is the narrator's abstention from commentary and interpretation and his self-limitation to the vantage point of one character. Or, as is sometimes the case, the third-person narrator will shift the focus to each of several characters in turn. This has been named multiple selective omniscience.[15] In any event, and whether focusing on one character or several, the third-person narrator remains neutral. He removes himself from the role of interposition between reader and story and by so doing creates a scenic or dramatic illusion. We see rather than listen; or if we listen, the voices we hear are the characters', not the narrator's. In sum, the difference between editorial and limited omniscience is that between the narrative methods of *Vanity Fair* and *Portrait of the Artist as a Young Man,* to name two extreme examples. *Dubliners* shows the mode of limited omniscience already developed to a high degree of sophistication, and no doubt Hemingway learned a good deal from it. But all this is familiar literary history which I summarize only to provide a foundation for the discussion of Hemingway's methods.

One of Hemingway's earliest stories, "Up in Michigan," one of the two pieces of his apprentice work to escape loss when a suitcase full of manuscripts was stolen in Paris in December 1922, demonstrates his competence in the technique of limited omniscience. Although in texture obviously indebted to Gertrude Stein and Sherwood Anderson, the point of view is not. This passage indicates the Stein-Anderson influence: Anderson in the naïveté of attitude, simple diction and the emphasis on the characters' emotions; Stein in the heavy repetitions.[16] Yet it also manifests Hemingway's effort to produce the effect of a subjective voice without actually using an I-narrator.

> Liz Coates worked for Smith's. Mrs. Smith, who was a very large clean woman, said Liz Coates was the neatest girl she'd ever seen. Liz had good legs and always wore clean gingham aprons and Jim noticed that her hair was always neat behind. He liked her face because it was so jolly but he never thought about her.
>
> Liz liked Jim very much. She liked it the way he walked over from the shop and often went to the kitchen door to watch for him to start down the road. She liked it about his mustache. She liked it about how white his teeth were when he smiled. She liked it very much that he didn't look like a blacksmith. She liked it how much D. J. Smith and Mrs. Smith liked Jim. One day she found that she liked it the way the hair was black on his arms and how white they were above the tanned line when he washed up in the washbasin outside the house. Liking that made her feel funny. (*The Short Stories*, p. 81)

In the second paragraph, through a combination of reiteration of key phrases and a sequence of short sentences of similar construction, Hemingway connotes the simplicity, the one-thing-at-a-time quality, yet also the obsessiveness of Liz's perceptions. The obsessiveness, of course, rises out of her unrealized but nevertheless urgent sexual attraction to the man. This much is apparent, even transparent. But what Hemingway pursues and captures in the whole story is a level of voice (not only diction but also intonation) and a vantage point which tend to transform the omniscient narrator into a first-person narrator. The speaker in the first paragraph is truly omniscient in what he knows, including what Jim notices about Liz and thinks about her, but the speaker's point of view in the broadest definition of that term—not just "narrative perspective" but *attitude*—is identical with that of the characters. Consequently, we discern no discrepancy, no distance, between narrator and characters even though he is not one of them.

By the same method the narrative voice in the Nick Adams stories which dominate *In Our Time* remains omniscient in the technical sense, but functions with subjective immediacy, because the depth of the narrator's perception rarely if ever exceeds that probable for the protagonist. The following excerpt from "The Three-Day Blow" illustrates how Hemingway used largely objective narration to delineate characters' emotional states:

"I'll get a chunk from the back porch," Nick said. He had noticed while looking into the fire that the fire was dying down. Also he wished to show he could hold his liquor and be practical. Even if his father had never touched a drop Bill was not going to get him drunk before he himself was drunk.

"Bring in one of the big beech chunks," Bill said. He was also being consciously practical.

Nick came in with the log through the kitchen and in passing knocked a pan off the kitchen table. He laid the log down and picked up the pan. It had

contained dried apricots, soaking in water. He carefully picked up all the apricots off the floor, some of
them had gone under the stove, and put them back
in the pan. He dipped some more water onto them
from the pail by the table. He felt quite proud of
himself. He had been thoroughly practical. (*The
Short Stories*, pp. 120–21)

Hemingway depicts the comic tipsiness of the boys in
two ways: in the objective action of Nick's spilling of the
apricots and his meticulous attempt to set things right,
and in the insistent description of the boys' intentions
as "practical." Although the term itself reflects an authorial interpolation, the narrative voice remains sufficiently
neutral and consonant with the characters' perspective
to convey almost the illusion of interior monologue. That
is, Hemingway plays off the contrast between the norm
of rational and well-coordinated behavior which is typical of the sober condition, and the passion for precision of
two intoxicated boys striving to conduct themselves with
dignity. The construction of the passage conjoins with
the narrative voice to produce this effect, for the series
of sentences specifying in detail how Nick retrieves the
apricots enhances the clumsiness of the action by setting
it against the control of the style. Too, in the episode of
the apricots Hemingway poses an objective epitome for
the domesticity Nick has tried to avoid in breaking his
engagement to Marjorie.

Hemingway only rarely lapses into authorial comment
on action and character in his short stories written in the
omniscient mode. I find discrepancies in but two stories,
and these would probably be overlooked by most readers.
"Soldier's Home" begins with an editorializing and even
occasionally didactic narrator (e.g., "Krebs acquired
the nausea in regard to experience that is the result of un-
truth or exaggeration") before it changes to limited omniscience and dramatic scene. "Mr. and Mrs. Elliott" un-
typically uses the editorial narrator throughout, with one
particularly blatant authorial intrusion in the story's first

paragraph: "Like all Southern women Mrs. Elliott dis-
integrated very quickly under sea sickness, travelling at
night, and getting up early in the morning." We can
only explain this lapse, but not excuse it, as a prefigura-
tion of the bad Hemingway of the early 1930s. In this
story it seems to have been aroused by Hemingway's
antipathy for the characters he was depicting, a distaste
too strong and reckless to be constrained by technique.

The opposite emotion produces the same result in
Across the River and into the Trees. The shifts in this
novel from neutral and limited omniscience to editorial
omniscience are much less frequent and obvious than
the corresponding first-person inconsistencies in *To Have
and Have Not*, but they signal a similar uncertainty in
the relationship between narrator and protagonist. Despite the differences in method and structure of the two
novels (although, curiously, *Across the River and into the
Trees* also began as a short story), Hemingway's desire to
aggrandize his hero again overcame his artistic good
sense. We also note a peculiar connection between Harry
Morgan and Colonel Cantwell; they are Hemingway's
least appealing protagonists. Thus when Hemingway intrudes to say of Cantwell, whose whole configuration
little recommends him, "He did not notice the old used
steel of his eyes nor the small, long extending laugh
wrinkles at the corners of his eyes, nor that his broken
nose was like a gladiator's in the oldest statues. Nor did
he notice his basically kind mouth which could be truly
ruthless," we believe the narrator even less than if he
had remained noncommittal.[17] Furthermore, although
Hemingway uses an ostensibly objective method to describe his protagonist, he relies excessively on Cantwell's
observations, musings, and interior monologues. This
concentration accentuates the novel's lack of action and
makes it by far the most static and least modulated of
Hemingway's long works.

In contrast to these evidences of Hemingway as med-
dling omniscient narrator, and much more typical of his
craft, is the perspective of "Big Two-Hearted River."

Here limited omniscience functions perfectly to connote both the geographical isolation of the protagonist and his emotional insularity. Hemingway's technique in this story, deliberately rigorous and narrowly focused to depict the cautious step-by-step operation of the protagonist's sensibility, has sometimes been interpreted or misconstrued by hostile critics as the writer's incapacity for complex thought and his distrust of intellection.[18] But the method is purposeful; it replicates the hero's condition. He must concentrate on little physical actions and on basic sensations, so that ideas and words are consciously avoided. As a result, the story attains an almost unbearable concentration. Its twenty-two pages of narration, virtually uninterrupted by dialogue, comprise one of the longest such sequences in all Hemingway's work. Passages of interior monologue, interwoven with objective narration, provide almost the only relief.

His mouth dry, his heart down, Nick reeled in. He had never seen so big a trout. There was a heaviness, a power not to be held, and then the bulk of him, as he jumped. He looked as broad as a salmon.

Nick's hand was shaky. He reeled in slowly. The thrill had been too much. He felt, vaguely, a little sick, as though it would be better to sit down.

The leader had broken where the hook was tied to it. Nick took it in his hand. He thought of the trout somewhere on the bottom, holding himself steady over the gravel, far down below the light, under logs, with a hook in his jaw. Nick knew the trout's teeth would cut through the snell of the hook. The hook would imbed itself in his jaw. He'd bet the trout was angry. Anything that size would be angry. That was a trout. He had been solidly hooked. Solid as a rock. He felt like a rock, too, before he started off. By God, he was a big one. By God, he was the biggest one I ever heard of. (*The Short Stories*, pp. 226–27)

But even in most such cases in "Big Two-Hearted River" the interior monologue is not so much conscious inner speech as articulated instinct or sensation. Just as in this passage, which hovers between outside and inside narration, moving alternately from the omniscient statement of concrete action and the protagonist's response to that action, to unvoiced perception, and at last to voiced perception, the final statement is not a "concept." This distinctive merger of omniscient and interior voices was a method Hemingway mastered early in his career and favored in much of his best work, a type of uncued interior monologue or *style indirect libre*. We have something of it in the sentence "There was a heaviness, a power not to be held, and then the bulk of him as he jumped," which sounds more like Nick's thoughts to himself than the narrator's address to us. As a consequence the entire method, point of view and style together, combines to render that experience without reflection, act without idea, which Nick seeks to restore his health. By employing so strictly limited an omniscience Hemingway abolishes all selfhoods and identities, the speaker's as well as the hero's.

At the other extreme from the almost unbearable concentration in the point of view of "Big Two-Hearted River" we have the multiple perspectives and varied methods of "The Short Happy Life of Francis Macomber" and "The Snows of Kilimanjaro." Although "The Snows of Kilimanjaro" does employ a limited omniscience quite consistently focused on the protagonist, it achieves an effect of broader scope by alternating dialogue, interior monologue, and interior flashback with a minimum of objective narration. "The Short Happy Life of Francis Macomber" smoothly integrates a prevailing neutral omniscience with quick selective glimpses into the minds of all the major characters, especially Macomber and Wilson, but also Mrs. Macomber and even, momentarily, a lion. This method not only produces an extraordinary rapidity of tempo, which accords with the violence and unpredictability of the action, but also holds the key to Mrs. Macomber's motivation in shooting her husband. The critical hubbub has died down now, but there has been much gratuitous argument claiming that Mrs. Macomber commits cold-blooded murder.[19] Such an interpretation ignores the text and superimposes the critic's ingenuity upon the conventions of narrative perspective. When an omniscient author makes an assertion from the vantage point of a particular character, we have no right to deny it. So Hemingway writes, in the crucial passage:

> Wilson had ducked to one side to get in a shoulder shot. Macomber had stood solid and shot for the nose, shooting a touch high each time and hitting the heavy horns, splintering and chipping them like hitting a slate roof, and Mrs. Macomber, in the car, had shot at the buffalo with the 6.5 Mannlicher as it seemed about to gore Macomber and had hit her husband about two inches up and a little to one side of the base of his skull. (*The Short Stories*, p. 36)

This objective statement is unequivocal and completely excludes a willful and deliberate act of murder. At most we can infer an unconscious desire on the lady's part to see her husband dead, and a concomitant deflection of her aim. Or, we can accept the text at face value and judge it sheer accident, caused by panic and careless gun-handling. Furthermore, such a reading, legislated by the point of view, yields a more profound characterization by throwing the emphasis back upon Wilson and showing just how tough he can be in a crisis. The imputation of murder is not Hemingway's but Wilson's, and whether or not he really believes it (since Wilson has not looked over Mrs. Macomber's shoulder and we have), it gives him the upper hand a true man must always have over a woman, if he is to enjoy the happy life proper to the authentic male. That is one of the story's basic messages, and control of narrative perspective is instrumental to it.

In both stories, each of them packed with enough substance to fill a novel, we observe most of the techniques Hemingway applied at length in *For Whom the Bell Tolls*. In that novel, as I have implied, the use of the omniscient mode enables the novel to open out to the epic magnitude congruent with its theme of the complete interdependence of man and mankind. Although the action centers largely on Robert Jordan, it deviates frequently enough in time, locale, and focus to accentuate the epic sense and provide a diversity of attitude and response. Accordingly, we get transient but illuminating insights into the minds of Pilar, Anselmo, Pablo, Maria, Andrés, El Sordo, Golz, and Karkov (an incomplete list), each of whose perspectives refracts the reader's view of the action and the hero. Perhaps more important, the multiple selective omniscience enables Hemingway to portray Jordan as a reflective man, one constantly apprised of the implications of what is happening around him, yet restrains the writer from adopting the invidious role of editorializing and didactic narrator.[20] This passage exemplifies Hemingway's method of incorporating action and reflection, the one originating spontaneously in the other:

> Robert Jordan sunk his elbows into the ground and looked along the barrel at the four riders stopped there in the snow. Three of them had their automatic rifles out. Two carried them across the pommels of their saddles. The other sat his horse with the rifle swung out to the right, butt resting against his hip.
>
> You hardly ever see them at such range, he thought. Not along the barrel of one of these do you see them like this. Usually the rear sight is raised and they seem miniatures of men and you have hell to make it carry up there; or they come running, flopping, running, and you beat a slope with fire or bar a certain street, or keep it on the windows; or far away you see them marching on a road. Only at the trains do you see them like this. Only then are they like now, and with four of these you can make them scatter. Over the gun sights, at this range, it makes them twice the size of men.[21]

Notice again here the inward drift from objective-omniscient statement of an external scene, to the transitional instant when the mind begins to internalize experience ("You hardly ever see them at such range"), to the interior monologue which becomes a stream of memory welding the past and the present into a single ongoing entity. As in *A Farewell to Arms*, the tactics of the change are simple and inconspicuous: a shift from third-person to second-person pronouns, an alteration in verb tenses from past to present.

Another passage illustrates the conjunction of action, dialogue, and shifting perspective within the same episode:

"I am glad to see thee," Anselmo said. "But I was just about to leave."

"Like hell you would have," Robert Jordan said happily. "You'd have frozen first."

"How was it up above?" Anselmo asked.

"Fine," said Robert Jordan. "Everything is fine."

He was very happy with that sudden, rare happiness that can come to anyone with a command in a revolutionary army; the happiness of finding that even one of your flanks holds. If both flanks ever held I suppose it would be too much to take, he thought. I don't know who is prepared to stand that. And if you extend along a flank, any flank, it eventually becomes one man. Yes, one man. This was not the axiom he wanted. But this was a good man. One good man. You are going to be the left flank when we have the battle, he thought. I better not tell you that yet. . . .

"Listen," he said to Anselmo. "I'm awfully glad to see you."

"And me to see thee," the old man said.

As they went up the hill in the dark, the wind at their backs, the storm blowing past them as they climbed, Anselmo did not feel lonely. He had not been lonely since the *Inglés* had clapped him on the shoulder. The *Inglés* was pleased and happy and they joked together. The *Inglés* said it all went well and he was not worried. The drink in his stomach warmed him and his feet were warming now climbing. (Pp. 199–200)

Actually, this episode (of which the excerpt is but an abbreviated part) incorporates several narrative voices speaking alternatively, each of about equal importance. The omniscient voice both provides the necessary exposition and makes comments that do not intrude because they belong within the perspective of the appropriate character ("that sudden, rare happiness that can come to anyone with a command in a revolutionary army"), and because the omniscient voice suddenly speaks in the character's very tones ("the happiness of finding that even one of your flanks holds"). Once inside Jordan's head, we remain there for a few moments and listen to his dialogue with himself. Next, we listen to a brief dramatic exchange, the audible voices of Jordan and Anselmo in conversation, which serves to shift the focus of attention to Anselmo. As with Jordan we begin with the omniscient voice ("He had not been lonely") and follow it as it blends into Anselmo's inner speech, the point of transition contained in the word "*Inglés*," native to Anselmo. This continues to be the leitmotif of Anselmo's discourse, retained even when the omniscient voice again enters, as the episode continues beyond the particular excerpt I have included here. In short, the passage demonstrates Hemingway's effortless movement back and forth between two different characters, two different perspectives, and objective and subjective presentation. Although we can isolate the technique and graph it in a study such as this, in the novel itself the reader would only be aware of the illusion of felt life.

The multiple perspective in *For Whom the Bell Tolls* also offers Hemingway the means to import a quantity of ideological material without transgressing the narrative convention or calling our attention to a break in continuity. Hemingway had failed to solve the same problem in *To Have and Have Not*, where, as we have

seen, the politics appear extraneous. But Jordan's political convictions and his concept of the significance of
the war are not only germane to the book's whole purpose and structure, they enter in a manner consistent
with method and point of view. By establishing Jordan
as the sort of character who evaluates a situation even
as he experiences it, a fact Hemingway makes emphatically clear early in the novel by merging objective action
with interior monologue in the manner I have demonstrated, Hemingway accustoms us to participate fully in
the workings of the protagonist's mind. However, he
carefully refrains from the discussion of politics until
we have become partner to Jordan's opinions on many
things: the impact of wealth on character, Spanish folk-
ways, duty, absinthe, killing, and so on. In fact, the first
passage of any length setting forth Jordan's ideology
does not appear until chapter 11, well after a hundred
pages. By that time, if the reader is at all sympathetic
he shares Jordan's perspective and regards him as a projection of himself. Technically, any narrative perspective could serve to communicate ideas, but the use of
limited omniscience avoids most of the risks: the artificiality and didactiveness of the traditional editorial-
omniscient narrator, the loss of immediacy and vibrancy
in the I-narrator mode if the speaker pauses too long to
tell us what he is thinking rather than what he is living.

The omniscient perspective of *The Old Man and the
Sea*, as appropriate to a work of its length and situation,
is narrowly focused and limited in order to concentrate
intensively on a single man and a single action. Yet,
within this method Hemingway also adopts some interesting variations. With a single exception, when we dip
quickly into the mind of the boy, Hemingway scrupu-
lously maintains the third-person voice during the book's
first twenty pages, which treat events on shore. We know
the contents of Santiago's thoughts by means of the
narrator's statement of them but we do not share in
them directly. However, once Santiago is by himself and
rows out to sea we enter his mind with increasing fre-

quency, sometimes moving from outside to inside by means of traditional cues ("he thought," "he said"), sometimes gliding over directly from third person into the subjective voice. In other words, we get to know Santiago better once we have him alone. The initial instance of Santiago's voiced thought is indicated by quotation marks; after that the text uses no typographical markers except for what is spoken aloud. Thus to the reader third-person and first-person narration seem visually the same, as they do aurally. Likewise, the seams of the narrative, the transitions in voice, are kept from intruding upon the reader's attention. This is a typical passage:

> The fish moved steadily and they travelled slowly on the calm water. The other baits were still in the water but there was nothing to be done.
>
> "I wish I had the boy," the old man said aloud. "I'm being towed by a fish and I'm the towing bitt. I could make the line fast. But then he could break it. I must hold him all I can and give him line when he must have it. Thank God he is travelling and not going down."
>
> What I will do if he decides to go down, I don't know. What I'll do if he sounds and dies I don't know. But I'll do something. There are plenty of things I can do.
>
> He held the line against his back and watched it silent in the water and the skiff moving steadily to the northwest.
>
> This will kill him, the old man thought. He can't do this forever. But four hours later the fish was still swimming steadily out to sea, towing the skiff, and the old man was still braced solidly with the line across his back. (Pp. 42–43)

Here we observe again that skillful merger of narrative modes at which Hemingway excels. The passage begins with third-person narration but with the writer so closely identified with the protagonist in time, place, and outlook, we cannot tell them apart: "The other baits were still in the water but there was nothing to be done." It then shifts to direct utterance, set off by the conventional punctuation and phrase, to be swiftly succeeded by a passage of uncued interior monologue ("What I will do"), another brief objective statement, and finally a paragraph integrating cued interior monologue ("This will kill him") and omniscient narration.

However, despite its artistry the novel commits one serious error in technique which damages its claim to the stature of miniature masterpiece. It is strictly an error in narrative perspective but it manifests Hemingway's occasional tendency to aggrandize his heroes beyond their earned value. In this case the writer cannot refrain from emphasizing a correspondence between his noble old fisherman and Jesus Christ, an association which ought to have remained implicit. Here is the mistake, which occurs late in the work: " 'Ay,' he said aloud. There is no translation for this word and perhaps it is just a noise such as a man might make, involuntarily, feeling the nail go through his hands and into the wood" (p. 107). Without this intrusion from an editorializing narrator who is alien to the story, the protagonist's character would be more, not less, impressive. It is a connection the reader might make for himself anyway, since the configuration of the entire work tends toward allegory. Moreover, once the equation has been announced, the later passage which details Santiago's painful climb up the hill to his shack, bearing the mast of his boat on his shoulders, would not seem so transparent an allusion to Christ's last ascent. We rarely conceive that simple editing could improve Hemingway, but this is a case where the excision of just a few words—at minimum everything after "involuntarily" in the above passage, or better, everything after "aloud"—would be much to the work's advantage.

The method of *Islands in the Stream* more resembles *The Old Man and the Sea* than *For Whom the Bell Tolls*. It is cast in the mode of limited omniscience and remains there consistently, with the characteristically fluent shifts between third-person narration and interior monologue. Hudson, a formidable protagonist, owes his quality to the writer's dramatization of him rather than to any superfluous praise from an editorializing narrator. Altogether, the novel is quite well crafted and offers many examples of tight, vivid writing and stirring action. Why, then, do we care less about Hudson than about Jordan and Santiago? I lack the critical acumen to answer the question authoritatively and I can muster no convincing formal or technical explanation. I am compelled to fall back upon impressionistic terms and say that I neither like Hudson very much, know him deeply, nor suffer any real grief when he is mortally wounded at the novel's conclusion. Somehow the answer, or part of it, probably does reside in point of view, the writer's relationship to his hero and his story; but at best I can only offer my intuition that Hemingway himself holds back from a complete projection into his protagonist, despite the character's resemblance to the novelist in many facets of personality and experience. It is as though a kind of schizophrenia operated here, with the protagonist as an image of his creator but the emotional investment, the soul, withheld. One stylistic cue to this phenomenon is Hemingway's persistent reference to the protagonist by his full name, Thomas Hudson, a habit which in the course of hundreds of such references generates an aura of formality and aloofness. Too, without making a careful tabulation, I estimate there are relatively fewer shifts into interior monologue and introspection than is the case both in *For Whom the Bell Tolls* and *The Old Man and the Sea*. Even when Hemingway does take us inside, he less often conveys the lowdown, no-holds-barred truth of the unblinking self-confrontations we have in his best heroes. The emotional range of this protagonist also seems more limited and rarely persuades us of Hudson's capacity either for rage or ecstacy, though Hemingway sometimes depicts him experiencing both. Yet this evasion may not be calculated. Probably it is unconscious—perhaps reflecting the writer's own wavering grip on reality, external and internal.

Consequently, although I am leaning heavily on biographical factors in this case, I suspect that biography holds the best reply to the problem of *Islands in the Stream:* why it is merely an acceptable book, not a good one. If such a judgment seems harsh, remember that the standards are those requisite to Hemingway. In *Islands in the Stream,* unlike Hemingway's other novels in which the technique is under control, mastery of craft represents not greatness but only high competence— perhaps the exception that proves the rule.

4

Hemingway's Dialogue

The dialogue is among the few aspects of Hemingway's work which has resisted the probes of even his most antagonistic critics. They usually leave it alone and look for weaker places to penetrate. Moreover, the dialogue has been perhaps Hemingway's most influential technique. Not only has it inspired a host of popular imitators, but such different and estimable writers as John O'Hara, J. D. Salinger, and Bernard Malamud have also taken valuable lessons from it. Indeed, the instructions on how to write dialogue which appear in a recent and highly regarded book addressed to aspiring creative writers are virtually a synopsis of Hemingway's methods, with Hemingway himself repeatedly cited as the model to be emulated. I quote portions of the relevant passages.

> In a dialogue scene the reader's attention should be drawn to what the characters are saying, and the words stand out better by themselves, as do the speakers, if the third person does not enter too often. When the speech is charged with emotional associations or significance, when it is loaded, as it should be, and requires the concentrated attention of the reader, stage directions might annoy, confuse, and fatigue him, especially if more than three people are talking. The reader can supply the gesture and intonation himself. Individualized speech in the authentic idiom of the speaker and in just the right tone makes descriptions of gestures and such third-person details

unnecessary. An occasional identification of the speaker is enough, and a highly significant gesture should not be omitted, but the writer should depend on the speech rather than on stage directions. . . . The dialogue should suggest, if not fully reproduce, the sharp, abrupt, disjointed nature of spoken English, with its stresses and slacks, its sudden bursts of explosive rhythm. English is a stress language and not a syllabic one in rhythm. . . . our test again is mimesis—the closest imitation of actual speech, or thought-speech, expressive of character and emotion at any given moment in the action. In dialogue also the part stands for the whole.

Dialogue should be dramatic, as in a play; not written obviously for information or the history of the characters in quotation marks; not routine small talk; not too long, or a series of set speeches, but short, pointed, loaded.[1]

In the absence of evidence to the contrary, we can deduce that Hemingway's skill in dialogue developed primarily out of a natural gift, an "ear," rather than as the result of an arduous apprenticeship under established masters. His earliest imaginative writing for the Oak Park High School literary magazine, the *Tabula*, demonstrated a reliance on dialogue and a facility in it that some able writers of fiction never attain. Furthermore, throughout his journalism for the *Kansas City Star* and the *Toronto Daily Star* and *Star Weekly* Hemingway frequently enlivened his stories with sprightly passages of dialogue, an unusual practice and one beyond the scope of most journalists. Here is a humorous passage from an early contribution to the *Toronto Star Weekly*, March 6, 1920, that illustrates Hemingway's facility and already carries some of the characteristics of his "signature." He is telling about a visit to a barber college for a free shave.

"Next," called one of the students. The others looked expectant.

"I'm sorry," I said. "I'm going upstairs."

Upstairs is where the free work is done by begin-
ners. . . .

"He's going upstairs," said a barber in a hushed
voice.

"He's going upstairs," the other echoed him and
they looked at one another.

I went upstairs.

As Charles Fenton has pointed out, Hemingway was
lucky in his employers.[2]

Whatever insights Hemingway derived from Gertrude
Stein about the "abstract relationships of words" and
the effects of repetition, he was already obviously much
more than a rank amateur before he came under her
tutelage. In the writing of dialogue the graces he gained
from others merely accentuated what seems to have been
his from the beginning. Too, by his own admission Hemingway found only dialogue easy to write; all the rest
came slowly and painfully. As he told Lillian Ross in
1950, "When the people are talking, I can hardly write
it fast enough or keep up with it." [3] Although there are
signs this facility could be deceptive and corrupting, on
the whole Hemingway's dialogue remains among the
accomplishments least blemished by time.

As more than one scholar has remarked, Hemingway's
dialogue most resembles, surprisingly, that of Henry
James. Both writers used dialogue to dramatize individual character consciousness and also theme. Furthermore, both employed a technique of brief exchanges
which tended to refer obliquely to the subject under
discussion rather than to name it outright. Another important technique common to both is incremental repe-
tion, or repetition-plus-variation, a type of stichomythia.
In this rhetorical scheme each speaker will pick up a
word or phrase from the other's speech and utilize it as
the basis for his own remarks, but adding, subtracting,
or changing, so that the dialogue continuously rehearses
itself yet evolves as it proceeds.[4] This conversation from
"The Battler" typifies the method of incremental repetition. I have italicized the reiterated words:

"Hello!" Nick said.

The man looked up.

"Where did you get *the* shiner?" he *said*.

"A brakeman busted me."

"Off *the* through freight?"

"Yes."

"I saw *the* bastard," *the man said*. "*He* went *through* here 'bout an hour and a half ago. *He* was walking along *the* top of *the* cars slapping his arms *and* singing."

"*The bastard*!"

"It must have made him feel good to *bust you*," *the man said* seriously.

"*I'll bust him*."

"*Get him* with a rock sometime when *he's* going *through*," *the man* advised.

"*I'll get him*."

"*You're* a tough one, aren't *you*?"

"No," *Nick* answered.

"All *you* kids *are tough*."

"*You* got to be *tough*," *Nick said*. (*The Short Stories*, p. 131)

Notice, too, in this exchange the use of several simultaneous patterns of repetition both of word and phrase, accentuated by such near-rhymes as busted/bastard, you/through/tough, he/me, him/man, cars/arms/are.

However, the comparison must not be overstated. There are two vital differences between James and Hemingway. First and most obvious, James depends on elaborate stage directions, surrounding his dialogue with constant cues not only to the characters' manner of speech but also to their appearance, gestures, the surroundings, and so forth. Hemingway's dialogue is at the other remove. As in the passage just cited, stage directions are banished except for minimal notation as to speaker and the sparsest reference to gesture and scene—which become all the more important because of their scarcity. Rarely does Hemingway cue us as to tone, inflection, tempo, or mode of delivery. The only such cue in "The

Battler" passage is the word "seriously," a hint less of tone than of the crucial fact, later to be revealed, of the speaker's madness. In these respects Hemingway's seemingly simple and candid dialogue demands as much from the reader's attention as James's, and with fewer visible resources. Second, the major thrust of James's characters' speech is toward the refinement and subtilization of perception or *intellectual* response; in Hemingway the incremental method tends to deepen and sharpen *emotional* response, feeling, or attitude. It may often include a vital intellectual component, but it really seeks more to move than to appraise. (Thus in the quoted passage above we intuit the presence of danger despite the surface camaraderie.) James's dialogue looks denser but it is also cooler. In sum, both writers attain extraordinary resonance, each his own kind, and in both the dialogue offers the opportunity for manifold interpretation.

Richard Bridgman has established that the clipped, repetitive, and incremental qualities of Hemingway's dialogue spring from the same roots as his characteristic style—vernacular American speech.[5] It is a colloquial style and a colloquial dialogue; thus it conveys an unsurpassed illusion of actuality. Of course, this is not a "real" speech but a fabricaton, a stylized version of real speech, for the patternings and reiterations of Hemingway's talk far exceed that in life. Again these traits are visible in the "Battler" conversation. They result not from a linguistic stammering or ineptitude, but from the opposite: discipline and control. The paradox of Hemingway's style is nowhere more evident than in his dialogue—an effect of random and spontaneous simplicity produced by the most deliberate and conscious craft. Part of this illusion is that of banality or irrelevance, but this is a ruse to mask the underlying meaning, as in life we use set phrases and stock responses for protective cover until we are securely positioned for authentic communication. Too, like the vernacular from which it derives, Hemingway's dialogue includes silence, and in its fragmentation and compression, shows a proclivity to culminate in silence.

One further generalization. The overall or synthetic impression created by Hemingway's dialogues is that of "durational realism," to borrow Sartre's phrase. That is, the conversations of Hemingway's characters not only seem to be reported from life, they appear to occupy the same amount of time and space as they would in life, as if they were actually overheard. But this too deceives. The realism is not durational but affective; the conversations do not comprise the sum of the characters' relationship, they represent its distillation, its quintessence. It is as though the reader were presented with a bare scenario which retained only the actors' speeches, and asked to do the work of writer and director in order to reconstruct the scene fully and dramatize it. Thus, it is left to the reader to add the pauses and interpret the dialogue for tempo, volume, tone, and inflection, and to decide the proper emphasis for setting, action, and gesture. The secret of Hemingway's dialogue is just this demand it makes on the reader, while at the same time it allows him to stage the scene in his own head as a perfect performance according to his own tastes and interpretation. Or, to borrow another analogy, each reader his own maestro.

I should now like to illustrate and amplify these generalizations and to make a number of additional observations about the functions and effects of the dialogue in the work itself. I will explore the varied uses of dialogue in structure, plot, and characterization, then look closely at some of Hemingway's special dialogue techniques.

Among the most radical and yet most noticeable features of Hemingway's short stories is their heavy reliance upon dialogue. No other important American writer of short fiction gave more weight to dialogue nor used it with greater frequency. No one had so fully exploited the dramatic method, nor does anything written before Hemingway explain the form of such stories as "The Killers," "Hills Like White Elephants," or "The Sea Change," which are composed almost exclusively of dialogue. In contrast, such works as "Mr. and Mrs. Elliott" and "Big Two-Hearted River," which have little or no dialogue, are rare in the Hemingway canon. The usual Hemingway mode, as we can observe merely by turning the pages of the volume of collected stories, is a short piece of narration or exposition, then almost continuous dialogue interspersed with a few other brief prose paragraphs. Or, sometimes the story begins with a dramatic scene and proceeds in dialogue until the end, where a succinct narrative section appears. As a result we often read Hemingway vertically rather than laterally, perhaps a factor in our pervasive sense of movement and tension, even in stories containing little action. Neither the eye nor the mind can remain fixed for very long in the vertical alignment of Hemingway's truncated conversations, unlike the static effect of paragraphs of massed prose.

It follows that upon dialogue falls much of the burden of setting, plot, character, and theme carried in other writers, for example Hemingway's contemporary Fitzgerald, by description, exposition, and narration. This intends no invidious comparison because Fitzgerald could also write superb dialogue and unforgettable dramatic scenes; it is simply a matter of difference in method. And in such radical instances as the stories named above, e.g., "Hills Like White Elephants," dialogue is all, in itself comprising plot, character, and theme. In short, to the large majority of Hemingway's short stories, dialogue is integral.

Let us consider several kinds of stories which illustrate the varied roles and significance of dialogue. First, in a relatively few cases the dialogue may highlight action, disclose hidden facets of character motivation, and provide ironic contrasts, but its function is still not primary. These stories really revolve around what happens rather than what is said—on *plot*, in the most conventional sense of that term. For example, "Indian Camp," "The Undefeated," "The Short Happy Life of Francis Macomber," and "The Capital of the World" are all essentially plotted stories which subordinate dialogue to action. This does not mean that dialogue is superfluous in them; only that it is ancillary to the objective and external events, the causalities, conflicts, and reversals without which there would be no "story." The obvious link between all these works is their dependence upon a specific violent action so extreme that it becomes an ultimate test of character.

We see this exemplified in "Indian Camp" toward the end of the story, when a few lines of dialogue juxtaposed against what actually happens, provide an insight into the character of Nick's father, a doctor who has just performed a surgical delivery of an Indian woman in protracted and agonized labor.

> "That's one for the medical journal, George," he said. "Doing a Caesarian with a jack-knife and sewing it up with nine-foot, tapered gut leaders."
>
> Uncle George was standing against the wall, looking at his arm.
>
> "Oh, you're a great man, all right," he said.
>
> "Ought to have a look at the proud father. They're usually the worst suffers in these little affairs," the doctor said. "I must say he took it all pretty quietly."
>
> He pulled back the blanket from the Indian's head. His hand came away wet. He mounted on the edge of the lower bunk with the lamp in one hand and looked in. The Indian lay with his face toward the wall. His throat had been cut from ear to ear. The blood had flowed down into a pool where his body sagged the bunk. His head rested on his left arm. The open razor lay, edge up, in the blankets. (*The Short Stories*, p. 94)

By contrasting the father's boastfulness with both the woman's pain preceding the boast and the horrible revelation of the man's suicide just after it, Hemingway makes us suddenly realize that the father's detachment from the situation, which we, like Nick, have assumed to be professional self-discipline, is also compounded of egotism and plain cold-heartedness. The doctor's phrase "these little affairs" now takes on an entirely different connotation: arrogance. Furthermore, Hemingway hints at a norm against which the doctor is to be judged, because George's sarcastic reaction and his glance at his arm (where he has been bitten by the Indian woman in the frenzy of her labor) express his sensitivity to the situation, unlike the doctor's callousness. Although the story's concluding dialogue partially reaffirms the doctor's humanity, it also points to an innocence he shares with his young son: "Is dying hard, Daddy?" "No, I think it's pretty easy, Nick. It all depends." From the standpoint of technique the thing to note here is that the longer passage quoted above fairly represents both the story's method, which intersperses dialogue and narrative in almost equal amounts, and its emphasis on what occurs. Words, and the cerebration they imply, take a subordinate place in the context of such events.

In "The Undefeated" the dialogue serves a dual function, exposition and emphasis. By opening the story with two scenes consisting largely of dialogue, Manuel in Retana's office and later in the café with Zurito, Hemingway sketches in the essential facts of the situation which will subsequently enter into the action: Manuel's recent wounds, his lack of favor with the fans, and the indifference of promoter and waiters to the destiny of a second-rate torero—the same reactions soon to be expressed by the bored critic during the story's central episode. Likewise, dramatic scene also brings out Manuel's qualities of character, his stubborn courage and professional pride, and thus foreshadows the story's outcome, for the sight of the bull's head in Retana's office and the waiters' banter about gored matadors are ominous prefigurations. However, once the locale shifts to the bullring, dialogue gives way largely to narrative and changes in its purpose from exposition to intensification, as very brief bits of conversation (or dramatized interior monologue) counterpoint and accentuate the increasing urgency of the action. Indeed, a triple contrast is effected by the earthy bullfighting idiom of the exchanges between Zurito, Manuel, and others, the inflated sports-jargon of the critic composing his review (which Hemingway renders as a form of dialogue), and the standard English of the narrative. At the end, with Manuel immobile on the operating table, the story again returns to dialogue to measure the protagonist's heroic self-delusion against what has happened to him, as he insists "I was going good." Once more, words ring hollow against actualities.

"The Capital of the World" is another story which turns on what happens rather than what is said. However, because it uses dialogue relatively sparsely, the conversations are thrown into especially sharp relief against one another and the ongoing action. In particular, two dialogues frame the story's climactic event, the fatal wounding of the young man Paco who has tried to prove his courage. In the first conversation Paco, taunted by Enrique, is supremely confident of his bravery. Then, after he has faced the "horns of the bull"—a pair of butcher knives tied to a chair—and taken one of them in his groin, he speaks in the wan voice of a man mortally stricken, yet one stubbornly clinging to his ideal of conduct. By alternating each segment of dialogue with a corresponding passage of narrative action, Hemingway builds tremendous concentration; by portraying Paco's last words as persistent in their idealism despite his condition, he achieves the starkest irony and completes the story's mordant mood. This tone is epitomized in the last bit of conversation between the dying boy and his accidental murderer:

> "I came straight," said Enrique crying. "All I wanted was to show the danger."
> "Don't worry," said Paco, his voice sounding far away. "But bring the doctor." (*The Short Stories*, p. 49)

This juxtaposition of "Don't worry . . . But bring the doctor" verges on the blackest of dark comedy.

As in these other instances, the dialogue in "The Short Happy Life of Francis Macomber" works to deepen character and enhance action, although this story, too, depends essentially upon plot. However, it introduces an additional dimension of dialogue in that the characters' very capacities or proclivities for speech become integral to their configuration and to the story's basic theme: the miracle of manly courage. Early in the story Macomber's cowardice in running from the lion is at once expressed in and compounded by his inability to keep his mouth shut about it and about such other highly disgraceful matters as his wife's infidelity. Margaret Macomber's remark, "Conversation is going to be so difficult," proves true in more ways than she suspects. Within the same ironic frame of reference Wilson's first piece of advice to Macomber about the protocols of conduct, "We never talk about our clients. . . . It's supposed to be bad form to ask us not to talk though," exposes one of the basic precepts Macomber must learn to become a complete man.

Accordingly, throughout the tale talking or not talking continues to be both a major aspect of character and a leitmotif in the dialogue itself, as in the exchange between Margaret and her husband when she returns from Wilson's tent during the night and repeats to his questions and helpless, bitter protests: "But please let's not talk, darling. . . . We don't have to talk about it, do we?" at the same time hinting at her sexual satiation with the repeated "I'm very sleepy." Once Macomber begins shooting well and experiences his miracle, he can accept Wilson's final lesson: "Doesn't do to talk too much about all of this. Talk the whole thing away. No pleasure in anything if you mouth it up too much." From that point in the story, when Macomber quells his wife, "If you don't know what we're talking about why not keep out of it?" to the very end, when Wilson forces Mrs. Macomber to beg for silence, true manhood is defined in part by the male's ability to blunt the female's deadliest weapon, her tongue.

The difference between the significance of dialogue in such stories as "Indian Camp" and "The Short Happy

Life of Francis Macomber" and the next group I will discuss is the difference between the important and the essential. That is, the greater number of Hemingway's stories use dialogue to do even more than thicken plot and amplify character. To cite an extreme example, so much is the depiction of a major character in "A Clean, Well-Lighted Place" affected by a single line of dialogue, it has taken several critics to puzzle out the *literal* meaning of the story, forcing some of them to conclude that either Hemingway's carelessness in composition or a printer's error produced a line out of order and thus an apparently incompatible combination of a character and his utterance.[6] In this instance Hemingway's habit of unspecific reference to a character at the beginning of the story as "one waiter," without clear indication as to which of two he meant, in conjunction with his typical reluctance to provide stage directions, resulted in confusion rather than complexity. Although the situation is not representative, and we rarely have trouble associating Hemingway's characters with their speeches even in long conversations, despite the lack of explicit identification, it does denote the crucial place of dialogue in Hemingway's work and the enormous responsibility carried by only a few words in an entire story. Or, to take a less problematic sample than a "A Clean Well-Lighted Place," Hemingway will use dialogue as almost the sole means of exposition and character depiction, accumulating the necessary information piece by piece as the work proceeds. "The Battler," "Cat in the Rain," "Ten Indians," "The Light of the World," "Homage to Switzerland," all represent this kind of story, frequent in Hemingway's fiction.

"The Battler" and "Ten Indians," two stories little discussed except for their place in the Nick Adams saga, illustrate Hemingway's substantive reliance upon dialogue and also his versatility of technique.

Although the first several paragraphs of "The Battler" are cast as narrative, the rest of the story of Nick's encounter with the demented ex-fighter and his Negro companion is rendered almost entirely in dialogue. The initial exchange between Nick and "the battler," part of which I quoted above, uses the curt, nearly monosyllabic speech natural to the fighter and imitated by Nick to present a hard-boiled exterior. Such key repetitions already alluded to as "bastard," "tough," and "bust" both delineate the level of speech and indicate the story's motifs of violence and social exile. The abruptness and coarseness of the fighter's manner of speech, his candor about his mutilated face, and his confession of his dementia fix him as a dangerous figure as the conversation proceeds, although he makes no direct threats to Nick at first. Of course, what he says also has the expository function of identifying him and accurately stating his condition. Most of the work of exposition, however, is performed by the third character who soon enters the story and subsequently dominates it: the Negro named "Bugs." Bugs also introduces a new element into the dialogue, for in contrast to the tough lingo of the fighter and the boy, Bugs speaks in a mellifluous combination of carefully polite diction and Negro dialect which is both comic and sinister. As Bugs speaks he fills in the background of the fighter and his own relationship with him, revealing an entire galaxy of experience Nick knows nothing about. But the remarkable aspect of this character's dialogue, whether or not his relationship with the fighter is homosexual—as Philip Young suspects—is how his gentle mode of address, which seems only to suggest and cajole ("May I offer you a slice of bread dipped right in the hot ham fat?"), really communicates a series of commands that compel obedience.[7]

To convey the pseudocourteous dialogue characteristic of Bugs, Hemingway gives him longer utterances than Nick and the fighter and writes his dialogue laterally, in contrast to the vertical arrangement necessitated by the terse remarks of the others. The very typographical appearance of Bugs's speech thus enhances the impression of a silky, continuous flow. At the same time his true hardness and control, his authentic self, is transmitted by the short sentences, active verbs, and vernacular expressions—("pull out," "thump")—all overlaid with the gloss of decorum. This passage from the end of the story typifies the Negro's delivery:

> "I can wake him up any time now, Mister Adams. If you don't mind I wish you'd sort of pull out. I don't like to not be hospitable, but it might disturb him back again to see you. I hate to have to thump him and it's the only thing to do when he gets started. I have to sort of keep him away from people. You don't mind, do you, Mister Adams? No, don't thank me, Mister Adams. I'd have warned you about him but he seemed to have taken such a liking to you and I thought things were going to be all right. You'll hit a town about two miles up the track. Mancelona they call it. Good-bye. I wish we could ask you to stay the night but it's just out of the question. Would you like to take some of that ham and some bread with you? No? You better take a sandwich." (*The Short Stories*, p. 138)

In "Ten Indians" we move into dramatic scene almost at once and remain in it throughout, although the story's concluding paragraph in the voice of the omniscient narrator gives the last little twist to character. Here dialogue acts as the agent of exposition in the special sense of disclosure or revelation, since what is hinted in the bantering of the Garner family in the story's opening scene—the infidelity of Nick's Indian girl friend—becomes explicitly stated at the end by Nick's father. Not that the Garners have exact knowledge that Prudence has been cheating on Nick. However, their jovially contemptuous remarks, caused by their stopping to remove nine drunken Indians from the road, point to the "low" status soon to be extended to the girl. She is the tenth supine Indian, not drunk like the others but also on the ground.

The contrast between the good-natured and relaxed Garner family and the prim father (once again the villain of the piece), which constitutes a material element in the story, comes mainly out of the dialogue. The Garners joke among themselves, their byplay connoting their sexual tolerance and their comfortable manner transmitted in loose and folksy speech ("Them Indians." "Girls never got a man anywhere. Look at your Pa." "Shucks."). On the other hand, Nick's father's delivery has a crisp correctness about it, even though there is nothing formidable about vocabulary or syntax. This quality of reserve and remoteness, despite the superficial goodwill of his remarks, gets through in the way he divulges what he had seen in the woods. In forcing Nick to learn the story by asking questions, one at a time, thus aggravating the revelation by delaying it, he inflicts the very hurt he purportedly tries to avoid. This method correlates with his careful choice of words and his use of euphemisms: "They were having quite a time," "I just heard them thrashing around," which again add to Nick's malaise by stimulating his imagination. Moreover, by stretching out the dialogue between Nick and his father and taking almost a full page to complete the question and answer process, Hemingway creates a sense both of the father's prudishness and the exacerbation of Nick's feelings. Too, the whole conversation is given an ironic tone in that it follows just after the father has greeted Nick cordially and served him some pie, so that we cannot be sure whether the report on Prudence (the name is ironic in itself) expresses the father's vengefulness toward his son's choice of friends or an honest attempt to perform his paternal duty.

There are many instances in Hemingway's stories in which the organization or texture of the dialogue exposes character rather than information. That is, dialogue operates as virtually the only mode of characterization and makes up most of the story's substance. For example, in "Cat in the Rain" we never do discover what is wrong between the two young Americans in their hotel, although the discord takes several forms: the objective detail of the rain, the wife's urgent yet whimsical wish for the cat outside, the husband's absorption in his book and general indifference to his wife's mood. What the dialogue emphasizes, and thereby suggests as the basis for the conflict, is the wife's childishness. The first thing she says cues the reader to this trait, "I'm going down and get that *kitty*" (my italics), and from that point on almost every statement she makes begins with the child's "I want." Without specifying by stage direction the tone or inflection of her speech, Hemingway catches the sound of the spoiled child's petulance and self-righteousness by intensive repetition and such characteristic terms as "now" and "fun":

> "I want to pull my hair back tight and smooth and make a big knot at the back that I can feel," she said. "I want to have a kitty to sit on my lap and purr when I stroke her." . . .
>
> "And I want to eat at a table with my own silver and I want candles. And I want it to be spring and I want to brush my hair out in front of a mirror and I want a kitty and I want some new clothes.". . .
>
> "Anyway, I want a cat," she said, "I want a cat. I want a cat now. If I can't have long hair or any fun, I can have a cat." (*The Short Stories*, pp. 169–70)

The most striking example of dialogue as a mode of character revelation in Hemingway's short stories appears in "The Killers." Without overt threat of violence or show of weapons the two hoodlums insinuate such menace in their manner and words alone that the men in the diner obey them abjectly. If something about their appearance evokes death, their speech nevertheless does most of the work of terrorizing the others. This depends less on *what* they say—because they do not announce their mission to kill Ole Andreson until after Nick, George, and the cook have obeyed—than on how they speak. Andreson's inability to run from his pursuers, baffling to Nick at the end of the story, only projects Nick's own helplessness before them. How does Hemingway create this atmosphere of danger?

We infer at once that these are no ordinary customers when the second man repeats almost verbatim the first man's words, establishing the formula of itemized repetition which persists throughout the dialogue of the killers: "I don't know," "I don't know what I want to eat." Our suspicion is heightened when one man orders his dinner with unusual exactitude, "I'll have a roast pork tenderloin with apple sauce and mashed potatoes," the way one would do it in jest, except that his next remark is belligerent: "What the hell do you put it on the card for?" Our suspicions are confirmed when, despite George's explanation, a second food order is given in the same scrupulous manner. Now it becomes clear that the men bait the proprietor and invite trouble, for this precise repetition of another's words is the method of mockery, a method we all learn early in our experience of speech. Next, they jibe at the town and then swiftly pick up George's little attempt at rejoinder as the opening for direct insult, the "bright boy" label they bestow on the others and use as a verbal club. They repeat that epithet twenty-five times in five pages of text.

The identical speech pattern of the killers, with their catch-phrases and rehearsed responses, duplicates their identical dress and enhances their deadliness by suggesting at once the falsely cheerful routine of a vaudeville act and the mechanical behavior of robots.[8] Everything they say indicates a habit of thought in which human beings are stripped of individuating differences, typed as "bright boy," "Swede," or "nigger," and transformed into items in an entertainment—stressed in the killers' references to movies and amusement. Men's lives hinge upon a whim, for only Max's casual remarks to Al save Nick, George, and the cook from death: "So long, bright boy," he said to George. "You got a lot of luck." "That's the truth," Max said. "You ought to play the races, bright boy" (*The Short Stories*, p. 285).

In "Hills Like White Elephants" and "The Sea Change" dialogue is not only essential, it is the totality. No external plot remains; the situation has been condensed to people talking. Moreover, unlike the stories just discussed in which there is at least some action and a change of scene (each of them uses a form of the inside /outside structure), these stay fixed in one place. Yet although the dialogue compresses the entire relationship of the characters into a single brief conversation, it supplies enough evidence to enable us to reconstruct the past. The dialogue in both stories also illustrates Hemingway's strategy of seducing the reader's attention by never being fully explicit about the subject of the conversation or the point of contention. In "Hills Like White Elephants" the abortion which threatens to disrupt the couple's union is alluded to only as an "operation" and "it"; in "The Sea Change" we learn about the homosexual liaison merely by references to "her," "vice," "perversion," and "it." This obliqueness is more than a trick, however, for it communicates in both cases the characters' attempts to maintain a semblance of control over the powerful emotions they feel. The sense of things unsaid permeates both dialogues and intensifies the impact of the actual utterance.

In "Hills Like White Elephants" the objective narrator supplies not a single cue to the delivery of the characters' remarks; all must be inferred from context and response. The first clear signal that something is amiss comes in the edged exchange over the girl's observation about the distant hills, an exchange that suddenly alters a seemingly cordial atmosphere:

> "They look like white elephants," she said.
> "I've never seen one," the man drank his beer.
> "No, you wouldn't have."
> "I might have," the man said. "Just because you say I wouldn't have doesn't prove anything." (*The Short Stories*, p. 273)

The conversation also plants the ironic phrase of the title, with its idiomatic sense of a thing now debased or devalued, the realization of a mistake.

Another deliberately polite chat follows, to be again

abruptly disturbed by bickering over the taste of absinthe, but again restored to politeness by a few lines of pleasantry. With the atmosphere now fully charged, the real conflict enters in the man's mention of the "operation," which he characterizes as "awfully simple," "just to let the air in," and "all perfectly natural." His description of the abortion reflects more than the attempt to minimize its pain and inconvenience for the woman; he really portrays it in the terms he wants for their relationship: to ventilate it and restore it to spontaneity. Once the subject is introduced, it monopolizes the rest of the conversation, infiltrating the girl's defenses and stimulating a little of the anger and turbulence she feels. At the same time she wants the man enough not to drive him away by assaulting him with all her rage and disgust. All this is contained in two lines, when she says in reply to his continued exhortation, "Would you please please please please please please please stop talking?" followed a moment later, when he utters yet another conciliatory remark, by "I'll scream." The "please" reiterated seven consecutive times without punctuation is the simple but effective device by which Hemingway communicates the sound of a woman's just barely restrained hysteria. Her subsequent smiles and assertion of well-being as the story concludes are further symptoms of her inner condition, producing an ending to the story we might describe as dynamically unresolved, not only "open" but with fuse lighted.

Something of the detail other writers provide in stage directions to cue the reader's response, Hemingway supplies by seemingly random and realistic bits of objective reference to setting and gesture. But though unobtrusive, these are carefully ordered and significant. The setting, a whistle-stop railroad station between two major cities, itself suggests the precariousness of the couple's present condition between a carefree past and an uncertain future. The fact that they sit outside in the heat connotes the pressure of the situation and prefigures the urgent feelings soon to be brought out but not dissipated. The barrenness of the treeless surroundings is also a significant detail. However, the gesture or simple act of *looking* makes the most important counterpart to what is said.

When the waitress brings the beer and looks at the couple we receive the first hint of tension—just as in "The Killers" Nick looks at the two men who enter the diner, and keeps on looking at them. The dialogue continues to be interspersed with portentous looks. The girl looks at the distant hills, the bead curtain, the ground, the curtain again, the river, and the hills once more. Each of these looks corresponds with a phase in the conversation. She looks at the remote hills (the vanished past as well as the bleak future) before the first flare-up of enmity, and the bead curtain (a transparent yet tangible barrier, or perhaps an image of the decorous front they maintain) just after it. She looks at the ground when he mentions the operation for the first time, at the faraway river and trees in talking about their future, and at the dry and remote hills when he persists in trying to persuade her about the abortion while simultaneously asserting his undying affection and fidelity. The man, in counterpoint, looks at the luggage that records their carefree and itinerant past (now at a standstill), at the tracks (escape), and at the people in the bar who are not arguing but "waiting reasonably for the train." There are other telling gestures also. When the girl removes her hat and places it on the table at the beginning of the story, this suggests the uncovering of emotion soon to come, at once "letting the hair down" and "putting the cards on the table." When the man picks up the two bags and moves them at the end, he indicates his desire both to shift the burden he feels and to run from the crisis he has provoked. Yet as influential as all these gestures are in the dramatic action of the story, they hide inconspicuously in the text, affecting us only subliminally during the actual experience of reading.

"The Sea Change" employs fundamentally the same dialogue technique, although it is a more ambiguous and probably less successful story. Here the tension builds from the first line and persists undiminished until almost the end. The unusual aspect of the dialogue is its power of insinuation, for such remarks as the girl's "We're made up of all sorts of things. You've known that. You've used it well enough," and the man's later statement "And when you come back tell me all about it," imply that the couple's relationship has been in some ways as "corrupt" as the homosexual affair to which the girl asks her lover's consent. As in other Hemingway stories where homosexuality is the subject, "The Sea Change" implies a general perversion of character, a deduction supported by the story's conclusion which hints at the man's degradation. By permitting the girl's adventure, he is more culpable than she in living it.

The technique of "The Sea Change" falls short of "Hills Like White Elephants" in that by shifting the focus from the couple to the man alone in the last few paragraphs Hemingway diminishes the dramatic effect of the dialogue and weakens the character emphasis. Neither the man's motivation solely, nor the woman's, has been the center of interest but their interaction. Further, the omniscient narrator shows his hand a little too openly. The contrast between the couple's appearance of beautiful youth and the subject of their dialogue smacks of the sensational, and the quick omniscient glimpses into the barman's mind and into the man's at the end distract rather than sharpen our attention.

The most evident example of the dramatic method in Hemingway's short fiction, a story consisting only of dialogue, is "Today Is Friday." However, we must view it as a tour de force, a bravura display of Hemingway's dialogue skills, rather than as a successful work in its own right. The three soldiers in the story (play, really) are all deeply moved by the suffering of the crucified Christ but each responds to it and expresses it differently. The first soldier, a tough veteran, admires Christ's courage as one seasoned professional respects another. His repeated "He was pretty good in there today" serves as incantatory refrain. The second soldier bluffs a façade of stoical indifference but his remarks often hint at a concealed empathy. Note, too, that he is the first to break off the drinking bout. The third soldier is ill from beginning to end, purportedly of stomach but more probably of spirit. His reiterated "I feel like hell tonight" comprises a second, heavily suggestive refrain. The Jewish wineseller is plainly intended as a generic type, struck off in his first speech: "Here you are, gentlemen. You'll like that. . . . That's a nice little wine." Indeed, this sort of cleverness is the story's problem. The dialogue reduces so much to stock responses, to attitude as caught in a key phrase, that Hemingway's method verges on self-parody.

In comparison to the distinctive quality of the short stories, Hemingway's use of dialogue in his novels cannot justly be called radical nor perhaps even innovative, although he certainly assigns to dialogue both greater space and larger responsibility than that given it by most novelists. As in the stories, to riffle the pages of the novels is to observe again and again the vertical typography which indicates people talking.

One of the less apparent features of Hemingway's novels is that those with strong plots and much overt action, such as *A Farewell to Arms, To Have and Have Not, For Whom the Bell Tolls,* and the first and last sections of *Islands in the Stream,* which would seem to fall naturally into the narrative mode, also place material reliance upon dialogue as a technique of narration. Rarely in a Hemingway novel will a narrative passage run on without dialogue for more than five or six pages, and even that is exceptional. Closer to the norm would be two or three pages of narrative prose, then dialogue; more common yet, a few paragraphs of narration alternated with equal or greater amounts of dialogue. Curiously, even in the books we tend to remember as essentially narrative and which contain a heavier concentration of narrative sequences (for example, *To Have and Have Not*), dialogue is still abundant in one or another form—sometimes as dramatic monologue with much the same effect as uttered speech. The obvious inference is that Hemingway adds to the customary function of dialogue in the novel, characterization, the tasks of narration and exposition. Nor should we overlook the place of dialogue in the structural pattern as a technique of alternation and counterpoint, a means to shape a book's proportions and vary its tempo and mood. Hemingway utilized dialogue for modulation in his nonfiction as well, most notably in the long discursive work *Death in the Afternoon,* where he specifically introduces the facetious conversations with the Old Lady to relieve the tedium of continuous exposition.

Let us approach dialogue in the novels by first looking into characterization.

One of the valuable yet subtle techniques of characterization through dialogue in *The Sun Also Rises* is the contrast drawn between public and private conversations. This contrast signifies the large opposition between the "in" and "out" groups of characters and is thus integral to theme. From the start Jake makes it plain that among his objections to Cohn and Cohn's crowd, the expatriate poseurs, is Cohn's inability to keep private feelings out of public conversations. We notice this at once when Cohn confesses his fears about the transience of life and his desire to go to South America before it's too late, exposing a juvenile attitude he ought to have concealed. The indictment against Cohn becomes really severe, however, when Jake witnesses the nasty scene in which Frances Clyne airs her resentments and ridicules Cohn while he sits there and takes it. In contrast, Jake's hopeless love for Brett and the agony it entails are restricted to scenes known to themselves alone. Publicly Jake and Brett converse in laconic exchanges made up largely of terse witticisms and cryptic allusions. The same contrast prevails through the novel, with a few interesting and notable variations.

When the in-group characters drink, they are liable to say too much and violate the protocols of restraint. This is exactly the situation in chapter 13, when, parallel to Frances's earlier, sober humiliation of Cohn, Mike launches into him and vilifies him in front of the others, shaming himself as well as Cohn by betraying emotions more properly kept under guard. Even Brett, consummate actress that she is in maintaining her bluff English stoicism, tends to let herself go in drink and become too noisy and a little abusive. We observe this in chapter 7, when Brett's jibes against Count Mippopopolous, "Don't be an ass. . . . You haven't any values. You're dead, that's all," rebound off the Count's imperturbable dignity to Brett's own discredit. In drink she can also be careless with Jake's feelings, as at the end of chapter 4.

Hemingway portrays the contrast between the characters drunk and sober not only by the content of their remarks but by quantity and diction as well. When Brett is sober and alone with Jake she tends to speak in clear and standard diction, and in complete sentences. In public, or tipsy, she lapses into fragmentary bits of speech, dropping subjects, verbs, or pronouns, and/or into British colloquialisms. Depending on the context, the effect is either mannered (public) or reckless (drunk). Mike is drunk from the beginning to almost the end, but before the Pamplona sequence he masquerades as feckless jester, asserting his presence with quips and witticisms. But in chapter 13 he steps front and center and delivers a barrage of remarks in consecutive volleys, punctuating his attack with the repeated reference to Cohn as a "bloody steer." Bill is another character who, sober, is normally terse and rather inconspicuous but ungrammatically magniloquent in drink, fixating on a word or phrase and worrying it endlessly.

Although Frances is perfectly sober in the scene in which she abuses Cohn, she is similarly out of control. Hemingway imitates her hysteria, duplicating in the form of the dialogue Frances's gamut of emotion, by the use of a steadily incremental process. When Frances first meets Jake and Cohn she pretends to be calm, and thus the shape of her speech on the page does not differ markedly from that of the other characters, although it is slightly longer. Then, as the scene and her emotion develop, and she pulls Jake aside to complain to him, there is a gradual inflation of her remarks, although individual

sentences remain short. Finally, when the three are together and she launches her main assault on Cohn, letting go all restraint, Hemingway writes her speech as an
uninterrupted burst, a succession of short, heavily repetitive sentences all interconnected into long paragraphs.
At the height of her tirade Frances carries on for five
unbroken paragraphs, the last running to thirty-one lines
of print, a full page, all the more visible and emphatic
because of the rarity of such passages in the novel. The
combination of brief, heavily stressed sentence units
within the continuous paragraph structure produces exactly the effect of unbridled fury Hemingway wants. No
other character in the novel even approaches an utterance of this length. (Mike's later attack, consonant with
his masculinity, is much more concise and open.) This
is a fair sample of the Frances monologue, about half
the final paragraph of her oration.

> "Listen, Robert, dear. Let me tell you something.
> You won't mind, will you? Don't have scenes with
> your young ladies. Try not to. Because you can't have
> scenes without crying, and then you pity yourself so
> much you can't remember what the other person's
> said. You'll never be able to remember any conversa-
> tions that way. Just try and be calm. I know it's
> awfully hard. But remember, it's for literature. We
> all ought to make sacrifices for literature. Look at me.
> I'm going to England without a protest. All for litera-
> ture. We must all help young writers. Don't you think
> so, Jake? But you're not a young writer. Are you, Rob-
> ert? You're thirty-four. Still, I suppose that is young
> for a great writer. Look at Hardy. Look at Anatole
> France. He just died a little while ago. Robert doesn't
> think he's any good, though. Some of his French
> friends told him. He doesn't read French very well
> himself. He wasn't a good writer like you are, Rob-
> ert?" (Pp. 50–51)

Something of this same method, what might be called
the rhetoric of hysteria, is employed in the story "A Way

You'll Never Be," when Nick's inability to control his thoughts, which sail off into flights of fantasy, results in a similar outburst of incoherence in the presence of an Italian officer. It, too, gathers force not only from what Nick says but also by his deviation from the caution and concision typical of Hemingway's protagonists.

Another technique of characterization through dialogue Hemingway practices in *The Sun Also Rises*, although hardly to the degree observable in later novels, is the contrast between English and other languages or that between English as spoken by foreigners and native speakers. Foreign speakers are credited with a candor and directness or pungency of speech not always given to those born to the language. So Count Mippopopolous sometimes makes faintly humorous grammatical blunders, but these only point up the essential honesty and openness of his remarks. Too, he speaks with conviction and care, qualities which expose some of the pretense in others, as I earlier noted. The same air of authority attaches itself later in the novel to both Montoya and Romero, whose natural dignity of manner shows up the sometimes flippant English and Americans. See, for example, the dialogue in chapter 16, where Hemingway plays off Romero's inherent simplicity and dignity against Mike's and Bill's garrulousness.

This contrast of tongues is pervasive though not yet highly stylized in *A Farewell to Arms*. Hemingway introduces the fact of contrast in the second chapter, when Frederic Henry tells us that the ribald bantering at the priest's expense by the officers was carried on in "pidgin Italian for my doubtful benefit," and the dialogue itself is written with deliberate awkwardness. Although the narrator obviously speaks fluent Italian, he thinks in English and relates the story to us in English, with the effect that Hemingway maintains a subtle yet persistent counterpoint, a sense of Henry's apartness and alienation from the locale he inhabits, which contributes to the novel's motif of the "separate peace." To compare Henry's conversations with his enlisted men, the priest, Rinaldi, the

Italian doctors, and Count Greffi, against the dialogues between Catherine and himself and against the articulation of his own thoughts, is to perceive that Hemingway uses at least four voices. Thus he reinforces in dialogue the choric effect we noticed in the treatment of narrative perspective. The hero's dialogues with his subordinates, the priest, and Count Greffi all share a certain formality of expression which hints at the protagonist's self-consciousness with them and his concentration in speaking the language correctly. Rinaldi's speech is formal, too, but exaggeratedly so and often undercut with a slangy term (for example, his habit of calling Frederic "baby"), so that the result is breezy and often comical. With Catherine, Frederic is direct but still more proper and less colloquial than he is either in his own thoughts or his narrative account, for although he and Catherine both speak the same language they speak different national dialects. This passage from chapter 5 documents what I have been saying about the interplay of voices:

> "Oh, darling," she said. "You will be good to me, won't you?"
>
> What the hell, I thought. I stroked her hair and patted her shoulder. She was crying.
>
> "You will, won't you?" She looked up at me. "Because we're going to have a strange life."
>
> After a while I walked with her to the door of the villa and she went in and I walked home. . . . Rinaldi was lying on his bed. He looked at me.
>
> "So you make progress with Miss Barkley?'
>
> "We are friends."
>
> "You have that pleasant air of a dog in heat."
>
> I did not understand the word.
>
> "Of a what?"
>
> He explained. (P. 27)

Here we observe three of the four voices: the protagonist's narrative and interior voice ("What the hell, I thought"); the more formal dialogue with Catherine;

the comic formality of the exchange with Rinaldi ("make progress," "pleasant air of a dog in heat"). We note, too, in this same passage that despite the illusion of durational realism Hemingway inserts a significant cue— "after a while"—which points both to an indeterminate lapse of time and an unspecified action, perhaps explaining Rinaldi's innuendo about Frederic's air of passionate unfulfillment. These subtle references to unseen gestures are a characteristic and effective Hemingway strategy.

Although I have alluded to it in some respects, Hemingway's practice of using dialogue to enlarge his characterizations and supply important information needs further explanation. To cite two cases in point, a sound understanding of the motivations of the lovers in *The Sun Also Rises* and *A Farewell to Arms* depends upon a close reading of the dialogue of their early encounters.

In *The Sun Also Rises* the whole mood of the opening chapters of the novel hinges on Brett's remarks at the end of chapter 3 and beginning of chapter 4, the first time she and Jake are alone. By her confession "Oh, darling, I've been so miserable" and the dialogue immediately thereafter, Hemingway banishes the superficial brightness and insouciant irony prevailing to that point and replaces it with exacerbated and unassuaged sexual anguish. What we learn from this conversation is that although Jake is impotent, he is hardly numb, and that Brett burns with an even hotter fire. Moreover, the dialogue advances the suggestion that Jake and Brett have attempted acts of love before, perhaps repeatedly.

> "Don't touch me," she said. "Please don't touch me."
>
> "What's the matter?"
>
> "I can't stand it."
>
> "Oh, Brett."
>
> "You mustn't. You must know. I can't stand it, that's all. Oh, darling, please understand!"
>
> "Don't you love me?"

"Love you? I simply turn all to jelly when you touch me."

"Isn't there anything we can do about it?". . .

"And there's not a damn thing we could do," I said.

"I don't know," she said. "I don't want to go through that hell again."

"We'd better keep away from each other."

"But, darling, I have to see you. It isn't all that, you know."

"No, but it always gets to be."

"That's my fault. Don't we pay for all the things we do, though?" (Pp. 25–26)

As I read the scene, such statements of Brett's as "You must know" and "I don't want to go through that hell *again*" (my italics), and the "that" in the later line, all evince an active sexual desire between the characters and the attempt to release it. With this element of un-requited passion added to the other factors in the char-acter configuration, their later behavior—as, for example, when Jake looks at his body in the mirror and weeps, his anger at Cohn for the weekend intimacy with Brett, his self-hatred when he sends Brett off with Romero—be-comes even more meaningful. The same desire for re-lease, to the degree of inducing temporary illness in Jake, is emphasized in the scene in chapter 7 when Brett visits Jake's apartment with the Count in tow. Part of that scene, with another conspicuous gap in the continuity of time and action cued by the narrator's phrase "Then later" (p. 55), hints once more at some sort of physical exchange. In other words, we must include a certain physiological stress among the other sorts of emotional pressure that the characters suffer.[9]

A scrutiny of the initial dialogues between Frederic and Catherine also uncovers levels of motivation which considerably enhance the characters' credibility. Com-mencing with *A Farewell to Arms* critics have often com-plained about the unreality of Hemingway's portrayal of romantic love. They have found particularly incredible the ease and rapidity with which Hemingway's men get their women into bed, and concluded that the heroines were all too cooperative and malleable. The issue has been too much debated to require much further comment, but I do wish to elucidate a few features of Catherine's motivation, as exposed in the dialogue, which prove her to be not so easy a conquest as some have read her.

What Hemingway brings out in all the early encounters between Frederic and Catherine is that she makes Frederic Henry a reincarnation of her dead lover, and that in transferring her affections to him she relieves herself of an intolerable burden of guilt and accumulated emotion. So much has she suffered that she lapses into intermittent moments of aberration, a fact both of them realize. She is emotionally primed to surrender herself to almost any sympathetic and attractive man, when Frederic appears fortuitously on the scene—supplanting Rinaldi who is about to take advantage of her shaky morale. This also helps explain the acerbic undertone in some of Rinaldi's later jests.

Catherine's state of mind is indicated almost from the first words she utters, for she no sooner says "How do you do?" than she asks at once (before Frederic has said a word), "You're not an Italian, are you?" hardly the conventional courtesy at the instant of meeting another. Her subsequent remarks also probe deeply; and then Frederic's inquiry about the riding crop she handles—suggestive in itself—opens the opportunity for Catherine to tell about her dead lover. After only a few minutes, with Catherine's total candor indicating her vulnerability and her need to tell her story, even to a stranger, Frederic is cued as to how he must behave if he is to receive what Catherine owes to her dead soldier-lover, her "all." In their second meeting, part of which I quoted above to illustrate the contrast of voices, what seems to the still insensitive Frederic a quick surrender ("Oh, darling, . . . you will be good to me, won't you?"), is actually the result of Catherine's struggle and moral decision *before* she meets Frederic. And in their next encounter, after Frederic has spent a few days at the front, his identification with Catherine's former fiancé is made explicit: "Say 'I've come back to Catherine in the night,'" followed soon by her blunt recognition of her disorder. But the emotional entrance has been gained and Frederic has begun to exist for Catherine in his own right.

These dialogue scenes in the novels, especially those just summarized in *A Farewell to Arms*, tend to deceive us if we think of them too strictly in terms of the "normal" passage of time. As in "Hills Like White Elephants," although they are realistic in their "probability of motive" and in their imitation of the authentic speech patterns of actual men and women, they represent quintessences—a kind of artistic shorthand for life. The extraordinary frankness between Frederic and Catherine at first encounter could be explained credibly by the pressures of war, the sense of living on borrowed time that makes people marry on first acquaintance during a weekend pass. But we must also imagine their meetings to be a metaphor of experience, a condensation of what happens over the span of weeks or months in real life. A different norm prevails in Hemingway's fictive cosmos, the norm which measures experience not by duration but by intensity, existential time, a concept explicit in *For Whom the Bell Tolls*. There is a relativity at work in these truncated dialogues that cover so much ground so quickly. Just as the characters' speech betokens a distillation of the way people talk in actuality, so their experience concentrates into small span what is dispersed in real life. Another kind of shorthand, dialogue as thematic summary, appears in the opening pages of *For Whom the Bell Tolls*, when Anselmo in chastising Pablo prefigures the significance of the entire action: "thee, with thy dwelling place to be undisturbed, puts thy foxhole before the interests of humanity."

The contrast of tongues in *To Have and Have Not*, in accord with the novel's social purpose, is based on class differences. Just as Hemingway's temporarily Marxist perspective led him to realign class structure into a moral order, with the wealthy as evil and the poor as virtuous, the most correct and elegant speech generally typifies the worst characters ethically. What Mr. Sing, the ruthless smuggler of alien Chinese, Frederick Harrison, the Washington official who wants to take the wounded Harry Morgan "into custody," and the rich homosexual Wallace Johnston all have in common is their cultivated English. In contrast the good guys, Harry Morgan, Albert, Marie, speak the uncouth vernacular of just plain folks. There is another group of medium-good, medium-bad people, for example Professor McWalsey and Helen Gordon, who speak correctly but forthrightly, as in the case of Helen's pungent diatribe against her husband's sexual conduct in chapter 21 (which uses the same construction as Frances's outburst against Cohn). Fortunately, Hemingway keeps a tight enough grip on the dialogue so as not to inflate the novel's already obvious characterizations. He modifies the speech patterns often enough to avoid stereotyping, as when he includes a rather rough-talking lady tourist among his aristocratic characters (chap. 15) and introduces a number of levels of diction into the night scene in Freddy's bar (chap. 22). In fact, the book's dialogue, together with some sequences of breathless action, goes a long way toward redeeming its faults.

Hemingway's most extensive experiment in dialogue, one I judge highly successful, is the transliteration of Spanish into English in *For Whom the Bell Tolls*. So far as I know, this is Hemingway's own innovation, the culmination of those effects he had ventured in *A Farewell to Arms* and such stories as "A Clean, Well-Lighted Place," which echo the sound of a foreign language. Whether or not Hemingway is entirely faithful or accurate in rendering Spanish idiom into the exact English equivalent makes an interesting but not wholly relevant question, and one answerable and important only to the bilingual reader. From the standpoint of craft and the concern of an English-speaking audience, the vital question is how the dialogue functions in the novel and what it contributes to the overall aesthetic effect. That is, we must assess how well the language strategy creates the illusion of reality.[10]

First, we note the congruity of the dialogue with the novel's situation. As with the expatriate protagonist of A *Farewell to Arms*, an alien in Italy, Robert Jordan knows the language of Spain well enough to speak it with great fluency but he continues to think in his native tongue. Thus, Hemingway suggests a linguistic counterpart to Jordan's politics. He shares the language and the cause with others, yet he retains his individuality and private mind. As a result, Hemingway creates at once a marked contrast of tongues and a double vision, the saying and the thinking, which add substantially to the novel's resonance. He emphasizes this duality by occasionally focusing Jordan's thoughts on the very differences in language and the cultural and psychological distinctions these differences connote. For example, in the first chapter he calls our attention to the pronunciation of names in Spanish and records that Anselmo's rebuke of Pablo is in an archaic dialect—in both of these instances hinting at Jordan's apartness from the others, the "foreigner" in him. Too, as the novel continues we are constantly reminded that Jordan speaks in Spanish and reflects in English by the overt use of unusual constructions and the incorporation of untranslated Spanish phrases.

But this transliteration is not so obvious or easily accomplished as it may seem. Further inspection locates a third element in the novel's contrast of tongues: brief narrative and expository passages in the omniscient mode which subtly carry over the Spanish flavor from the adjacent dialogue. We would expect these to be in standard English since, as we have seen, the omniscient perspective tends to merge with the protagonist's. But as a technique of modulation, and perhaps to intimate that Jordan sometimes lapses into Spanish in his very thoughts,

Hemingway inflects even the omniscient voice. To take a frequent example, there is the reference to Pilar as "the woman of Pablo" but always within a compatible context, as in " 'And thou,' the woman of Pablo said to Pablo almost viciously. 'With thy talk of safety' " (p. 82).

The immediate impact of the Spanish-English transliteration will register upon anyone who reads the novel, as it did upon virtually every reviewer and won almost unanimous praise from them. Nor is it a mere gimmick. As more than one critic has written, it participates in the novel's epic illusion. This occurs in three ways: it makes the characters and their circumstances seem even more distant from the normal run of things, and thereby more fascinating; it confers a sense of antiquity or timelessness upon them; it elevates the language of common men to a dignity consonant with the extremity of the action in which they engage. This involves more than the use of archaic pronouns and verb forms ("thee," "hast"); it means the rather risky reliance upon a deliberately contorted rhetoric, e.g., "Thinkest thou that thy entry carries importance?" (p. 221). Such a technique is inherently artificial and could become obtrusive, if not carefully managed, as our illusion of reality collapses when James Fenimore Cooper's eloquent Indians begin to orate, to cite the worst case I can think of. How does Hemingway evade the problem?

By those supple practices, alternation and counterpoint. The kind of sentence just quoted appears often, yes, but it is not the rule. In fact, most of Hemingway's dialogue consists of terse, concentrated, colloquial statements whose diction and syntax deviate very little from standard English. Perhaps one sentence in twenty is cast from the Spanish mold, while others communicate the foreign flavor by blending a Spanish word or phrase into a familiar English construction. This passage is typical:

> "We will have good weather for it, Inglés," Pablo said to Robert Jordan.
> "We," Pilar said. "We?"

"Yes, we," Pablo grinned at her and drank some of the wine. "Why not? I thought it over while I was outside. Why should we not agree?"

"In what?" the woman asked. "In what now?"

"In all," Pablo said to her. "In this of the bridge. I am with thee now."

"You are with us now?" Agustín said to him. "After what you have said?"

"Yes," Pablo told him. "With the change of weather I am with thee." (P. 222)

Although the overall level here is perhaps slightly elevated over a comparable passage in *The Sun Also Rises* or *A Farewell to Arms*, surely it is not radically different. Moreover, Hemingway escapes the temptation to be sententious in his dialogue. If on one occasion a character utters a lofty sentiment in an appropriately formal manner, evocative of Spanish, as in Anselmo's figurative opposition of the foxhole and the interests of humanity, another time profound things will be said in the simplest ways, e.g., Pilar's "Life is very curious. . . . I would have made a good man, but I am all woman and all ugly. Yet many men have loved me and I have loved many men" (p. 97). Another of Hemingway's contrapuntal techniques is to insert a slangy English construction into the Spanish transliteration, usually in Jordan's speech, as when he says to Pablo, "How's business?" (p. 51).

Nor must we neglect a basic condition of dialogue, its appropriateness to the speaker. Other than the variations already noted, the novel's dialogue (even though "in Spanish") differs with the character, reflecting personality, age, education, and so on. A salient reason why Pilar comes through as so vivid and engaging a character is her linguistic range. In telling one of her splendid stories she mounts naturally to greater formality and eloquence, but in conversation she is blunt, pithy, vulgar. Anselmo, nature's nobleman, expresses himself always with unaffected dignity, the style as the man. Pablo is unpolished but clear and concise. Maria, as befits her background and her youth, speaks with simple propriety. The mercuric and complex Agustín explodes again and again into untranslatable bursts of obscenity, all the more emphatic and comical by their elaborateness: "Thy duty. . . . I besmirch the milk of thy duty. . . . Where the un-nameable is this vileness that I am to guard?" (p. 92). And the ludicrous quality of the too-serious and conventional Fernando gets through to us in his penchant for jargon: "I am agreed that it is perhaps best that he should be eliminated in order that the operations projected should be insured of the maximum possibility of success" (p. 219). Another sort of example of the modulation within the Spanish-speaking characters themselves appears in chapter 11, when the deaf El Sordo, on first meeting Jordan, speaks to him in pidgin-Spanish, and then, as the dialogue proceeds, addresses Pilar fluently, and finally turns to Jordan and converses not only easily but with force. Although the omniscient narrator cues us to these changes, the effect is self-sustaining. By it Hemingway unfolds El Sordo's character gradually, deepening it as the speaker grows steadily more verbal. Too, Hemingway augments the dramatic value of the scene by paralleling El Sordo's revelation of his true capacity for speech with his growing trust of Jordan, despite the brevity of their meeting. The dialogue duplicates the action.

Nothing Hemingway wrote after *For Whom the Bell Tolls* registers any advance in his craft of dialogue. Indeed, we discern a trend in which the ripeness of the dialogue style in *For Whom the Bell Tolls* sometimes degenerated into mannerism. This is especially true of *Across the River and into the Trees*, where the obliqueness of reference and laconic delivery which flow naturally out of character and attitude in the earlier books become self-conscious posturing. Furthermore, there is little range in the talk of his protagonist. Colonel Cantwell's repertoire seems limited to three styles: arrogant toughness for his subordinates and enemies, sentimentality for Renata—more, not less, effusive because of its show of stoicism—and pretentious gravity or mock-gravity with his friends. The contrast of tongues, in this novel the transliteration of Italian, appears labored in some instances.

The dialogue in *Islands in the Stream* is generally more skillful and gains a greater illusion of naturalness, particularly in Hudson's conversations with his sons, but it also goes bad on occasion. Much of the novel's middle section, "Cuba," its talkiest part, is also the least convincing. Although Hudson's monologues with his cats achieve some humor, I find them particularly tedious. Moreover, throughout the novel Hudson's dialogues with women are less credible than those with men. Certainly this is true of the episode in which Hudson makes love to a former wife, a character reminiscent of Hadley, Catherine Barkley, Maria, Martha Gellhorn, and Marlene Dietrich, synthesized and all at once.

Finally, we observe the inclination in these two novels toward too much dialogue, the kind of excess one could hardly have predicted from the writer of "The Killers." The lovers' talk in *Across the River and into the Trees* meanders on interminably, and I have been told that the deletions in the manuscript of *Islands in the Stream* consisted almost entirely of dialogue.[11] The same fault dogged the long novel titled "The Garden of Eden" which Hemingway worked at recurrently over the last fifteen years of his life, but, according to Carlos Baker, never brought to publishable condition. Baker refers to a narrative method greatly dependent upon dialogue but with page after page of the characters' talk devoted to trivialities.[12]

However, lest we leave the subject with the impression that the master, grown old and sick, had completely relaxed his hold on his craft, we should recall the countervailing cases, *The Old Man and the Sea* and *A Moveable Feast*, wherein Hemingway's dialogue exhibits its customary expertise. In *The Old Man and the Sea* the hero's simple eloquence in his dialogues with the boy and in his dramatic monologues during the struggle with the fish reminds us of such characters as Pilar and Anselmo.

Although the Spanish transliteration is more muted than that in *For Whom the Bell Tolls*, it attains the same conviction and authenticity. The style and structure of *A Moveable Feast* make it, in my judgment, Hemingway's best work of nonfiction, and its dialogue contributes substantially to its quality. Such scenes as those with Gertrude Stein and Fitzgerald are as graphic as anything in *The Sun Also Rises*. If the dialogue conveyed a less intense illusion of reality or if it were less comically resonant, we would be repelled by Hemingway's vindictiveness. In these two books, at least, we have evidence that toward the end Hemingway could still handle one of his sharpest tools with unerring skill.

5

Further Observations on Style and Method

The title of this chapter is deliberately expansive so as to collect in one loose and baggy container a variety of related topics. By "style" I mean essentially language and rhetoric; by "method" I have in mind such matters as Hemingway's use of detail, sometimes metaphorically or symbolically, the technique with which he created landscapes, and a few analogies between his practices and those of musical composition. Some of these points have been treated in passing in other contexts, but I return to them here to give them proper emphasis in the whole range of Hemingway's craft and to develop them more fully. Other topics will be considered in this chapter for the first time.

In regard to style I am happy to withdraw the claim that Hemingway's craft has been neglected. It is the one area of his art which has elicited a depth and quantity of commentary comparable to that lavished upon the Hemingway Hero and the Code. Although the earliest close textual analyses of Hemingway's style date from the 1940s, the reviewers of his beginning work recognized the distinctiveness of his language and rhetoric. Even those who deplored his choice of character and situation and doubted his future significance, acknowledged the originality and appeal of his style. In the past twenty years there have been a number of searching studies of the style by Harry Levin, Frederic I. Carpenter, John Graham, Charles Fenton, Philip Young, Carlos Baker,

Earl Rovit, and Tony Tanner, to name only the most notable. Richard Bridgman and Walker Gibson have each chosen Hemingway's style as exemplary of certain important characteristics of American language and have examined it with valuable results, especially Bridgman. Too, linguists are now turning to Hemingway's style as material for comparative and transformational analysis, although not yet with conclusions immediately applicable to practical criticism. I must therefore start by synthesizing and summarizing established positions before I can build upon them. What follows for the next few pages is a composite view of Hemingway's style, modified by my own perceptions.[1]

No important writer of prose in English has ever written in a style at once so individualized and seemingly so artless. Its basic characteristics are sufficiently prominent for every reader to discern for himself. The majority of sentences are short and declarative, arranged in a straightforward sequence determined by the internal logic of the action or situation. Simple or compound sentences predominate, with the coordinating conjunction "and" used to the degree that it becomes almost incantatory. Consequently, there is a minority of complex or compound-complex sentences and relatively little subordination. The succession of relatively short sentences produces a sense of rapidity or dynamism, or at times a staccato effect. This dynamism and illusion of movement is augmented by the use of almost entirely active verbs. Another technique Hemingway uses to create the effect of vitality is to play off active verbs against static ones, or employ gerundive or participial forms. The gerunds and participles are especially important in conveying the impression of ongoing action.

Like the sentence structure, the diction is also quite elementary and favors plain familiar, and monosyllabic words. Fewer adjectives and adverbs appear than in most literary styles or in real-life discourse. The adjectives vary from highly specific and concrete terms such as names, numbers, colors, to the generalized and subjective, e.g., *fine*, *lovely*, *good*. Nouns carry the greatest weight, and by their frequency and in combination with the definite article *the* produce a strong suggestion of "thingness" and exactitude. In its diction Hemingway's basic method has been said to resemble Haiku, in that both depend upon the smallest possible units of language to provoke response and attain meaning.[2] However, this similarity can be explained by Hemingway's indebtedness to Pound and the precepts of Imagist poetry rather than his own direct contact with Oriental verse. I should add that although Hemingway's diction is generally so accessible a child could understand it, he seasons it with a sprinkling of foreign words, an occasional exotic or offbeat usage, and the strategic placement of unexpected adjectives or adverbs—techniques which forestall monotony and preserve the necessary element of surprise.

The simplicity of Hemingway's syntax parallels the other simplicities. Perhaps his most obvious and celebrated stylistic technique is that of repetition, although we must be reminded that repetition was, and remains, a natural attribute of colloquial speech. Gertrude Stein was the first American writer to fully appreciate that fact and try to capitalize upon it in her work. Hemingway brought her experiments to fruition and made it a major resource of his style; thus, the initial point to be recorded about Hemingway's repetition is that it imitates actuality. However, as a stylistic device he uses it in several ways. There is the basic repetition of a key word or phrase, together with subtle shifts in emphasis and hints of new meanings (this is the usage we saw clearly in the dialogue between Nick and the ex-fighter in "The Battler," cited in the previous chapter). Another type is syntactical repetition, wherein Hemingway aligns several phrases or clauses of similar grammatical structure in a sequence, again with small incremental modifications. Or, he may expand the repetition into a rhetorical pattern by building it into a series of like sentences, perhaps with identical openers. Or, he may combine one or more of these methods into an intricate design running to paragraph length and beyond. The horrendously vivid description of the behavior of a hyena when hit by a rifle bullet, a passage which extends to three long paragraphs in *Green Hills of Africa* (pp. 37–38), illustrates the remarkable effects Hemingway could contrive from patterns of repetition.

Hemingway's paragraphs do not seem as distinctive of his signature as individual sentences and for this reason have attracted little comment from students of the style. Yet their role is significant. I argue that the power of Hemingway's sentences is cumulative, arising not so much from the single statement as from the progression or montage of sentences in the paragraph, and the corresponding progression of paragraphs. This is why Hemingway's style is so easy to imitate or parody one sentence at a time, but so difficult to reproduce in the large—or to excel. The imitator or parodist misses the coherence of the order of sentences and paragraphs. Furthermore, the size, structure, and relationship of the paragraphs are integral to the overall effect. Short paragraphs emphasize or highlight shifts in character or mood. Long paragraphs recreate the flow of thought or reproduce the continuity of a single action. Hemingway also gains the impression of immediacy by often combining different activities or changing focus to different characters within the same grammatical or structural unit, both sentence and paragraph. Transitional markers between successive paragraphs tend to be unobtrusive. One of Hemingway's favorite tactics, perhaps a carry-over from a basic practice in journalism, is to begin a paragraph with a sentence pinpointing time and place. Another is to repeat the name of a central character or an appropriate pronoun reference. As a result, in Hemingway's work, unlike Faulkner's, we always know who is doing what to whom, where, and when. Anything that smacks of intellectual process or "interpretation"—*however, therefore, accordingly*—is avoided. This is true even of such expository and discursive works as *Death in the Afternoon* and *A Moveable Feast*.

Although at our initial experience of Hemingway's style it seems at the furthest remove from poetry and much less suited to reading aloud than Faulkner or Fitzgerald, it does contain its own kind of lyricism. Its music is of two types. There is the occasional formal lyricism we associate with literary masterpieces of tradition, a lyricism gained through allusion, the conscious exploitation of a resonant and stately diction, or derived especially from involved patterns of harmonic repetition. In contrast and more commonly, there is the accidental music of ordinary speech, or its literary counterpart, free verse.[3] Hemingway's most characteristic rhythms are thus the choppy rhythms of colloquial language rather than the sonorous measures of a latinate high style. Again, the central technique of repetition often determines the beat, and in certain crucial action passages, as I will demonstrate, Hemingway employs varied rhythmic structures to emulate the intrinsic tempo of the activity itself. Likewise, he uses sound discreetly rather than habitually, saving it for special effects. For example, he makes some onomatopoeic correspondence between the sounds of words and the actions they denote. He quite frequently creates a subtle echo-effect or a muted rhyming as the spontaneous product of the method of repetition. There are also instances of purposeful alliteration, assonance, and consonance. Yet, all these devices are more subliminal than apparent, so that our reaction to the texture of Hemingway's prose remains dominantly visual rather than aural. In contrast to the mellifluous prose of Melville, Faulkner, Fitzgerald, or Wolfe, Hemingway sounds dissonant. It takes careful listening to hear his music. I will develop this point later.

What I have been describing as Hemingway's style is, in fact, the early or "classic" style, that epitomized in "Big Two-Hearted River," a work often chosen by critics as exemplary but which I see as extreme. Although the style of that story is truly unique, even dazzling in its effects, it teeters on the edge of mannerism. Actually, Hemingway's style underwent gradual change in the direction of greater fluency and variety. Some of this is already manifest in *A Farewell to Arms*; it is much more evident in the two brilliant African stories of the mid-1930s, and it culminates in *For Whom the Bell Tolls*. In that novel the sentences are much longer and often complex in structure, the diction and syntax more elaborate (and not only because of the Spanish trans-literation), the lyricism more frequent and pronounced, and rhetorical devices more varied and abundant. However, although I consider the style of *For Whom the Bell Tolls* a triumph, no work after it fully reproduced or repeated that style. *Across the River and into the Trees* unsuccessfully attempted a hard-boiled version of it. *The Old Man and the Sea* utilized some of its dialect techniques but kept to the simple mode in diction and syntax—with excellent results, I must add. *A Moveable Feast* returned to the style of *The Sun Also Rises*, renewing it gracefully and subtly. *Islands in the Stream* synthesizes the early and the late: looser and more eloquent than the early, yet still more restrained than the late. Consequently, while it is not quite accurate to speak of "Hemingway's style" as though it were a fixed entity, his method retained sufficient similarity and unity of purpose to permit valid generalization about it.

Almost without exception the commentators on Hemingway's style have extrapolated from the hallowed dictum that "the style is the man." That is, they have construed technique as world view or attitude. To our profit, this approach has produced a coherent and trenchant appraisal of the impact of the style upon our consciousness, and a deep insight into technique as a form of utterance—the merger of the writer's method and vision, or method as vision. The liability in such criticism, as I have earlier noted in brief, has been the tendency to exploit the style to judge the writer's mentality by academic criteria or by other sets of purportedly humanistic principles. Thus the paradox arises that Hemingway's style, among the most "objective" in modern fiction, i.e., among those in which ethical statement is least overt, was almost from the beginning interpreted by critics as a "moral" style. By the 1940s this had become a truism of Hemingway criticism. In 1941 Mark Schorer wrote presciently: "The style which made Hemingway famous —with its ascetic suppression of ornament and figure, its insistence on the objective and the unreflective (for good fighters do not talk), its habit of understatement (or sportsmen boast), the directness and the brevity of its syntactical constructions, its muscularity, the sharpness of its staccato and repetitive effects, 'the purity of its line under the maximum of exposure,' that is, its continued poise under the weight of event of feeling—this style is an exact transfiguration of Hemingway's moral attitude toward a peculiarly violent and chaotic experience. His style, in effect, is what he had instead of God." [4] At about the same time Joseph Warren Beach remarked that although Hemingway's style consciously evaded intellectual processes, it was perfectly suited to "the aesthetic projection of images." [5]

Most subsequent criticism, some of it brilliant, is an elaboration of these basic insights. Harry Levin pointed out that the appeal of Hemingway's technique was essentially visual, linear, "cinematographic," attaining its vividness and fluidity by the careful ordering of impressions in a particular sequence, each separate image momentarily holding the reader's attention as it passes. Philip Young traced the origins of the style and stressed its illusion of reality and objectivity by means of its close focus upon a narrow range of experience. Young saw that much of Hemingway's irony results from the method of understatement, the depiction of harrowing experience in quiet little words. Young also concluded that the tautness of the style expressed the writer's attempt to subdue his inner traumas by the application of an external discipline of technique. Carlos Baker compared Hemingway's method with T. S. Eliot's theory of the "objective correlative," and emphasized the governing principle of Hemingway's search for "truth" through the rigid suppression of emotion and subjectivity. F. I. Carpenter, John Graham, Earl Rovit, and Tony Tanner, have all tried to account for the special intensity of Hemingway's rendition of physical and sensory experience, the "perpetual now" effect of his prose, his use of selective detail, and his treatment of the act or instant of perception itself. Tanner's treatment is especially cogent. Hemingway's syntax, he resolves, "works to disentangle each precious single sense impression: it is . . . the syntax of sensation." [6]

The problem with much of this criticism is its predilection, even in the sympathetic critics, to bend the style to the service of something else and thus distract us from the way the style actually functions. What they have really been after is that elusive entity, Hemingway's "mind." In the pages to follow, I should like to restore the emphasis to technique qua technique, as appropriate to this particular study, and thus direct my attention to process and result. The aspect of Hemingway's mind I want to illuminate is that of the craftsman. To this end I will select a number of passages typical of various aspects of Hemingway's style and analyze them closely. I hope to demonstrate that Hemingway was a more resourceful and versatile writer than has commonly been admitted.

Critics generally agree that Hemingway's portrayal of physical action ranks among his greatest strengths. I will state the case even more enthusiastically and say that this is an area of achievement in which Hemingway is unsurpassed in English prose fiction. Hemingway himself stressed his need to understand and master the essentials of action-writing as a foundation for his style. In the best-known expression of it, a passage with which much commentary on Hemingway's style necessarily begins, he said:

> I was trying to write then and I found the greatest difficulty, aside from knowing truly what you really felt, rather than what you were supposed to feel and had been taught to feel, was to put down what really

happened in action; what the actual things were which produced the emotion that you experienced. In writing for a newspaper you told what happened and, with one trick and another, you communicated the emotion aided by the element of timeliness which gives a certain emotion to any account of something that has happened on that day; but the real thing, the sequence of motion and fact which made the emotion and which would be as valid in a year or ten years or, with luck and if you stated it purely enough, always, was beyond me and I was working very hard to try to get it. (*Death in the Afternoon*, p. 2)

The essence here, Hemingway's action-formula, so to speak, is "the real thing, the sequence of motion and fact which made the emotion." And by "real" I think Hemingway implies more than the obvious contextual definition of genuine, authentic, durable; he also means *actual, tangible*. Again, as Carlos Baker and others have remarked, there is a striking similarity between Hemingway's view and Eliot's definition of the objective correlative: "a set of objects, a situation, a chain of events which shall be the formula of that particular emotion; such that when the external facts, which must terminate in sensory experience, are given, the emotion is immediately evoked." [7]

Hemingway's other allusion to his method which I believe pertains directly to action-writing is the tantalizing reference in *Green Hills of Africa* to what he calls the "fourth and fifth dimension" of prose—a prose "much more difficult than poetry" (p. 27). What I think Hemingway is talking about may be otherwise named in Robert Frost's phrase "the sound of meaning." That is, beyond the perception of a particular fact or image and its placement in the proper arrangement with other facts or images (as Hemingway went on to cite in the *Death in the Afternoon* passage his perception of the exposed thigh bone and soiled underwear of a gored matador as "the real thing"), there is the control of language itself: the ordering of words in the sentence, their groupings into phrases and clauses, their syllabic lengths and combinations—whether gliding into or jarring against one another, and the organization of the whole sentences into the right sequence, so that the progression and rhythm of word, phrase, clause, and sentence, duplicate or reproduce the duration and tempo of the action.

As our first example, consider this sentence from "Chapter IX" of *In Our Time,* which dates back to Hemingway's earliest published work: "The second matador slipped and the bull caught him through the belly and he hung on to the horn with one hand and held the other tight against the place, and the bull rammed him wham against the wall and the horn came out, and he lay in the sand, and then got up like crazy drunk and tried to slug the men carrying him away and yelled for his sword but he fainted" (*The Short Stories,* p. 159). Hemingway's manipulation of language and syntactic structure illustrates style-as-action and documents many of the observations made above.

Most familiarly there is the unbroken succession of sparsely punctuated coordinate clauses coupled by "and" —Hemingway's so-called "paratactic style." Thus, the continuity and intensity of the action are immediately conveyed by the uninterrupted duration of the prose unit. Just as the action depicted is the most concentrated in "Chapter IX," so the sentence containing it is the longest—amounting to almost half the entire sketch. The sequence of events exactly duplicates the order of occurrence, with no discernible narrative mediation or rearrangement. Complexity or density derives not from any difficulty in apprehending what is happening but from the need to keep it all in the mind's eye at the same time, especially as the focus fluctuates back and forth from man to bull, with the bull dominating the middle of the sentence just as he renders the man most helpless during that part of the action. The quantity of material packed into the single sentence (74 words) strains our responses and augments the effect of un-abated force. The sparsity of the punctuation adds to the strain; we must read through four clauses, each detailing a separate action, before we can pause, and then four more as the sentence ends. The use of thirteen consecutive active verbs also creates a tremendous sense of movement.

The punctuation, though minimal, has two purposes: to aid in the shift of focus to the bull and isolate the single most dramatic moment of the action, and to indicate the same syntactical pause or interval as the action itself contains. That is, the clause "and he lay in the sand" is surrounded by commas because there is truly a pause in what happens. The commas mark what has been left out, the matador's act of falling and rising, an omission calculated to add to the intensity of the movement. The "pause" thus constitutes a kind of interpretation—a wholly unobtrusive kind. Yet another technique in controlling the speed is to vary the length of the individual clauses. The first clause has four words, the second eight, and the third ten, producing an *accelerando* effect. Then, as the sentence winds down, we have the corresponding *retardando* of steadily shortening units, with the lengths of the last three clauses as nine, five, three. The use of the conjunction "but" to introduce the brief final clause contrasts sharply with the prevailing "and," thereby helping to terminate the sentence abruptly and imitate the same halt to the action: "but he fainted."

With one vital exception the language in the sentence is unadorned and unmusical, but at exactly its center point—which is also the center of the action—Hemingway posits one rhythmic and heavily euphonious clause: "and the bull rammed him wham against the wall." In order to fix this moment most firmly in the reader's memory Hemingway accents its visual appeal with an additional call upon the auditory sense, a type of "pedal effect." The startling "wham" is also the sole deviation in the sentence from normative diction and syntax. It's a small device, once we have seen it work, but all we need do to dissipate its power would be to punctuate it. Simply add a couple of commas, "and the bull rammed him, wham, against the wall," and the effect is much weakened. Although only the rhymed and consonantal phrase "rammed him wham" catches our immediate attention, it is but one of several operative poetic devices. There is the assonance and consonance of *and/rammed, wham/against*, the consonance of *bull/wall*, and the reiterated *the/the*. There is also a measurable under-rhythm of two anapestic feet succeeded by two iambic feet which provides a rapidity and fluidity of tempo appropriate to the action:

> x x /   x   x   / x /   x /
> and the bull rammed him wham against the wall

Another kind of action sequence which approaches the fourth and fifth dimensions by techniques less evident than the coordinate clause-*and* method depends upon intricate syntactical and sound patterns. This is the sentence from "Fathers and Sons":

> In shooting quail you must not get between them and their habitual cover, once the dogs have found them, or when they flush they will come pouring at you, some rising steep, some skimming by your ears, whirring into a size you have never seen them in the air as they pass, the only way being to turn and take them over your shoulder as they go, before they set their wings and angle down into the thicket. (*The Short Stories*, pp. 488–89)

The acceleration effect which is perhaps the most unusual feature of the sentence is enhanced in context by two shifts in voice, from third person narration to direct address, and from the controlled, rational, grammatically correct lecturing voice to that so rapt in the action it discards linguistic convention to find its own kind of order. The montage of the lengthening clauses, conjoined with the jumbled burst of language which imi-

tates the basic movement of the birds' flight and communicates the speaker's excited participation in it, can
be more clearly observed if we paste together a leaf
from Hemingway's contemporaries William Carlos Wil-
liams and E. E. Cummings and rearrange the prose as a
bit of free verse. This is what the sentence might look
like if we used space to emulate the action, building in
the approach, culminated in the instant of passing, and
diminished in tempo and distance as it concludes:

In shooting quail
you must not get between them and their habitual cover,
once the dogs have found them,
or when they flush
they will come pouring atyou,
steep

g
n
i
s
i
r

some
some   skimmingbyyourears,
whirringintoasizeyouhaveneverseenthemintheairastheypass,
the only way being
to turn and take them over your shoulder as they go,
before they set their wings
and a
n
g
l
e
d
o
w
n
intothethicket.

That is, I have crudely tried to suggest here the modulation and timing of Hemingway's sentence, especially its

"whoosh" effect, the phenomenon of a flying object which seems to gain speed as it approaches, attaining a movement so rapid it blurs precisely at the instant it is closest to us and thus produces a sensation of suspended animation. However, my reordering of a prose passage into the vertical progression of free verse does violence to one extremely important fact of the prose—its lateral movement. The prose experience I labor to describe, particularly the instant of culmination, depends upon the eye being driven *across* the page (like the birds' flight) with increasing quickness, so that the words seem to run together to simulate the visual illusion of "the real thing." Notice, too, that the punctuation in the passage has an important part in controlling duration and distinguishing the measured pace of the opening clauses from the hectic continuity of the central action. Other important devices are the consonance of the *s*'s and *r*'s and the deployment of four successive participial verbs, *pouring, rising, skimming, whirring.*

We can name such sentences "imitative form," the effort to parallel the structural design of an utterance with its lexical message so that the reader apprehends two kinds of meaning simultaneously, the one translatable or paraphrasable in logical terms, the other sensory or emotive. Hemingway's work contains enough instances of such complex structures to deter us from lapsing into a superficial view of his style as resembling the simple-minded utterance of child or savage. For example, *Green Hills of Africa* (pp. 148–50) contains a single sentence of approximately four hundred and fifty words which by its elaborate periodicity duplicates the overt extended metaphor of the Gulf Stream. The continuity and contiguity of its clauses and the slow, stately rhythms of the rhetorical pattern reproduce the sense of the uninterrupted flow of a deep ocean current. This is yet another variation of the action style, although the topic of the sentence has nothing to do with violence; rather, it deals with the writer's politics, his choice of literary material, his life-style, and his relationship with the critics.

So far, we have examined single sentences illustrative

of the action-style, but on occasion Hemingway integrates a series of such sentences into one or more paragraphs to create an extraordinarily palpable rendition
of violent physical experience. A passage from "The Undefeated" provides a case in point.

> Zurito watched. The monos, in their red shirts, run-
> ning out to drag the picador clear. The picador, now
> on his feet, swearing and flopping his arms. Manuel
> and Hernandez standing ready with their capes. And
> the bull, the great black bull, with a horse on his back,
> hooves dangling, the bridle caught in the horns. Black
> bull with a horse on his back, staggering short-legged,
> then arching his neck and lifting, thrusting, charging
> to slide the horse off, horse sliding down. Then the
> bull into a lunging charge at the cape Manuel spread
> for him. (*The Short Stories*, p. 252)

This paragraph incorporates some of Hemingway's
favorite methods with others less often utilized.

Gone is the familiar series of coordinate clauses and
linking conjunctions. There are but four instances of
"and" in the paragraph, and only one introduces a main
clause. Hemingway has eschewed his characteristic construction for the simple reason that the action itself is
not connected and successive but unpredictable, frenzied, chaotic. The bullfight here is out of control, the
basic fact reflected in the broken syntax with its juxtaposition of short, fragmented sentences. Everything is happening at once, as indicated by the stream of participial
verbs: *running, swearing, flopping, standing, dangling,
staggering, arching, lifting, thrusting, charging, sliding,
lunging*. In this case, and contrary to the conclusions of
some commentators on Hemingway's style, the number
and kind of verbs do bear primary responsibility in the
re-creation of violence. The crowding of brief units into
short, heavily punctuated sentences also intensifies the
illusion of speed and power run amuck.

Although the paragraph has no single consistent rhythmic pattern, the staccato beat coming naturally out of

this syntax is modulated and enhanced in two important places. The reiterated lines "And the bull, the great black bull, with a horse on his back. . . . Black bull with a horse on his back" collect additional force from their conjunction of anapestic and iambic rhythms, with the anapest dominant, just as the effect of the successive participles "lifting, thrusting, charging" is amplified by their intrinsic trochaic measure. Alliterations and internal rhymes (black bull, black/back) and the strong consonance of the *t* sounds in the participial group contribute further to the effect. If Hemingway's attempts at verse produced little of value at the beginning of his career, it can be seen in his prose, especially his action-style, that he took some useful lessons from the experiment. We should also note in the above passage how, as in the examples previously cited, the action speeds up from the static opening "Zurito watched" into breathless rapidity, decelerates in the longer line of the concluding sentence, and returns to stasis in the first sentence of the next paragraph: "The bull was slower now, Manuel felt."

Of all the action writing in Hemingway, I know of none more accomplished than the paragraph in *For Whom the Bell Tolls* which depicts El Sordo as he looks through the sights of an automatic rifle at an approaching Fascist officer. I find it an astonishing display of craft because although the character himself is perfectly immobile, Hemingway reproduces an illusion of dynamic movement by structuring the duration, order, and tempo of El Sordo's reactions to keep pace with the bold stride of the oncoming figure.

> Only one, he thought. We get only one. But from his manner of speaking he is *caza mayor*. Look at him walking. Look what an animal. Look at him stride forward. This one is for me. This one I take with me on the trip. This one coming now makes the same voyage I do. Come on, Comrade Voyager. Come striding. Come right along. Come along to meet it.

Come on. Keep on walking. Don't slow up. Come right along. Come as thou art coming. Don't stop and look at those. That's right. Don't even look down. Keep on coming with your eyes forward. Look, he has a moustache. What do you think of that? He runs to a moustache, the Comrade Voyager. He is a captain. Look at his sleeves. I said he was *caza mayor*. He has the face of an *Inglés*. Look. With a red face and blond hair and blue eyes. With no cap on and his moustache is yellow. With blue eyes. With pale blue eyes. With pale blue eyes with something wrong with them. With pale blue eyes that don't focus. Close enough. Too close. Yes, Comrade Voyager. Take it, Comrade Voyager. (P. 319)

Although another detailed analysis would be unwarranted, in brief what we have here is perceptual process, including the exercise of the rational and evaluative faculties, portrayed as though it were direct physical action and communicated in the mode of dramatic monologue. Moreover, the whole passage takes on the quality of poetic utterance or incantation both by the urgency of its rhythm and the richness of its language, the style embellished by syntactical inversion ("this one coming now"), epithet ("Comrade Voyager"), and the exotically foreign (*"caza mayor"*). Finally, there is the intricate interweaving of incremental repetitions throughout: one reiterated word or phrase momentarily dominant, replaced by another, then another, then the first and second reappearing in altered form, and so on. Indeed, I find at least eleven different motifs of repetition working concurrently in the paragraph, culminating in the climactic sequence of the six "with" clauses, and the whole action released in the unfolding final triplet of expanding units of two, three, and four: "Too close. Yes, Comrade Voyager. Take it, Comrade Voyager." No primitive ever composed so complex a harmonics. As the concluding fillip, Hemingway uses the following paragraph for the actual instant or commission of the violence, employing the killing itself to relieve the almost unbearable tension: "He squeezed the trigger of the automatic gently and it pounded back three times against his shoulder with the slippery jolt the recoil of a tripoded automatic weapon gives."

Among the significant permutations of the action-style is its adaptation to replicate the bodily movements and responses of physical love. I find the two earliest examples of it in *A Farewell to Arms,* the first in chapter 3 when Frederic recalls with mixed feelings the drunken one-night stands with prostitutes during his leave. As part of the rhetoric of a long paragraph, imitative of the protagonist's stream of memory, Hemingway conveys the impression of intercourse with a simple repetition: "sure that this was all and all and all" (p. 13). Late in the novel there appears another less apparent imitation of the sexual rhythm in which the style travels subtly from the depiction of mental states to physical sensations, suggesting in order and with increasing intensity: memory, urgent desire, physical response to desire, the mindless relief of desire, and the subsequent disappointing return to full awareness of self and surroundings. This occurs at the start of chapter 32, just after Frederic has escaped the battle police at the Tagliamento.

> I could remember Catherine but I knew I would get crazy if I thought about her when I was not sure yet I would see her, so I would not think about her, only about her a little, only about her with the car going slowly and clickingly, and some light through the canvas and my lying with Catherine on the floor of the car. Hard as the floor of the car to lie not thinking only feeling, having been away too long, the clothes wet and the floor moving only a little each time and lonesome inside and alone with wet clothing and hard floor for a wife. (P. 240)

In this paragraph the protagonist's self-awareness, enforced not only by the rational structure of the syntax of the opening clauses but also by the repeated personal pronoun "I," vanishes into his involuntary physical responses aroused by the movement of the train. The sexual impulse takes over at precisely the point where the pronoun disappears ("only about her a little") and is emphasized by the subsequent repetition ("only about her"), the montage of lengthening clauses, and the scrambled syntax and participial verbs of the second sentence. The passion abates or is spent somewhere after the first clause of that sentence, because with "having been away too long" and the reiteration of "wet," "lonesome," "alone," and "hard floor," we are back in the world of rational consciousness. The emphatic declarative opening of the next paragraph makes this clear: "You did not love the floor of a flat-car."

The technique of communicating sexual action through stylistic pattern, though Hemingway was to extend and experiment with it in *To Have and Have Not* and especially in the lyrical lovemaking of Jordan and Maria in *For Whom the Bell Tolls*, can be observed in brief but essential form in "Fathers and Sons." It combines incremental repetition, syntactical montage, and accelerating staccato rhythm to gain its effects.

> "It's hard to say," Nick Adams said. Could you say she did first what no one has ever done better and mention plump brown legs, flat belly, hard little breasts, well holding arms, quick searching tongue, the flat eyes, the good taste of mouth, then uncomfortably, tightly, sweetly, moistly, lovely, tightly, achingly, fully, finally, unendingly, never-endingly, never-to-endingly, suddenly ended, the great bird flown like an owl in the twilight, only it daylight in the woods and hemlock needles stuck against your belly. (*The Short Stories*, p. 497)

Again Hemingway frames the rapturously unthinking moments of the sex act with a coherent prose of reason, leading us from reflective memory into acutely empathic re-experience, down to the awakening and back to the point of initial awareness. With all the sources scholars have located to explain various facets of Hemingway's style, no one has accounted for such writing as this. For better or worse it entered English prose with Hemingway himself, with the result that all writers who come after him must consider his practice when they attempt to portray the same experiences.

We must not overlook the importance of stylistic technique in Hemingway's presentation of sensory data, the way things look, sound, feel, taste, smell. Hemingway uses a variety of methods in such presentations. As a major technique, he will arrange a series of concrete details which comprise the specifics or components of the sensation—its stimulus, so to speak—but leave the actual mechanism of response to the reader, sometimes suggesting the appropriate intensity of the response with a surprisingly generalized adjective, sometimes providing a precise cue. For example, in chapter 7 of *The Sun Also Rises* Hemingway culminates Jake's narration of the process of chilling and serving champagne with the unspecific but impressive assertion "It was amazing champagne," the word *amazing* allowing the reader to react to the limits of his own capacity. In contrast, there is Nick's response to his first bite of hot supper in "Big Two-Hearted River," which climaxes the point-by-point description of the preparation of that supper: " 'Chrise,' Nick said, 'Geezus Chrise,' he said happily." The slurred enunciation of the oath copies the cautious, deliberately slack contouring of the mouth when a person eats something hot and tries to say something at the same time; it also provides a delightful moment of comic relief. Too, the choice of exclamation is a clear index to the pleasure of the response. The most elaborate passage of cued sensory response in Hemingway's work, one too long to quote, is the depiction of the smell of death in chapter 19 of *For Whom the Bell Tolls*. The use of a series of graphic particulars to evoke an olefactory reaction is a technique I have not seen elsewhere before Hemingway, and after him ordinarily only in imitators or disciples (for example, Norman Mailer's evocation of smell in *An American Dream*). Since odor has no visual or audible equivalent, Hemingway stimulates the imagination by supplying a set of vivid dramatic situations, each of which contributes one element to the smell of death: the reek of a storm-tossed ship, the breath of old women who have drunk blood, the scent of dead flowers mixed with the effluvium of spent human sperm. We also observe that in its depiction of the smell of death by specific procedures which the listener is asked to perform, the impact of the whole passage on the reader is dynamic and approximates the effect of the action-style, even though the style itself does not rely upon unusual devices of diction, syntax, or rhythm.

Another technique gets even closer to the anatomy of sensation by employing sound to simulate tactile experience. For example, there is the cue to the intrinsic quality or texture of a food and the imitation of the noise of eating it in this sentence from *For Whom the Bell Tolls*: "He crossed the stream, picked a double handful, washed the muddy roots clean in the current and then sat down again beside his pack and ate the clean, cool green leaves and the crisp, peppery-tasting stalks" (p. 9). In this, the saying of *cool green leaves* and *crisp, peppery-tasting stalks* evokes both the minty flavor of watercress and the moist crunching of it. Then there is a similar but more abstract type of gustatory suggestion which I can cite but not really explain, except to guess that it works by the precision of the adjectives and the syllabic interaction of the words chosen, as, for example, in "The wine was icy cold and tasted faintly rusty" (*The Sun Also Rises*, p. 121). I surmise, without knowing why, that the conjunction of *wine/icy/faintly* and the presence of so many liquid and sibilant sounds approximates the effect of coldness and the act (sound?) of drinking.

Of course, as I have tried to emphasize, the method underlying Hemingway's depiction of sensory experience is simply one aspect of the general technique responsible throughout his work for the rendition of a constant, tangible, and urgent reality: the method of selective detail. And at this juncture I embark on the second of my major topics in this chapter. As we have seen in the study of narrative perspective and dialogue, and as any number of critics have attested, Hemingway's characters do have inner lives, fantasies, nightmares, self-colloquies, and so on. But they draw their primary ability to penetrate our imaginations and lodge there permanently from their earthly, physical selves. Accordingly, no other modern writer offers a fiction comprised of a thicker and firmer texture of reality than Hemingway, a texture woven from physical detail. Yet I assert again that this is more than a dense layer of verisimilitude; it serves metaphorically and symbolically as well. The detail I am especially concerned with is that of perception, movement, and gesture—the detail which sets Hemingway's people "in the world" and constantly reconfirms their existential selves, the *thingness* of their bodies and lives. However, this thingness is not so much a matter of knowing a great deal about what the characters look like or what they wear. Hemingway is surprisingly reticent in such details. Instead, we always know *where* they are; what they see, touch, taste; what they do and how they do it; and the time, weather, and terrain.

In my discussion of individual works in previous chapters I have shown that the detailing of some little, seemingly insignificant gesture or movement—detail which in context melts into the overall verisimilitude of the work (for example, the closing of gates in "The Doctor and the Doctor's Wife")—really performs the important function of cueing unstated emotion or attitude. This is a type of objective correlative, or, to recall E. M. Halliday's apt phrase, objective epitome. However, even though the practice has already been noted, it is so pervasive in Hemingway's writing and yet so easy to overlook I want to return to the method and study it here at somewhat greater length. Two incidents in *A Farewell to Arms* will support what I have been saying about the tangibility of Hemingway's fictive world and demonstrate how detail manifests character and theme.

At the beginning of chapter 3 the protagonist returns from leave to his quarters near the front:

> The room I shared with the lieutenant Rinaldi looked out on the courtyard. The window was open, my bed was made up with blankets and my things hung on the wall, the gas mask in an oblong tin can, the steel helmet on the same peg. At the foot of the bed was my flat trunk, and my winter boots, the leather shiny with oil, were on the trunk. My Austrian sniper's rifle with its blued octagon barrel and the lovely dark walnut, cheek-fitted, *schutzen* stock, hung over the two beds. The telescope that fitted it was, I remembered, locked in the trunk. The lieutenant, Rinaldi, lay asleep on the other bed. He woke when he heard me in the room and sat up. (Pp. 10–11)

Other than the necessary function of the passage to firmly reestablish Frederic in a military environment, why is such vivid and particular treatment given to the sniper's rifle, especially inasmuch as it is never mentioned again? Why the sharp focus on it, in a prose so carefully controlled and so wary of excess? The answer: because it tells something important about the protagonist.

Most obviously in the whole passage there is the pleasure in the order of things, the neat and precise disposition of objects in the immediate physical environment. We might call it Hemingway's pervasive desire for "a clean, well-lighted place." [8] This satisfies our predilection for order and helps us preserve the illusion of control over the threatening unruliness of the cosmos. So much we can share with Frederic Henry. But that military equipment, especially the deadly rifle, should be depicted in almost aesthetic terms ("lovely"), reveals an attribute or attitude in Henry never spoken in the novel and, indeed, contrary to his mission in the ambulance unit as a saver of lives. What this episode really intimates is Frederic's boyish love of guns for their own sake and his lack of awareness of what guns do to human bodies. Consequently, Hemingway's momentary focus on the rifle returns us to the pre-Catherine, pre-separate peace, pre-reflective narrator condition of Frederic Henry, and suggests an unconfessed motivation for his military service at a time when his sensibility was on the same level as his gear: the boy's fascination with war, its adventure, and its accouterments.

Another little sequence of details, innocuous on the surface, appears soon after the opening of the novel's last chapter. Frederic has brought Catherine to the hospital and her labor has commenced. All proceeds normally and the mood is optimistic as Frederic goes out to get breakfast. On his way back to the hospital there is this seemingly lighthearted encounter:

> Outside along the street were the refuse cans from the houses waiting for the collector. A dog was nosing at one of the cans.
> "What do you want?" I asked and looked in the can to see if there was anything I could pull out for him; there was nothing on top but coffee-grounds, dust and some dead flowers.
> "There isn't anything, dog," I said. (P. 325)

But the true function of the passage belies its superficial cheerfulness. The mention of garbage cans and the scavenger dog strikes ominous warning notes: the cans and their contents are objective epitomes for the end of the tranquil domesticity the characters have briefly shared (coffee grounds), the demise of their love and of Catherine herself (dead flowers), and man's fate at large (dust). We might extend the symbolism just a little further and see the unsuccessfully searching dog as representative of Frederic himself, the narrator sifting through the debris of the past for something nourishing. Thus, the objective epitome does the work of a philosophical commentary on the vanity of human wishes— and also delineates the protagonist's altered condition —without the obtrusiveness and tedium of an actual commentary. By the use of objective detail, technique becomes a form of thought, translated into dramatic metaphor.

As I mentioned in the first chapter, selective details functioning symbolically are particularly efficacious in the short stories. One such instance perfectly illustrates what Ezra Pound meant, in articulating the Imagist aesthetic, when he defined an image as "that which presents an intellectual and emotional complex in an instant of time." [9] In "Soldier's Home" the protagonist's mother lectures him on goodness and duty:

> "I've worried about you so much, Harold," his mother went on. "I know the temptations you must have been exposed to. I know how weak men are. I know what your own dear grandfather, my own father, told us about the Civil War and I have prayed for you. I pray for you all day long, Harold."
>
> Krebs looked at the bacon fat hardening on his plate. (*The Short Stories*, p. 151)

The trivial detail of the congealing bacon fat is, of course, an imagistic summary of the whole scene: the mother's no longer digestible moralizing, his own queasy response to it, and his feeling of entrapment in a sticky domesticity. To translate the image literally is to accurately describe the protagonist's situation and state of mind: what was once nourishing remains only in the form of a slightly repulsive residue.[10]

In "Out of Season" the objective detail of the wife's walking behind the two male characters, and her reluctance to join them even when called, signifies the marital tension which is never explicitly named but nevertheless must be understood for the story (and its title) to be meaningful. Once the reader's attention is awakened, closer inspection uncovers a number of parallels and correlatives for the discord between the American man and woman: the fluctuating and unpleasant weather, the aloofness of the townspeople, the murky river with its adjacent dump heap, the wife's persistent chill despite layers of clothing, and, at last, the entire abortive fishing expedition. In "Banal Story" the gesture with which the story begins, the eating of an orange and spitting out of the seeds, is the subtle counterpart (and subtlety is rare in this sardonic sketch) of the prevailing contrast between the tangy representation of life as "adventure" by popular magazines and its ineluctible realities of suffering and death. "Now I Lay Me" uses at least two important details. First, there is the noise of the chewing silkworms which contributes to the protagonist's insomnia not because of the noise itself but because it subliminally evokes the deeper fear of death which keeps him awake, the devouring of the body by the grave's worms. Second, there is a parallel between the episode in his memory, when he recalls his father's attempt to rake together the fragments of his collection of mementos, destroyed by fire, and his own present attempt to collect the fragments of his psyche. Finally, in the story "Fathers and Sons," Nick's act of discarding his father's underwear because it smelled repugnant to him (although it had been freshly laundered) is directly related to the rejection of his father's constricted morality and his subsequent sexual initiation by the Indian girl.

One of the most valuable functions of selective detail in Hemingway's work is to indicate the significant conditions of setting or locale, for in Hemingway the description of season, weather, climate, terrain, and chronological time almost invariably carries symbolic import, or, at minimum, helps to create mood. For example, to cite a generalized strategy, darkness, cold, rain, and snow, either singly or in combination, usually signify impending disaster, moral or emotional deprivation, or, simply, melancholy. We can observe this in the scenic detail—sometimes only a sentence or two—of such stories as "Indian Camp," "The Killers," "Cat in the Rain," "In Another Country," "The Light of the World," and "One Reader Writes." The technique is even more consistent in the novels, as generations of critics have remarked of the rain in *A Farewell to Arms*. In this technique Hemingway's craft consists not so much of invention, because these are, after all, archetypal associations and properties, but rather of the unassuming naturalness or congruity of the physical detail with action and theme. Again because I have already treated this concept in another connection, my discussion at this point will be brief and synoptic.

Two early stories, "The End of Something" and "The Three-Day Blow," illustrate a basic version of Hemingway's method. In the first story the description of Horton's Bay during its heyday as a bustling lumbering center is fuller than Hemingway's usual exposition of setting, and by its amplitude tends to disarm us as a bit of local history and as the immediate source for the story's title. But it is also a paradigm for the romance of Nick and Marjorie, once-thriving like Horton's Bay yet now about to perish. It will appear that it, too, has fallen victim to nature, man's nature to chafe under female domination and reject it, for this seems to be Nick's motivation in ending the relationship. The connection between locale and action is unwittingly voiced by Marjorie, who says in the story's first line of dialogue, "There's our old ruin," referring nostalgically to a part of the town and its former usefulness. Nick's remarks, in turn, point both to an objective element in the situation and serve as portent. "They aren't striking," he says about their fishing, but also talking about himself. He, like the elusive trout, has no intention of getting hooked. In "The Three-Day Blow," the sequel to "The End of Something," the details of setting in the first paragraph of the story—rain, wind, choppy lake—correspond to Nick's desolate mood after the termination of his romance. His forlorn condition is also suggested by the now-barren orchard through which he walks. But his capacity for recovery, his *joie de vivre*, expresses itself in the spontaneous action of retrieving a fallen apple and putting it in his pocket. Like the storm, his grief will be of short duration.

Furthermore, the opening scene of "The Three-Day Blow" depicts a recurrent landscape in Hemingway, or landscape experience, one with symbolic or prophetic qualities. Just as does Nick in this story, Hemingway's characters often walk along roads bordered by trees or on paths among trees, beyond which can be seen a river or lake. What this symbolizes, I think, is the thematic progression of one of Hemingway's basic patterns of action, the youth's encounter with experience in his movement toward maturity and fulfillment, although the water can also represent immolation or death. That is, the configuration of this archetypal Hemingway landscape embodies the motif which Philip Young has seen as central to Hemingway's work. *Across the River and into the Trees* articulates this symbolic pattern in its title but reverses the order of experience, just as the narrative itself recounts a return to the scene of the protagonist's youth. Often, the road-tree-river landscape is extended to mountains which rise in the distance, likewise extending the experiential equivalence toward some kind of ideality or ultimate wisdom. Here we are reminded of Carlos Baker's theory of the mountain-plain antithesis, which remains another of the basic insights into Hemingway's symbolic method.

Among the most intricate of Hemingway's scenic techniques is the portrayal of setting through the use of the action-style and the evocation of a sensory response. I do not mean the delineation of setting so that we can see it; that is standard procedure in many writers. I mean rendering it so that we can *feel* it. This example from "The Undefeated" illustrates my point.

> He went down the stairs and out of the door into the hot brightness of the street. It was very hot in the street and the light on the white buildings was sudden and hard on his eyes. He walked down the shady side of the steep street towards the Puerta del Sol. The shade felt solid and cool as running water. The heat came suddenly as he crossed the intersecting streets. Manuel saw no one he knew in all the people he passed. (*The Short Stories*, p. 239)

This passage uses the rhythmic and onomatopoeic effects we have observed in the action-style to imply the very texture of heat and cold and their impact on the character's nerves. The flowing, quick-tempoed line "He went down the stairs and out of the door" runs up suddenly against "hot brightness of the street"—a sequence of hard-to-say words whose careful enunciation abruptly breaks the flow and rhythm. The next sentence, "It was very hot in the street and the light on the white buildings was sudden and hard on his eyes," likewise demands a slow, careful reading and, because of its monosyllabic construction, a heavy staccato accent. The very weight of the heat and the desolation of the scene is hinted by the frequency of the hard consonant sounds and the acute vowels. The relief provided by the shade in the next sentence has its counterpart in the resumption of a quicker tempo and the series of alliterative *s* sounds and liquid *l*'s. Then we are jolted back to the labored effect by the unrhythmic and cacophonous "The heat came suddenly." As a result of Hemingway's use of counter-rhythms and juxtapositions of consonance and dissonance, the reader sensitive to the passage will have participated in its sensations to some degree, and have shared something of Manuel's temporary mood of debilitation as connoted by physical setting. Another version of the same technique, but emphasizing the visual effect, occurs in the first taxi scene in *The Sun Also Rises* (p. 25). In that scene Hemingway counterpoints the flicker of light and darkness upon Brett's face against the movement of the taxi through the streets of Paris (a movement simulated in the sentence rhythms), with both light and movement as objectifications of the surging and waning of the characters' emotions.

The method of utilizing setting to abet character and action, without distorting or aggrandizing the authentic thingness of place, persists through to Hemingway's last work with undiminished skill. The opening scene of *A Moveable Feast*, for example, not only places us amidst the sights and sounds of Paris, but presages the book's underlying motif and final mood. The emphasis on the bad weather of winter, with its wet and cold, correlate, with the elegiac tone of the book's closing pages, wherein the writer rues the lost innocence of his first love and the corruption of his clean way of life. Too, in the same opening section the pungent detail of Hemingway's account of the emptying of cesspools may be the objective epitome—although perhaps unintentional, so self-hating is it—for the book's dredging up of old hatreds, jealousies, and secrets. Similarly, the first paragraph of *Islands in the Stream*, the description of Hudson's house as high, alone, and positioned between harbor and sea, says a good deal about the hero: its location and solidity both indicative of the conflicting strains in his nature, subject to great tempests yet enduring. I make all this a parable of the artist's personality and talent.

> The house was built on the highest part of the narrow tongue of land between the harbor and the open sea. It had lasted through three hurricanes and it was built solid as a ship. It was shaded by tall coconut palms that were bent by the trade wind and on the ocean side you could walk out of the door and down the bluff across the white sand and into the Gulf Stream. The water of the Stream was usually a dark blue when you looked out at it when there was no wind. But when you walked out into it there was just the green light of the water over that floury white sand and you could see the shadow of any big fish a long time before he could ever come in close to the beach.

Although no serious reader of Hemingway can neglect the importance of scenic detail in his work, and particularly the frequency and vividness of his landscapes, the process by which those landscapes are made has not been very carefully studied until recently. In addition to the techniques of syntactical and structural montage we have already surveyed, there is an essential visual method as well, and here we look to painting rather than to poetry or music for possible sources and parallels. In depicting the hero of his last novel as a painter, Hemingway manifested a kinship with that other art which goes back to his formative years. Almost from the start there was a painter's eye at work in Hemingway's landscapes.

Among the writer's most generous acknowledgments of indebtedness were those he gave to painters, and particularly Paul Cézanne. Hemingway's admission of this influence in *A Moveable Feast*, as he recalled his apprenticeship in Paris, only recapitulated what he had already said on many occasions: "I went there [the Musée du Luxembourg] nearly every day for the Cézannes and to see the Manets and the Monets and the other Impressionists that I had first come to know about in the Art Institute at Chicago. I was learning something from the painting of Cézanne that made writing simple true sentences far from enough to make the stories have the dimensions that I was trying to put in them. I was learning very much from him but I was not articulate enough to explain it to anyone. Besides it was a secret." Writer's secrets are notoriously difficult to fathom, but let us conjecture about what Hemingway meant, especially by the more precise statement he gave Lillian Ross in 1950: "I learned how to make a landscape from Mr. Paul Cézanne." [11]

First, we recognize certain overall similarities between the two artists which place them in the same aesthetic movement. Both were men of strong feeling who conspired to keep the naked statement of such feeling out of their work, and sought instead to embody it in technique. Moreover, both were men of keen intellect who deliberately abstained from abstractions and ideas in their subject matter; Cézanne's definition of the true spirit of art as that which "gives concrete shapes to sensations and perceptions" applies equally well to Hemingway's method and intent.[12] Both drew from earlier artists but saw their own work as fundamentally a departure from the past. Both meticulously revised their work in the quest for perfection. Both were anti-Romantic not only in their suspicion of obtrusive emotion but also in their penchant for leanness and sharpness of technique—the attempt to reduce things to the elemental. Too, neither hesitated to introduce subjects abhorrent to the polite audience. Cézanne's "The Autopsy" and "Le Grog au Vin" were as shockingly anti-genteel to his audience as Hemingway's treatment of violence, sexuality, and blemished human nature appeared to many of his readers.

More important, Hemingway's painter's vision, refined by his association with Gertrude Stein and Picasso during the period of his most rapid growth, can be compared to Cézanne's mode of seeing. From Cézanne Hemingway probably learned how to lead a reader's eye into a scene and control it throughout. Furthermore, Hemingway's landscapes share some of the same basic characteristics as Cézanne's, in perspective, construction, color, and use of line. Like Cézanne's, Hemingway's landscapes do not "compose" the lines of the scene into artificial symmetries and conjunctions but seem to follow the natural contours of the terrain. That is, earlier artists imposed an abstract pattern, often with an extrinsic or allegorical point, upon the scene; in Cézanne the eye wanders along the "realistic" figuration of the scene until the whole painting has been explored, producing an effect of fullness and naturalness rather than a "message." We perceive something of the same technique, in simple form, even in so early a Hemingway story as "Up in Michigan": "A steep sandy road ran down the hill to the bay through the timber. From Smith's back door you could look out across the woods that ran down to the lake and across the bay. It was very beautiful in the spring and summer, the bay blue and bright and usually whitecaps on the lake out beyond the point from the breeze blowing from Charlevoix and Lake Michigan" (*The Short Stories*, p. 82). The angle of vision here is that of the uninitiated young girl whose eye spontaneously travels out, guided by the shape of the actual scene, yet also in its outwardness and perception of the open, pleasing vistas of the lake, intimating her inner condition as well: innocence, optimism, the ambition for a happy future. In *The Islands in the Stream* passage the eye is led from the house as focal point down toward sand and water, and from green to dark blue as the water deepens. There is also a double vision which consists of first seeing the scene as a static whole, and then a dynamic fragmentation and re-ordering of it as it is set in motion, or into cinematic color, with the suggestion of moving underwater shapes. That is, Hemingway's landscapes, like Cézanne's, also express inscape, the *Gestalt* or essential form underlying the surface appearance.

Another of Cézanne's basic techniques was to use a succession of planes (or scenic elements) merging into one another, often alternating different components of the landscape (earth, trees, houses, mountains) in such a way that each is distinct as the eye focuses upon it separately, yet tends to blend into the next as the whole composition is viewed. Hemingway employs the same method consistently, as in the Hudson-house passage with its contrasting but integrated zones of house, beach, and water, or in the superb opening landscape of A *Farewell to Arms*, which juxtaposes a foreground of river, stones, road, and trees, and a middle distance of ripe plains and orchards, against a backdrop of bare mountains. Furthermore, the scene is observed, as are many of the versions of Cézanne's Mont-Ste.-Victoire paintings, from a kind of medium elevation somewhere between the level of plain and mountain. We might infer that not only the visual perspective of Hemingway's landscape but also the arrangement of its elements demonstrate Cézanne's influence. Recurrently in Hemingway's landscapes, e.g., *The Sun Also Rises*, "Hills Like White Elephants," "Wine of Wyoming," "The Snows of Kilimanjaro," as in Cézanne's, we look across a plain to a distant mountain. It, together with the road-tree-water scene, seems intrinsic to Hemingway's imagination.

There are yet other techniques in common. Both artists use color simply and consistently. Houses are white or brown, often with red roofs. The land is brown or green, the mountains blue, white, or brown. Add to this Hemingway's green or blue water, and we have virtually all the colors on his palette. The repetition of these few colors makes for a forceful panoramic effect, undistracted by a multiplicity of elaborate detail. Like Cézanne Hemingway avoids strong emphasis on shapes, attaining form mainly through color and juxtaposition. Like Cézanne Hemingway sometimes adopted the practice of enlarging the landscape by drawing the eye across it with strong horizontal lines. Hemingway also follows Cézanne's method of patching or quilting contrasting blocks of color, as Cézanne did to extreme in the near-Cubism of some of his late paintings. The patching technique can be glimpsed in the Hudson-house landscape, while such extended descriptions as that of Jake's approach to Roncesvalles in chapter 11 of *The Sun Also Rises* utilize most of the practices I have summarized.

Another vital technique which may owe something to Cézanne's example, although we have located a number of possible sources for it, is the writer's attempt to find and portray the psychological center of a scene by selecting the crucial detail which contained its emotional essence. This is perhaps the literary equivalent to Cézanne's search for the point of most striking light as the axis of the object or mass to be painted. Neither artist hesitated to change perspective, distort, or eliminate parts of the mass in his quest for the essence. It might also be conjectured that the sense of movement in Cézanne's work, rising mysteriously out of a flat, immobile painting, is what Hemingway meant in his own work when he alluded to those extra dimensions, the fourth and fifth.

The discussion of similarities between Hemingway's method and that of the pictorial artist could be greatly extended, but Emily Watts's recent book, *Hemingway and the Arts,* now renders it superfluous here. She analyzes not only Cézanne's influence on Hemingway but also that of such other artists as Goya, El Greco, Klee, Brueghel, and Miró. If her arguments do not always fully persuade, they are invariably interesting to any student of Hemingway's craft. As Edmund Wilson observed a half century ago in one of the earliest reviews of Hemingway's writing, and as Mrs. Watts demonstrates at length, the affinities between Hemingway and Goya seem especially striking.[13]

Equally strong analogies could be drawn between Hemingway's writing and musical composition. Although it is beyond my ken to treat the matter at all expertly, there is too much correspondence between the writer's basic techniques and certain kinds of musical form simply to ignore or strike off with a few words in passing. I will conclude, then, with a brief commentary which should be received as suggestive rather than definitive.

We have already remarked Hemingway's deference to Bach. His blunt assertion to George Plimpton in the *Paris Review* interview is even more emphatic and worth repeating: "I should think what one learns from composers and from the study of harmony and counterpoint would be obvious." [14] It is less obvious than Hemingway declared, but nevertheless his use of contrapuntal devices, as well as the fundamental method of repetition, can be perceived as analogous to musical technique. His employment of them reminds me not only of Bach's polyphonic style but also of Mozart. Hemingway's reliance upon repetition parallels Mozart's skillful habit of exploiting his economical harmonic vocabulary by means of slight but infinitely varied incremental repetitions. Hemingway's special use of incremental repetition in such a passage as the El Sordo-Fascist officer paragraph is thoroughly Mozartian; it also evokes Mozart's extraordinary ability to enhance his harmonies by means of "suspensions," delayed musical progressions producing transient discords.

Other Hemingway techniques elicit yet other correspondences. Hemingway's occasional onomatopoeic associations between the sounds of words and the actions they denote is a characteristic of such early musical forms as the virelai and madrigal. The silences in Hemingway's prose, its peculiar spareness as well as the pauses indicated by selective omissions both in dialogue and in exposition, are equivalent to *rests* in polyphonic voices. The writer's deployment of series of "and" clauses (the paratactic style) resemble what in music is called "eye music" or "running passages." Hemingway's imitative form, or the attempt to correlate the syntactical structure of a passage with the action depicted, is like "musica reservata," or the vivid musical expression of moods and images suggested by the text. His technique of increasing the intensity and tempo of an action passage by a series of participial verbs and control of syllabic quantity, as in the rendition of sexual intercourse, reminds us of the fugal technique of *stretto*, used to produce climactic conclusion. Even the painterly device of contrasting blocks of color can be equated with the composer's method of setting off block chords against one another.

Although very much a child of the twentieth century in that the characteristic effect of his prose upon the ear seems closer to dissonance than to the sweetly or strongly melodic, in musical terms Hemingway is nevertheless a "classical" composer: objective, restrained, in pursuit of the ideals of order and simplicity. Whatever the depth of feeling elicited or communicated, it is rigidly controlled by form. Such terms as "chastity of style" and "balance of phrase" used to define the classical in music also seem perfectly appropriate to Hemingway. However, where Hemingway sharply deviates from the classical, it is in the concept of *convention*. On the contrary, his prose seemed radical when it first appeared.

In this regard he is better aligned with such antiromantic, antiemotional, anticonventional "neoclassical" composers as Stravinsky and Prokofief, who emerged at around the same time as Hemingway in the early decades of the century during the period of enormous activity and innovation in all the arts. Like them he could be defined as a neoclassical artist, at least in the formal sense: one who reacted against the excesses of the nineteenth century by subduing sentiment within the confines of a tight artistic structure. His literary language was like their musical language: keenly dissonant and rhythmically complex, seemingly "simple," random, and artless in style and structure, but actually very accomplished. It could also be said of Hemingway, as it has been of modern music, that the loss of God is reflected in the loss of key centers, i.e., the loss of tonally-directed melody. Thus rhythm became for modern music the main unifying device in a composition, as tempo is perhaps the most powerful and basic of Hemingway's "musical" techniques.

Although, as I have said, Hemingway's prose is chromatically much less highly colored or melodious than Fitzgerald's or Faulkner's, such passages as the opening chapter of *A Farewell to Arms* or the first paragraph of "In Another Country" could be analyzed musically as tone poems. I quote the initial paragraph of "In Another Country":

> In the fall the war was always there, but we did not go to it any more. It was cold in the fall in Milan and the dark came very early. Then the electric lights came on, and it was pleasant along the streets looking in the windows. There was much game hanging outside the shops, and the snow powdered in the fur of the foxes and the wind blew their tails. The deer hung stiff and heavy and empty, and small birds blew in the wind and the wind turned their feathers. It was a cold fall and the wind came down from the mountains. (*The Short Stories*, p. 267)

The very title "In Another Country" is like a key signature, cueing the audience both to the somberness and the strangeness of what is to follow. These qualities, especially the sense of alienness, are verified by the experience of the language itself—the sound of meaning—emphatic and incantatory, and the deliberate and measured tempo which emphasizes the sadness of the mood. Although there are minor audible harmonies created by the repetitious interplay of consonant and vowel sounds, notably *i, n, t, a, w, r, o, l, s*, and the reiteration of individual words such as *in, fall, it, and, the, cold, wind*, the strongest effects derive from the cadences of similar phrases:

in the fall	it was cold	the wind came down
in Milan	it was pleasant	the wind blew their tails
in the windows	it was a cold fall	small birds blew in
in the fur		the wind
in the wind		

And the device of incremental repetition is so apparent as to need no comment.

Both in theme and technique the whole paragraph is a miniature a b á sonata form. There is the exposition of the opening sentences: "in the fall," "it was cold," "the war," which state the bleakness of season and the motif of impending disaster. This is followed by the development, or the temporarily mediating and mitigating interval of the comforts of Milan: "the electric lights came on," "it was pleasant," which also becomes threatening as the carcasses of animals and the encroaching season again arouse fear. Finally, there is the recapitulation, which returns to the opening phrases but now modified to include the major element that has entered during the development section—the wind: "It was a cold fall and the wind came down from the mountains." In effect, the wind has taken the place of the war; thus the passage concludes as it began: dissonantly, polyrhythmically, somberly.[15]

Other, more musically knowledgeable readers of Hemingway are henceforward invited to treat his work more fully in that context, as Mrs. Watts has done for Hemingway and the plastic arts. As for myself, I feel at this point that I have exhausted my prerogative as well as my information. Whatever illuminating correspondences remain to be established between the writer, the painter, and the composer, for the present I am driven back to one firm conviction: that the true artist can be recognized by his contribution to his own proper medium. After all, what we call *style* is just that singularity of craft, that inimitable shape the authentic artist gives to his materials. As no student of painting could fail to identify the work of Cézanne, or the serious listener the music of Mozart, so no reader with even a modicum of sophistication could mistake Hemingway's writing for any other.

6

Hemingway's Humor

At the end of the first chapter of *For Whom the Bell Tolls*, as Robert Jordan accompanies Pablo and Anselmo into the mountains to carry out the mission that could kill him, he counteracts his gloomy forebodings with a joke to himself and then goes on to formulate a principle for right conduct: "All the best ones, when you thought it over, were gay. It was much better to be gay and it was a sign of something too. It was like having immortality while you were still alive." Unquestionably Jordan speaks for Hemingway here and states a belief the writer himself strove to practice. In fact, there is a plenitude of gaiety in Hemingway's work, expressed in a comic vein which reaches from one end of his career to the other: from the contributions in high school periodicals to the posthumously published *A Moveable Feast* and *Islands in the Stream*. Furthermore, not only is this humor a vital attribute in those of Hemingway's characters who, like Jordan, exhibit grace under pressure, it is an important aspect of his craft. Yet with a very few exceptions the critics have neglected it.[1] Let us therefore attend to it as our final concern in this study.

Hemingway's humor encompasses a rather wide range of types, subjects, and moods. He was a skilled parodist and mimic who exercised his gift early and late. He wrote considerable satire, about equally apportioned between the gentle Horatian and the savage Juvenalian. Although much of his humor is dark—indeed so black it inhibits laughter—a good deal of it is also spontaneously and boisterously funny, with its major result the release of high spirits. He could be heavily and crudely obscene or profane, and just as delicately and subtly witty. In a few instances in his fiction the comedy seems forced and excessive, but in the main it is tightly integrated into the overall method and structure of the work and contributes significantly to its total achievement.

Hemingway's primary technique of humor, a technique which in itself articulates the comic vision, is that of incongruous juxtaposition. By this method contrasting or grossly unlike elements of attitude, language, action, or identity are placed in close proximity or paired in various combinations, so that surprise and laughter inevitably result from the absurd relationships and distortions produced by the unexpected arrangement of mismatched constituents. For example, one of Hemingway's favorite comic situations might be called nationality farce, which is really a version of the archetypal confusion-of-identity plot, wherein an American is mistaken for a German by an Italian, and so on. Another is to play off different speech patterns, modes of utterance, or language norms, and then capitalize on the attendant cacophony or misapprehension. The language-humor may collaborate in the nationality farce or it may function independently, as in the case which juxtaposes highbrow speech against the vulgate, or uses magniloquent terms to describe a low-down action or object. Another method stresses a character's silly or erratic behavior in circumstances which call for restraint and poise. Yet another technique sets incompatible values or attitudes side by side, usually so as to expose banal, pompous, or insincere thinking and conduct through the contrast with the frank, spontaneous, and earthy. All these techniques will be further defined and illustrated as we proceed.

Although there are special instances in Hemingway's work of an entire piece which is deliberately and wholly comic, notably *The Torrents of Spring*, more typically Hemingway's humor functions as one component (albeit an important one) in an artistic whole. As a factor in characterization it adds depth and roundness. In plot it provides relief and foreshadowing. Structurally, it is a way to modulate and gain symmetry. Ultimately, of course, we must understand that Hemingway's humor is more than a mere device, stratagem, or overlay; it is integral to the particular image of life his work creates and fundamental to his mode of response.

So much for the introduction. On to the thing itself.

Great stylists often display a flair for mimicry and find their own distinctive voices by first imitating others. In literature the mimic impulse frequently results in parody, as it did in Hemingway's writing. He first demonstrated both his urge to humor and his talent for parody before he graduated from high school in Oak Park, by composing jocular poems in the manner of Kipling or James Whitcomb Riley and during his senior year contributing a series of funny and sometimes satirical columns à la Ring Lardner to the school newspaper. In the Lardner imitations, as Charles Fenton has pointed out, Hemingway was also working toward his own style through the exercise in colloquial idiom and the practice in simple dialogue.[2]

Hemingway's next parodies of note were inspired several years later by Gertrude Stein and Sherwood Anderson during the period of his serious apprenticeship. The Stein parody appeared in the form of a poem published in a German literary magazine, *Der Querschnitt*, in the fall of 1924. Although Hemingway and Miss Stein were still on good terms at this time, Hemingway's aggressions —already obtrusive in his personality—are evident beneath the poem's seemingly boisterous and feckless obscenity. I quote a portion of the first stanza to exemplify its general method:

THE SOUL OF SPAIN
[In the manner of Gertrude Stein]

In the rain in the rain in the rain in the rain in Spain.
Does it rain in Spain?

Oh yes my dear on the contrary and there are no
  bullfights,
The dancers dance in long white pants
It isn't right to yence your aunts
Come Uncle let us go home.
Home is where the heart is, home is where the fart is.
Come let us fart in the home.

If we can extrapolate from A *Moveable Feast*, Hemingway is not only parodying Stein's style (with an aside
to Dada), but also, perhaps, mocking her distaste for
dirty words. He may even be making an oblique allusion
to her sex life. The poem continues in the same mode
of excremental humor, progressing from flatulation to
defecation in the second stanza and enlarging the scope
of the ridicule to include democracy, dictators, H. L.
Mencken, Waldo Frank, *Broom* (Harold Loeb's little
magazine), and Jack Dempsey, and in the final stanza
concluding with mock-homage to another of Hemingway's mentors, Ezra Pound.[3]

Hemingway disposed of Sherwood Anderson with a
parodic *nouvelle*, *The Torrents of Spring*, which served
multiple purposes. It castigated Anderson for what Hemingway felt to be the unforgivable deterioration of the
older writer's art in *Dark Laughter*. It brought about
Hemingway's release from his contract with Horace Liveright and allowed him to go to the more prominent
Scribner's. It announced the apprentice's complete liberation from the influence of the master. As a by-product
it also angered Gertrude Stein by adapting one of her
titles for its own uses and because it attacked one of her
close friends and associates. Although *The Torrents of
Spring* was turned out in several days during November
1925 (by Hemingway's account written "to cool out
. . . after I had finished the first draft of *The Sun Also
Rises*") and plainly exhibits its slapdash composition, in
many respects it is a tellingly ludicrous indictment of
some of Anderson's worst deficiencies.[4]

Anderson's romantic primitivism, and especially the

blood-knowledge and sexual spontaneity he mystically attributes to Negroes in *Dark Laughter*, are burlesqued by Hemingway as he transforms Negroes into Indians and sexy, knowing Negro laughter into war-whoops. The marital maladjustment and the yearning restlessness of Anderson's middle-aged characters have their humorous counterpart in Hemingway's Scripps O'Neil and his strange relationships with astonishingly well-read waitresses. Anderson's Middle West becomes Hemingway's northern Michigan. Hemingway's characters, like Anderson's, frequently behave out of primal impulse, drifting aimlessly in answer to some inner call and shedding their clothing as they wander. Like Anderson's people Hemingway's indulge in supposedly profound musing and philosophizing, ceaselessly posing questions about the nature of human existence, civilization, reality. In the manner of Anderson Hemingway makes all sorts of loose associations and illogical connections in his exposition and narration, and in ridicule of Anderson's habit of interrupting his stories with direct addresses to the reader Hemingway intrudes several hilarious interjections. All of this is erected upon the fundamental burlesque of Anderson's style, with its self-conscious simplicity, artificial naïveté, heavy repetitiousness, and tendency toward syntactical fragmentation. This is typical:

Spring was coming. Spring was in the air. (Author's Note.—This is the same day on which the story starts, back on page one.) A chinook wind was blowing. Workmen were coming home from the factory. Scripps' bird singing in its cage. Diana looking out of the open window. Diana watching for her Scripps to come up the street. Could she hold him? Could she hold him? If she couldn't hold him, would he leave her his bird? She had felt lately that she couldn't hold him. In the nights, now, when she touched Scripps he rolled away, not toward her. It was a little sign, but life was made up of little signs. She felt she couldn't hold him. As she looked out of the window, a copy of *The Century Magazine* dropped from her nerveless hand. *The Century* had a new editor. There were more woodcuts.[5]

As the passage shows, *The Torrents of Spring* also pays a good deal of facetious attention to literary matters, with epigraphs from Fielding and references to dozens of other writers, critics, and periodicals. Under the guise of spoofing, it parades Hemingway's sophistication in such matters. We are reminded, too, of Auden's perception that literary parody by its very nature is a backhanded compliment, for a writer can only parody the style of an author he admires.[6]

I surmise, without being able to prove my hunch, that some of the characterizations in the early chapters of *The Sun Also Rises* contain considerable parody of the speech-patterns of the characters' real-life prototypes. The substantiating evidence as well as the full appreciation of such parody would belong only to those who knew the people and had heard them talk. However, in some scenes, as for example the rendition of the homosexual group's dialogue in chapter 3, the parody is self-explanatory and requires no key. The same is true to some degree of Frances's excoriation of Robert Cohn at the end of chapter 6 (a passage which I quoted earlier), a double-edged parody both of her personal style of speech and of Cohn's literary pretensions. There are also moments of parody included in Bill's two comic-satiric orations in chapter 12. The first parodies the fashionable clichés of literary criticism ("irony and pity") and jingoistic newspaper editorials ("You're an expatriate. You've lost touch with the soil."). The second is a burlesque sermon in the evangelistic manner of William Jennings Bryan, then at his most prominent because of his role in the Scopes Trial. In giving these parodic speeches to Bill, Hemingway was following actuality, for the character was in part modeled on Donald Ogden Stewart, an accomplished humorist and parodist who had recently published *A Parody Outline of History*.[7]

Between *The Sun Also Rises* and *A Moveable Feast* the main inspiration for Hemingway's parodic humor was not so much individuals as attitudes embodied in certain kinds of utterance. For example, to name the most striking case in the short stories, there is the bleakly unfunny parody of the Lord's Prayer in "A Clean, Well-Lighted Place." In *Death in the Afternoon* the sequence of dialogues with the Old Lady, avowedly brought in for modulation and comic relief, depend essentially on parody. Although the Old Lady is herself a rather lovable character, her stilted formality, moral earnestness, and puzzled response to vulgar and unpleasant subjects comprise an extended parody of those academic and/or genteel readers and critics who had complained about Hemingway's crudity. Hemingway accentuates the parody of propriety by adopting a level of speech even loftier than the Old Lady's, occasionally swooping down to undercut it with a snatch of obscenity, or by juxtaposing the politeness of their style of conversation with such impolite topics as the prevalence of venereal disease among matadors or the practice of stuffing disemboweled horses with sawdust. "A Natural History of the Dead," an extended and overt attack upon genteel critics, first emerged as one of these conversations. In it Hemingway parodies the propriety and objectivity of the field naturalist or travelogue writer (and, by association, the literary critic) by adopting the manner of sober decorum to describe the smell and posture of corpses on the battlefield and similar matters. In another of these conversations Hemingway paid an indirect compliment to William Faulkner, then of far smaller reputation than Hemingway, as a writer *par excellence* about whorehouses.

The most insidious of all Hemingway's parody appears in *A Moveable Feast*, where among others Gertrude Stein, Ford Madox Ford, and F. Scott Fitzgerald are parodied not in their literary practices but as individuals. That is, in each instance Hemingway gets at his victim by the *ad hominem* method, ridiculing personality and attitude rather than manner and style. Yet these comic portraits also qualify as parody because they purport to precisely reproduce the person's words as part of a dramatic scene, with Hemingway himself in the role of innocent interlocuter and objective reporter. Gertrude Stein is devalued because she first defends homosexuality as a viable way of life, a defense set down in dignified and sophisticated terms as though recorded verbatim, and then is later shown crawling abjectly before her lover. (Curiously, under the guise of fastidiousness, Hemingway does not report the second conversation but only hints at its substance.) Ford's pretensions to the status of gentleman are demolished by the word-by-word rendition of his petty bullying of a waiter and by his insupportably snobbish declarations. Hemingway ridicules Fitzgerald in the long anecdote about Fitzgerald's self-pitying hypochondria, and in the briefer but more devastating episode wherein Fitzgerald seeks Hemingway's reassurance about the adequacy of his sexual equipment. Although Hemingway takes care in all these scenes to avoid blatant exaggeration of personal mannerisms of speech, lest satire become burlesque and character lampoon, they are parody nonetheless. Much of this is amusing, even hilarious, but it is contemptible, too, in light of our knowledge that these were Hemingway's friends and sponsors. As a result we find ourselves in the uncomfortable predicament of despising Hemingway in the very moment that we laugh with him.[8] The dialogue with Ford, which exploits the incongruous juxtaposition of Hemingway's feigned innocence and Ford's worldliness, and Hemingway's straight-faced use of preposterously obsolete and clichéd terms against Ford's genuine belief in them, exemplifies his comic method in these episodes. I quote a small portion of it (Ford has just "cut" a man he mis-identifies as Hillaire Belloc):

> "Tell me why one cuts people," I asked. Until then I had thought it was something only done in novels . . .
> "A gentleman," Ford explained, "will always cut a cad."

I took a quick drink of brandy.

"Would he cut a bounder?" I asked.

"It would be impossible for a gentleman to know a bounder."

"Then you can only cut someone you have known on terms of equality?" I pursued.

"Naturally."

"How would one ever meet a cad?"

"You might not know it, or the fellow could have become a cad."

"What is a cad?" I asked. "Isn't he someone that one has to thrash within an inch of his life?"

"Not necessarily," Ford said.

"Is Ezra a gentleman?" I asked.

"Of course not," Ford said. "He's an American."

(P. 86)

It is obvious, then, that Hemingway liked parody and did it well. However, as we have implied, parody really belongs to a broader comic dimension in Hemingway's work: satire. Each of Hemingway's novels contains at least some satire and it also recurs in a number of short stories. His targets are those satirists have ever aimed at, affectation and hypocrisy; his tone ranges from mild ridicule to scathing denunciation; his motive is exposure rather than improvement. I say this, that his satiric bent was more often than not destructive, to embarrass or indict rather than reform, because he had no plan or program to rectify the faults he revealed other than a generalized ideal of manly conduct. But this is not to say that his satire is any the less effective thereby. Swift had no social program either.

The urge to uncover folly and humiliate the foolish is clearly visible in *The Sun Also Rises*, which is, as Jackson Benson has verified, an extensively satirical book. Although the main butt of the satire is Cohn, even the protagonists Jake and Brett are made to seem a little foolish at times. If Cohn and other sentimentalists and litterateurs of his ilk behave fatuously, Jake and Brett also commit egregious errors of judgment and conduct, as I have earlier argued. Indeed, of the whole cast of the novel's characters only Montoya and Romero wholly escape Hemingway's satirical depiction because they alone adhere consistently to their principles and conduct themselves with dignity. There are also moments of wide, overt, and jocose satire such as that in chapter 19, in Jake's reflections upon the difference between French and Spanish waiters, and by implication, between French and Spanish values.

But despite such humorous interludes in the novel, and there are many, the ultimate effect of the book and its satire is not merely amusing. In this we reiterate a basic truth about both Hemingway's satire and his "humor" at large. Theoretically, we can define *The Sun Also Rises* as comedy in the strict literary sense of that term: it concentrates on folly and misconduct; its characters are somewhat buffeted about but remain alive and well at the novel's conclusion—at least as well as they began; it displays the discrepancy between what is and what ought to be, or between the visionary and the actual; it focuses upon man in his social aspects; it shatters the illusions imposed by artificial or impractical standards; and it finally affirms the life-urge and man's thrust to survive and continue. But two crucial factors intervene to inhibit laughter. First, there is the intangible element of tone, or the cumulative effect of the nuances of style, dialogue, and gesture—and the pervasive tone of *The Sun Also Rises* is decidedly not merry. Second, there is the theme, as reinforced and articulated by the action, of frustration and loss. Or it could be said very simply that a novel whose plot and character relationships depend upon a man's sexual mutilation and a woman's compulsive promiscuity is unlikely to produce a feeling of exhilaration in its readers. Yet neither hero nor heroine really qualify as tragic. They do *function*, in their way. What we need to accurately name *The Sun Also Rises* is a word unavailable in our critical vocabulary. Properly speaking, the book is neither a tragedy nor a comedy but an Irony.

The same bleakness (or blackness) inheres in several other prominent examples of Hemingway's satire. I will deal with these before going on to what is genuinely humorous in Hemingway's work. As a rule, Hemingway's black satire depends upon blunt sarcasm.

The most violent satire in Hemingway's writing appears in *To Have and Have Not*. Virtually everything said about the rich, about would-be proletarian novelists, and about most of the characters apart from Harry Morgan, his family, and friends, is either outspokenly derogatory or coarsely and bitterly satirical. This excerpt is representative of the novel's mode of ridicule by frontal assault:

> On the *Irydia IV*, a professional son-in-law of the very rich and his mistress, named Dorothy, the wife of that highly paid Hollywood director, John Hollis, whose brain is in the process of outlasting his liver so that he will end up calling himself a communist, to save his soul, his other organs being too corroded to attempt to save them, are asleep. The son-in-law, big-framed, good looking in a poster way, lies on his back snoring, but Dorothy Hollis, the director's wife, is awake. (P. 241)

And as the passage continues, Dorothy lapses into a long, self-pitying interior monologue and finally solaces herself by masturbating. The story "Mr. and Mrs. Elliott" employs a similar kind of derision by blatantly transforming the characters' sexual impotence into a dramatic metaphor for their sterility of imagination and spirit. These characters, we should add, were based on friends of Hemingway's first wife, just as those in *To Have and Have Not* are only thinly-disguised portraits from life. The portrait of André Marty in *For Whom the Bell Tolls* is another that Hemingway etched in acid, arousing the protests of those members of the International Brigade who had befriended Hemingway during his sojourn in Spain and shared their confidences with him as a comrade. They felt betrayed by the novel's derogation of Marty and other Loyalist leaders. Likewise, to settle a personal score Hemingway directed his venom against the aging and sick Sinclair Lewis in *Across the River and into the Trees*, defaming Lewis's talent and emphasizing the repulsiveness of his personal appearance. Hemingway spared Lewis (and perhaps escaped libel) only by not naming him outright.[9]

None of this is laughable. Whatever their impact upon the individuals under fire, Hemingway's black satires fail of humor not only because they exude malice but also because they lack finesse. With the exception of some clever innuendo achieved through repetition in the Elliott story, the technique of these sarcastic vignettes is undistinguished. The essential ingredients of compression and surprise are missing and we are told openly what we should spy out for ourselves. The main task Hemingway leaves to the reader is the guesswork involved in pairing the literary portrait with the real-life counterpart, and even this sort of surprise is limited for most of us to the detection of the famous prototype. That is, the identity of most of these characters may have been familiar to Hemingway and his circle but not to the common reader. Thus the satire remains an "in-joke," a variety of comedy Hemingway was too fond of for his own artistic good. Moreover, for the denunciation of individuals to outlast the cases in point and the contemporaneous scene, it must involve characteristics of type, class, personality, or profession which apply to all. But Hemingway's depiction of these people offers too little chance for transference and projection; it is just too topical.

However, I represent Hemingway's overall accomplishment as a satirist unfairly if I leave the impression that he was limited to a single mode. An excellent example of satire which surpasses mere topicality and is at once humorous and artistically successful occurs in chapter 15 of *A Farewell to Arms*. It treats one of the satirist's preferred subjects, pompous and incompetent physicians. The three doctors who first examine Frederic's wounded leg in the Milan hospital affect a solemn demeanor and use impressive medical terminology, but do not know how to handle the injured limb without hurting the patient, cannot tell the left leg from the right in an X-ray, and concur in the asinine diagnosis that surgery should be postponed for six months. In contrast, later in the chapter a good doctor comes bustling in overflowing (like Rinaldi) with gusto, compliments Catherine's beauty even as he examines Frederic's leg, gladly shares a drink with him, and plans to operate the next morning. The effect produced by the first group of doctors is ludicrous; the good doctor's visit is uproarious. The comic incongruity in the first instance derives from the juxta-position of professed competence with proven incompe-tence. The incongruity in the second springs from the delightful surprise produced by a doctor who talks and acts like a playboy rather than another officious puppet, yet exudes confidence and authority. Hemingway rein-forces the different comic effects by appropriately varied methods of presentation. The initial episode is spread over several pages and employs carefully spaced and de-liberate dialogue, replete with cues to ponderous pauses. The latter occupies a single page and portrays the doc-tor's speech and movements with a rapid, almost breath-less pace. (His opening remarks are compressed into a single rapid-fire monologue.) Accordingly the variation in space and tempo differentiates one form of comedy from the other and helps direct the appropriate response to each: intellectual satire in the first case, slapstick ex-uberance in the second.

Another engaging example of humorous satire aimed at a common aspect of human behavior rather than a particular individual appears in *For Whom the Bell Tolls* in the character of Fernando. Although Fernando is sufficiently well delineated to be credible as a single character, he functions more importantly in the novel as a type of universal figure: the utterly conventional, practical, unflappable man who persists in believing only in literal fact and the taste of his stew while the world falls to pieces around him. I surmise that in Fernando

Hemingway intended to strike off a likeness not only of a trait of Spanish character but also that species of stubbornly prosaic man who exists in all cultures. Whatever Hemingway's satiric purpose, the several dialogues between the stolid Fernando and the volatile Pilar—all splendidly funny—represent two completely incongruous approaches to living. At one extreme Pilar will try, do, or say anything that smacks of zest or joy, no matter how improper or dangerous. At the other Fernando affirms decorum, moderation, and restraint above all else. Obviously Hemingway means us to prefer Pilar and her way, but there is something admirable and even lovable about Fernando too, despite his extravagant sobriety. In Pilar's words he stands as a monument to "as usual."

Hemingway intensifies the comic juxtaposition of Pilar and Fernando by emphasizing the obvious distance between their attitudes with a less immediately apparent disparity in their modes of speech. Although both talk in the novel's formalized Anglo-Spanish transliteration, Fernando's speech is unswervingly punctilious and correct, bereft of all ornament and metaphor, and moving, like his train of thought, along a straight track of commonplace usage (although sometimes entangling itself in verbose jargon). In contrast to his manner Pilar's utterances soar on long eloquent flights of high rhetoric or suddenly plunge to pithy oaths and raffish invective. A small sample:

> "The melon of Castile is better," Fernando said.
> "*Que va,*" said the woman of Pablo. "The melon of Castile is for self abuse. The melon of Valencia for eating. When I think of those melons long as one's arm, green like the sea and crisp and juicy to cut and sweeter than the early morning in summer." (P. 85)

As parody is but one method of satire, satire itself comprises only a category, although a major one, of Hemingway's humor and not the whole of it. While we probably cannot distinguish exactly where satire ends and farce, burlesque, or some other comic mode begins, we can differentiate many instances of humor in Hemingway's work which are neither parody nor satire. But rather than continue with a list of comic types or modes and try to document each, I think it would be more profitable to name and describe the principal subjects or situations Hemingway found humorous, analyze the techniques he used to develop them, and discover to what purposes he put them. In all these subjects and situations some variation of the process of incongruous juxtaposition is instrumental to the production of the comic result.

To work from what has already been established, we observe, as implied in the Fernando-Pilar contrast, that a fertile source of humor is the juxtaposition of incompatible perspectives. (By "perspective" in this connection I mean attitude, creed, or opinion rather than narrative voice.) I will offer another example from *For Whom the Bell Tolls* to illustrate the humor of incompatible perspectives.

Although throughout the novel strong belief and emotional force collect around the agency of the supernatural as a factor in the characters' fates, thus validating superstition as an important form of truth, in one place Hemingway exploits this very dread to inspire laughter. This occurs in chapter 19, just after Pilar's ghastly exposition of the smell of death. In response to her overwhelming evocation of the great dark unknown which surrounds us, Jordan enters the dry little voice of reason.

"All right," Robert Jordan said. "And you say Kashkin smelt like that when he was here?"
"Yes."
"Well," said Robert Jordan gravely. "If that is true it is a good thing that I shot him."
"*Olé*," the gypsy said. The others laughed. (P. 256)

The technique here is that of *reductio ad absurdum* because Jordan's reply rebuts an attitude which communicates the cosmic, remote, bizarre, and fantastic as the ultimate reality, with a version of truth as small, near-at-hand, familiar, and pragmatic. In short, Jordan reduces Pilar's peroration to an epigrammatic joke: Anyone who smells like death is better off dead. The dark underside of the joke, shared in private and in silence by both Pilar and Jordan, is that he, too, smells of death. His amusing rejoinder is also the expression of his sanity and his courage, which allow him to keep going despite his prescience. Furthermore, and here I urgently endorse Jackson Benson's observation that the full impact of Hemingway's humor often depends upon oral delivery, the incongruous juxtaposition of the lyrical eloquence of Pilar's description, which has risen to the level of incantation and would impose a stunned hush upon its audience, with the quiet, terse, ordinary, and feignedly innocent tone of Jordan's riposte, is integral to the total comic effect.

Hemingway's humor of incompatible perspectives is at its best in the peculiar little story "A Pursuit Race," which, like so many other of Hemingway's offbeat tales, seems to have evaded critical attention. Although finally we would have to classify it as an Irony rather than a comedy, it centers around some very funny dialogue. The basis of the humor, and simultaneously of the sadness, is the contrast between the businesslike, sober, and well-adjusted Mr. Turner ("Sliding Billy") and the collapsed, drunken, drug-addicted wreck William Campbell. From this juxtaposition we might expect ridicule of one or the other character, depending on where the author located his sympathy, but no satire is forthcoming because the narrative sympathy extends almost equally to both. Turner pities Campbell and wants to help him but can not comprehend the sort of desperation that brought him to his breakdown. In contrast Campbell, despite his temporary and artificial euphoria, can intellectually analyze the difference between Turner's adjustment to stress and his own surrender to it, but can not do anything about it. ("You're called 'Sliding Billy.' That's because you can slide. I'm called just Billy. That's because I never could slide at all.") Where, then, is the humor in this pathetic situation?

The humor consists of the technique by which Hemingway juxtaposes the one character, Turner, who stands self-possessed and upright throughout the story, speaking sensibly and directly to the point, against the other who lies helplessly inert in bed and babbles on. The juxtaposition insinuates that although both men are adults, one is really the father and the other the child. Furthermore, Campbell wallows in his childishness and deliberately uses it to entertain himself and to irritate Turner (precisely as a recalcitrant child irks a demanding parent) by having a prolonged fantasy-romance with his bedclothing. This romance is the most vivid action in the story, described in an incremental series of hilariously explicit stage directions. These are characteristic, excerpted from different sequences of the continuing dialogue:

> He found he liked to talk through a sheet.
> "I love it under a sheet," he said.
> William Campbell breathed in and out through the sheet.
> "I just love sheets."
> "Dear sheet . . . pretty sheet. You love me, don't you, sheet?"
> "Be careful of my sheet."
> "Dear sheet," he said. "I can kiss this sheet and see through it at the same time." (*The Short Stories*, pp. 351–53)

It is authentically comical when a grown man plays infant and intersperses his conversation with another adult by all sorts of tricks with a bedsheet. (Try reading this aloud to savor it fully.) But it is Hemingway's special sort of dark humor when the man behaves so because he is coming apart at the seams. Again the story reveals a deeper layer of decidedly unfunny incongruity, for underneath the irrelevance of Campbell's meandering remarks, for example his peroration on various kinds of offal (with the pun on "sheet"), we discern the stark recognition of life's terror by those exhausted souls who stop running. This is also implied in the story's title, which shares the multivalent suggestiveness of many of Hemingway's titles. In short, the humor produced by the work's dramatic scene and juxtaposition of characters is reflected off the same dark backing of pessimism which dominates "A Clean, Well-Lighted Place."

Although it is not strictly an incongruity of perspective, one droll scene in *A Farewell to Arms* exemplifies the same technique by which an essentially serious conversation is turned farcical through the strategy of playing off the dialogue against a piece of comic business. In chapter 16, just before the operation on Frederic's knee, he and Catherine exchange some lovers' banter whose jocular tone only sharpens the characters' sincere feelings for one another, especially Catherine's. However, behind the dialogue and while it ensues, Catherine is also performing her professional duties as nurse by preparing Frederic for surgery—an action Hemingway cues so unemphatically that many readers would pass it by. That is, at the same time that Frederic and Catherine are exchanging seriocomic jests about their romance and speaking with endearment, Catherine is scrubbing and shaving him and administering an enema. Accordingly, her statement "Now you're all clean inside and out" refers dually and with comic ambiguity both to the condition of Frederic's body and to the revelations each has made to the other.

One of Hemingway's most enjoyable variations upon the situation of incompatible or incongruous perspectives is the drunk scene, sometimes involving antic stage business, as for example Nick's spilling and retrieval of the apricots in "The Three-Day Blow." The drunk scene can manipulate two kinds of contrast for comic ends: between an abstemious character and an intoxicated one (as in "A Pursuit Race"), or between characters who commence as sober and then proceed into inebriation. In the second type of scene, more frequent and usually

funnier than the first, the comic technique is modeled
on what happens in life. As he imbibes, the customarily
laconic and hard-bitten Hemingway hero waxes conspic-
uously talkative and/or confessional (e.g., Thomas Hudson in the "Cuba" section of *Islands in the Stream*),
pronouncing opinions on divers matters, unburdening
himself of confidences, or telling his listeners exactly
what he thinks of them. These revelations are all the
funnier because they tend to be iconoclastic, bawdy,
and well-salted with obscenity. Simultaneously, the characters' long-windedness may get completely out of control and result in marathon monologues which combine
totally unrelated subjects, diverse levels of speech, and
the voices of more than one speaker. The absurdly jumbled three-way conversation at the end of chapter 12 in
A Farewell to Arms, involving Frederic Henry, Rinaldi,
and the Major from the officers' mess, illustrates this
mode of humor operating with commendably zany results. Beginning seriously enough on the subject of politics, raised by America's recent entry into the war, the
conversation becomes lubricated with brandy and swiftly
degenerates into a sort of comic chorus:

> The Japanese want Hawaii, I said. Where is Hawaii?
> It is in the Pacific Ocean. Why do the Japanese want
> it? They don't really want it, I said. That is all talk.
> The Japanese are a wonderful little people fond of
> dancing and light wines. Like the French, said the
> major. We will get Corsica and all the Adriatic coast-
> line, Rinaldi said. Italy will return to the splendors of
> Rome, said the major. I don't like Rome, I said. It is
> hot and full of fleas. You don't like Rome? Yes, I
> love Rome. Rome is the mother of nations. I will
> never forget Romulus suckling the Tiber. What?
> Nothing. Let's all go to Rome to-night and never come
> back. Rome is a beautiful city, said the major. The
> mother and father of nations, I said. Roma is femi-
> nine, said Rinaldi. It cannot be the father. Who is
> the father, then, the Holy Ghost? Don't blaspheme.

I wasn't blaspheming, I was asking for information. You are drunk, baby. Who made me drunk? I made you drunk, said the major.

There are too many other comic incongruities of perspective in Hemingway's work even to list them all. For example, to cite only a few of the most important in the short stories, "The Light of the World" juxtaposes an argument between two whores over a dead prizefighter, whom both claim as their lover, against repeated allusions to scripture and Jesus Christ; "Homage to Switzerland" purports to ridicule an elderly European's credulous pride by setting it against a younger American's disenchanted spoofing but instead discredits the American; "God Rest You Merry, Gentlemen" builds a very black comic plot upon the themes of religious fanaticism and sexual mutilation, contrasting those who suffer because they are too sensitive or idealistic with those who avoid pain by being stupid and callous.

Perhaps because of his situation first as an American in the Italian army, then soon after as a foreign correspondent and expatriate, Hemingway was extraordinarily sensitive to a humor provoked by the differences between cultures or national identities. We can label this "nationality farce" because Hemingway tended to enlarge those differences and exaggerate existing prejudices or misconceptions to the point of total confusion, with comedy of errors or farce as the product. For example, in "Che Ti Dice La Patria?" the Italian waitress (who is really a prostitute) mistakes the two American travelers for Germans, an error which the narrator gleefully perpetuates, affirming that they are "South Germans . . . a gentle, lovable people," meanwhile speaking to the waitress in Italian and translating into English for his friend, Guy—although the waitress apparently thinks they speak German. During all this the nationality confusion is abetted by the burlesque business of the bosomy waitress's attempts to embrace Guy, so that the dialogue jumps helter-skelter among the three characters from the topic of nationality to sexuality. Other significant examples occur in *A Farewell to Arms,* when Frederic is twice mistaken for something else. In chapter 9, just after he has been wounded, a British ambulance driver identifies Frederic to the Italian field surgeon as "the only son of the American ambassador" but the surgeon somehow misapprehends Frederic to be French. In chapter 14 the Italian barber called to the hospital in Milan to shave him behaves oddly, to Frederic's puzzlement, because he believes him to be an Austrian. Yet though these episodes in story and novel are comical in themselves, they enhance the prevailing and more somber motifs of confusion of identity, deception, and betrayal. In "Che Ti Dice La Patria?" the mistake constitutes one buoyant and harmless moment in the characters' unhappy experience of a country which professes reform but is actually getting worse. In the novel the two amusing errors about the protagonist's nationality foreshadow the later, near-tragic episode at the Tagliamento, where the battle police assume Frederic to be a German spy and prepare to execute him.

The dialogue strategy of the contrast of tongues sometimes works together with the nationality farce and enriches it, or it can provide an independent source of humor. The contrast of tongues, it will be recalled, is the technique Hemingway used to highlight character and expose differences in attitude by dramatizing a conversation between speakers with diverse native languages, even though they can speak to one another in the same language. As in life such Hemingway conversations lean in the direction of comedy (unless one or both speakers is truly bilingual) because they bring out the discrepancy between the conventional and idiomatic use of the language by its native speaker and the quaint, picturesque, or aberrant expression of the foreigner. Or, Hemingway manipulated such conversations to comic ends by juxtaposing the mode of expression of the other language against the norms of American English. In sum, the situation itself engenders incongruous contrasts and surprises. Although Hemingway was hardly a trained linguist or a faultless speaker of any foreign language, he had a gift for the quick acquisition of a working knowledge of foreign tongues, a keen ear, and a considerable fluency in French, Italian, and Spanish, especially the latter.[10] Thus he had the necessary tools to play off one language against another for comic purposes.

There is a cogent example of this in *The Sun Also Rises*, in the novel's closing pages, after Jake has come to Madrid in response to Brett's telegram and inquires for her at her hotel:

> "Muy buenos," I said. "Is there an Englishwoman here? I would like to see this English lady."
>
> "Muy buenos. Yes, there is a female English. Certainly you can see her if she wishes to see you."
>
> "She wishes to see me."
>
> "The chica will ask her."
>
> "It is very hot."
>
> "It is very hot in the summer in Madrid."
>
> "And how cold in winter."
>
> "Yes, it is very cold in winter."
>
> Did I want to stay myself in person in the Hotel Montana?
>
> Of that as yet I was undecided, but it would give me pleasure if my bags were brought up from the ground floor in order that they might not be stolen. Nothing was ever stolen in the Hotel Montana. In other fondas, yes. Not here. No. The personages of this establishment were rigidly selectioned. I was happy to hear it. Nevertheless I would welcome the upbringal of my bags.
>
> The maid came in and said that the female English wanted to see the male English now, at once.
>
> "Good," I said. "You see. It is as I said."
>
> "Clearly."

Notice that this dialogue between Jake and the proprietress employs two variations of the technique: the direct reproduction of what is said, which accentuates the formality of the Spanish (however, observe that Jake's usage is closer to English than the proprietress'); the I-narrator's summary of what is said, purposely literal. By changing momentarily from the dramatic mode to narrative summary, Hemingway is able to call greater attention to the English-Spanish contrast and bring out the comic exaggeration inherent in the ceremoniousness of such phrases as "rigidly selectioned" and "upbringal." These twists and turns of language, the deviations from the norm which disclose the norm's capacity for endless ramification, partake of the essence of wit. The dialogue also conveys the jokester's distance from his material, for throughout the scene Jake's awareness functions on a double level, both as a participant in the conversation and as an amused observer. Underneath the proper and polite surface of the discourse Jake indulges in some of the pleasureful play that Freud maintains is the mechanism of language-humor.

We can locate another variation of the same basic technique at the other end of Hemingway's career in *The Old Man and the Sea*. Although it is a serious book, it is not inveterately a solemn one. For example, Santiago's reflections upon Joe DiMaggio furnish some interludes of comic relief and enlarge the protagonist's character by exposing his childlike credulity. It is humorous that this aged man, locked in combat with a huge fish, should worship a baseball player as perhaps his greatest hero and attribute to him a demigodlike fortitude. The humor of this incongruous juxtaposition of baseball and the contest with insuperable natural forces really depends, however, on the English-Spanish disparity. By transforming baseball lingo into his native Spanish, Santiago effectively exalts it to the necessary epic stature: the big leagues become *Gran Ligas*, New York's current opponent the *Tigres of Detroit*, and DiMaggio's bone spur *Un espuela de hueso*, which Santiago imagines to be a condition of agony beyond his own power to endure. Other examples of the comic results possible in the contrast of tongues appear in "Wine of Wyoming," especially in Madame Fontan's wonderful Anglo-French synthesis ("Il y a trop de Polack. Et, my God, ils sont sales, les Polacks."), and most notably of all in *For Whom the Bell Tolls*, which contains dozens of mirth-provoking juxtapositions of English and Spanish.

The short story I would choose as exemplary of the broadest range and strongest impact of Hemingway's humor within the smallest space is "The Gambler, the Nun, and the Radio," a work which interweaves both light and dark comedy of several types with remarkable effect. Not only does it demonstrate how Hemingway could stimulate laughter from a situation seemingly hostile to comedy, it also manifests his use of some of the most important subjects and methods I have been describing. Yet the comedy does not obliterate or dilute the story's intrinsic seriousness.

On the face of it the story's locale, a hospital, and its situation, the acquaintanceship between an American, Frazer, recovering from a broken leg, and a Mexican, Cayetano Ruiz, brought in with two bullets in his stomach, seem hardly conducive to the reader's sense of amusement. Hospitals, fractures, and abdominal wounds do not ordinarily provoke jollity. However, although Hemingway never allows us to lose sight of these sober matters, or such others as Frazer's despondency and disillusionment, we are recurrently distanced from them by a series of comic scenes, dialogues, and characters with ludicrous traits. In both scene and character Hemingway employs the methods of incompatible perspectives and the contrast of tongues to attain his comic effects. In each instance the incongruity of perspective brings into operation a corresponding incongruity of language.

The story's beginning, which intermixes disaster and farce in rapid succession and then unfolds into a comical dramatic scene, typifies its entire structure. The comedy originates with the assertion by the victim of the shooting, Cayetano (who may be mortally wounded, as we have already been told in the first few lines), that the shooting itself was an "accident." This assertion is ab-

surdly juxtaposed against the detective's rhetorical question: "An accident that he fired eight shots at you and
hit you twice, there?" At this point a choric dialogue
ensues including four speakers: Cayetano, the detective,
an interpreter, and Frazer (who is also the narrative persona). As the dialogue progresses, the completely opposed perspectives of detective and victim are further
aggrandized and complicated by the victim's sardonic
asides ("An accident that he hit me at all, the cabron"),
the interpreter's very free rendition of the victim's re-
plies and his own original contributions to the interview,
Frazer's more reliable but nevertheless slightly amended
translation, and the detective's inability to understand
anyone except Frazer. This excerpt from the earlier part
of the dialogue, before Frazer gets into the act, is representative of the entire paradoxical interview:

"Tell him to tell the truth, that he is going to die,"
the detective said.

"Na," said Cayetano. "But tell him that I feel
very sick and would prefer not to talk so much."

"He says that he is telling the truth," the interpreter said. Then, speaking confidently to the detective, "He don't know who shot him. They shot him
in the back."

"Yes," said the detective, "I understand that, but
why did the bullets all go in the front?"

"Maybe he is spinning around," said the interpreter.

"Listen," said the detective, shaking his finger almost at Cayetano's nose, which projected, waxen yellow, from his dead-man's face in which his eyes were
alive as a hawk's. "I don't give a damn who shot you,
but I've got to clear this thing up. Don't you want the
man who shot you to be punished? Tell him that," he
said to the interpreter.

"He says to tell who shot you."

"Mandarlo al carajo," said Cayetano, who was very
tired.

"He says he never saw the fellow at all," the interpreter said. "I tell you straight they shot him in the back."

"Ask him who shot the Russian."

"Poor Russian," said Cayetano. "He was on the floor with his head enveloped in his arms. He started to give cries when they shoot him and he is giving cries ever since. Poor Russian."

"He says some fellow he doesn't know. Maybe the same fellow that shot him." (*The Short Stories*, pp. 468–69)

On the one level, then, there is the comedy which arises spontaneously when people are talking past each other because one of them refuses to be coherent and another is deliberately obfuscating; on the second there is the additional comedy when such a conversation is taking place in two languages, with the miscommunication and differences in perspective multiplied by the variance in diction and syntax; on the third there is a comic discrepancy in the fact that two of the speakers, Cayetano and Frazer, are intelligent and sensitive, and the other two are a bit thick. This latter disparity is also hinted in the juxtaposition of the detective's hard-boiled English, Frazer's higher style, both in English and Spanish, and Cayetano's elegant Spanish.

Moreover, the linguistic contrast signifies a deeper contrast not only of mental alertness and acuity but also of value and attitude, for the scene evokes an important contrast between knowledge and ignorance, or between the long view and the short. To the detective the episode is simply a routine scrape involving a "spick," and he cannot understand why the wounded man won't cooperate. Wholly a pragmatist, the nearest he can approach to an understanding of Cayetano's motivation is to see it as some kind of make-believe: "This isn't Chicago. You're not a gangster. You don't have to act like a moving picture. It's all right to tell who shot you. Anybody would tell who shot them," the detective argues as the conversation continues. But to Cayetano the refusal is not extraordinary or heroic, only a part of the standard he lives by as a gambler—a sort of occupational hazard. Thus, his concept of the right and natural thing to do under the circumstances is wholly antithetical to the detective's. Frazer lends emphasis to the contrast and enhances the linguistic aspect of the comedy by translating the detective's banal exhortations into terms Cayetano can respond to: "One can, with honor, denounce one's assailant." Too, just as Frazer's ability to mediate between detective and victim adds to the dialogue comedy, his sympathy with Cayetano's values rather than his countryman's brings resonance to the whole scene and the characterizations it creates. Finally, the scene is sharpened as well as framed by the probability and constant reminder that Cayetano, the source of the comedy, may die. This is announced at the outset, reiterated emphatically during the dialogue, and underscored at the end by his confession of weakness and pain. Yet even in his duress Cayetano's own sense of the ridiculous remains active; witness his droll characterization of the "poor Russian."

The juxtaposition of tragic and comic elements persists throughout the story and, together with the alternation of dramatic scene and narrative exposition, comprises its structural design. Hemingway either combines both the serious and the funny in the same scene, as in his later dialogues with Cayetano, or counterbalances a humorous scene (or passage) against a sober one. He also extends, with appropriate variations, the same comic techniques utilized in the opening scene. The character of Sister Cecilia, for example, continues the detective's role except that she is portrayed not as obtuse but as innocent. She inspires three kinds of comic juxtaposition: her bubbly enthusiasm and speech contrasts with Frazer's terseness and weary detachment; her credulous passion for sports and prayers for her favorite teams ("Oh lord, may he hit it out of the lot!"), as though the games embodied cataclysmic encounters between good and evil —to her the Notre Dame football team is the champion of "Our Lady"—is ludicrously measured against the mundane reality of sport as hard competition and business; she aspires to the condition of sainthood, with exactly the same burning ambition as others aspire to be movie stars, surgeons, or poets. In addition to the comedy provoked by Sister Cecilia, the three Mexicans who come at the command of the police to visit Cayetano and who are not friends of his, but, ironically, of the man who shot him, also provide several very funny moments. They furnish Hemingway the chance to write some small-talk dialogue with amusing mock-gravity in the Spanish manner and to enhance the story with three entertaining character vignettes.

Interspersed with these scenes are the authentically grave matters not only of individual suffering, Cayetano's and Frazer's, but also hints of the impending universal pain of social upheaval and violence. In the story's last section Frazer's imagination wanders away from the pleasant diversion of picturing the ballrooms and cities, where his radio programs originate, and develops into an increasingly sardonic conjuration of apocalypse. Even the music goes bad: "When they wanted to know what he wished played, he asked for the Cucaracha, which has the sinister lightness and deftness of so many of the tunes men have gone to die to." As the narrative ends, Frazer engages first in an acidly comic interior-monologue parody of the Marxian dictum that "Religion is the opium of the people" (from which he produces a new maxim, "Bread is the opium of the people"), next in a serio-comic dialogue with the most radical of Cayetano's visitors, and at last concludes with a tacit endorsement of revolution. In sum, from start to finish "The Gambler, the Nun, and the Radio" is a microcosm of dark comedy.

I want to stress two other important points about Hemingway's humor. First, as I said at the beginning of this chapter, all Hemingway's major characters and many of his minor ones possess a sense of humor—including such villainous figures as Pablo. Perhaps the most conspicuous exception is Robert Cohn, who utters not a single phrase nor performs a single action which could properly be called funny. However, as the provocation and target of humor from others he, too, shares indirectly in the immortality bestowed by gayety. We must also notice that Hemingway's supposedly superficial and fantasy-concocted females participate in the same reward. Certainly Brett, Catherine, and Pilar have very lively comic instincts. We never like Catherine better nor believe in her more fervently than in chapter 37 when, during the harrowing night escape down the lake to Switzerland, she bursts into laughter at Frederic holding the blown-out umbrella and then offers him as much water as he can drink. The same is true of Hemingway's protagonists, even of such rugged types as Harry Morgan and Colonel Cantwell. In them the humor runs somewhat grim and harsh, or to the obscene, but it is there nevertheless and helps shade in otherwise flat characters. "Some nigger," Harry comments succinctly on the prowess of a man who has just killed three others with submachine gun and shotgun. In contrast, Colonel Cantwell delights in the bombast appropriate to his farcical observance of the rites of The Order of Brusadelli, which he has invented and named "after a particularly notorious multimillionaire non-taxpaying profiteer of Milan, who had, in the course of a dispute over property, accused his young wife, publicly and legally through due process of law, of having deprived him of his judgment through her extraordinary sexual demands." And for Jake Barnes, Frederic Henry and Robert Jordan the capacity for laughter is as natural to them as the capacity to draw breath.

It follows that comedy is not only an ever-present element in Hemingway's novels but also woven into their structural designs. Surely this is true of the three best: *The Sun Also Rises, A Farewell to Arms, For Whom the Bell Tolls.* In them humorous scenes, dialogues, or interior monologues set off the tragic elements, contrasted—and yet interlocked—with them in a way I think is singularly typical of Hemingway and integral to the special tone of his work. They provide in the structure the traditionally valuable service of "comic relief" and more. Note, for example, that among the several patterns of alternation and counterpoint which organize *For Whom the Bell Tolls*, humor is central. Once we look for it, we find it everywhere. I will give only a brief and partial summary.

In chapter 1 the danger of the bridge is juxtaposed against Golz's jokes about names, and Pablo's treachery is played off against Jordan's punning about the Jockey Club. In chapter 2 humorous exchanges with the gypsy and Pilar intersperse with continual allusions to death. In chapter 3 Jordan's profound conversation with Anselmo about the morality of killing is immediately succeeded by Agustín's luridly funny obscene outburst. In chapter 4 the tension aroused by Pablo's opposition to the mission of the bridge dissipates during Pilar's hilarious monologue about bullfighters. Chapter 6 lightens the serious subject of politics by means of Maria's *malentendus*. In chapter 8 Fernando's stupidity and Pilar's joyful account of Valencia help overcome the threat of the Fascist aircraft and the disheartening news that the secret attack is a subject of common gossip. And so on throughout the novel, although with a necessary diminution in the amount and frequency of the comedy as the action accelerates to its tragic finale. Yet even near the end the accumulating disaster is modulated by the frenzied humor of Andrés's attempt to get through the Loyalist outposts, against the opposition of sentries who want to settle the whole question of his identity by shooting him or tossing a hand grenade. Like "The Gambler, the Nun, and the Radio" this episode (chapter 36) could stand as a model illustration of the term "dark humor," for it is at once a travesty and of the utmost seriousness.

We could apply the same kind of analysis to *The Sun Also Rises* and *A Farewell to Arms*, with similar results in our discovery of the frequency, range, and intensity of humorous passages and humorous modes: from the clever comedy of manners in Jake's conversation with a pretentious young American novelist affecting British accent and suavity, to the black irony of Frederic Henry unawarely ordering a second helping of food and beer in a café while Catherine lies dying in childbirth. But there is no need to continue. The evidence can be found in the work by anyone who searches for it.

I have noticed a tendency in recent writing about Hemingway, perhaps influenced by the sad physical and mental deterioration of his last years, the ugly manner of his death, and the revelation of the less admirable facets of his personality, to conclude with the depiction of him as a ruined and tragic figure both as a man and as an artist. I prefer to end with a different emphasis, one that I hope will be increasingly justified by the perspective of time. I think he was above all a magnificent craftsman, and among his prime virtues was the ability to laugh.

The Manuscripts of A *Farewell to Arms* and *For Whom the Bell Tolls*

Although a definitive study of Hemingway's manuscripts and their relation to his published work must await the time when Mrs. Hemingway can fulfill her generous intention to deposit his papers in the John F. Kennedy Library (to be constructed in Cambridge, Massachusetts), and thus the papers become available to scholars, my examination of photostatic copies of the manuscripts of A *Farewell to Arms* and *For Whom the Bell Tolls*, currently deposited at the Houghton Library of Harvard University, led to some interesting discoveries. If these can be only tentatively advanced at present because the complete evidence is not accessible to me, i.e., the typescripts, galleys, and page proofs which would enable us to trace the work through the entire publication process and to determine accurately what changes were made at what stage, the discoveries are nevertheless of sufficient importance to justify a commentary. I will begin with a simple description of the manuscripts and then proceed to a discussion of such matters as organization, textual alterations, and characterization.

The manuscript of A *Farewell to Arms* is completely in holograph, written in a neat, easily readable hand, on unlined paper. The lines of handwriting run parallel to one another but in a consistently downward slant. The length of the paragraphs is very similar to that in the published work, although occasionally greater. Likewise, the punctuation of the manuscript is somewhat sparser than in the novel. In place of periods Hemingway uses a tiny *x*, after the journalistic practice. Additions, deletions, and revisions are all clearly marked either between lines or as marginal notations. In sum, the holograph offers almost no visual difficulty to the reader. Despite the illusion of roughness or tentativeness created by the appearance of a handwritten document, the experience of reading the holograph version of *A Farewell to Arms* is essentially that of reading the novel itself. Indeed, with a few significant exceptions which I will treat below, the manuscript is remarkably finished. Although Hemingway wrote slowly, we infer that what did get on the page was very likely to get into print. Obviously much of the process of composition was internal, at least in the case of *A Farewell to Arms*.

The manuscript of *For Whom the Bell Tolls* consists of a combination of typescript and holograph, with most of the latter half of the manuscript in holograph. I have the impression that the typescript pages are more heavily corrected than the holograph leaves, especially toward the beginning of the manuscript. I also conjecture that some of the typescript pages represent a second draft, for although they are integrated with the holograph pages in the correct numerical sequence there is a note at the beginning of manuscript chapter 10 (chapter 11 in the published work) which says: "should rewrite this whole chapter." The typed pages in this chapter are manifestly a second draft because they are marked as "insert." Hemingway's handwriting in the manuscript is identical to that in the earlier work in the shape of letters and words, and with the same characteristic downward slant; however, because the writing is much larger each page holds far fewer words than the manuscript of *A Farewell to Arms*. Similarly, the paragraphs are often much longer than in the published novel, where they have been divided both for the reader's eye-relief and for rhetorical effect. Again, the manuscript punctuation seems sparser and less careful than in the printed version. An exhaustive collation of manuscript with the finished work might reveal some deliberate pattern of revision in these details, but at present it appears to me that they comprise only the sorts of changes we would expect in any novelist's work in its transition from manuscript to print, toward the end of greater precision and coherence. It is also conceivable that some of the changes in punctuation and paragraphing were made at the advice of an editor.

Both Hemingway manuscripts testify to his practice of working continuously once embarked on a project and of keeping a careful record of his progress. Each manuscript includes pages interleaved at various intervals which list day-by-day word counts and cumulative totals. Such pages are especially frequent in the *For Whom the Bell Tolls* manuscript, where the count ranges from zero words on some days to over a thousand on others, with the norm at around six hundred words a day.

In a strictly quantitative sense both manuscripts are, then, substantially like the published novels. Although the *A Farewell to Arms* manuscript contains a number of passages of goodly length which have been deleted from the final work, these would altogether comprise only about ten pages in a total manuscript of 652 pages — or less than 2 percent. Of course, as I will demonstrate, these revisions attain a cumulative and qualitative significance that cannot be assessed merely by treating them as a simple problem in arithmetic. There are also many smaller discrepancies between manuscript and novel in phrasing and detail. The disparity between the manuscript of *For Whom the Bell Tolls* and its final form is, quantitatively, even less than 2 percent. The one conspicuous exception, the passage occupying pages 167–69 in the published version (the original 1940 Scribner's edition) — Jordan's musings on the possibility of condensing a whole life's experience into a few days — doesn't exist in the manuscript. Otherwise the differences consist mainly of variations in individual sentences and paragraphs, and rarely more than a line or two.

In organization manuscripts and novels are virtually

identical, with the result that the reader can place printed text beside the manuscript and follow both simultaneously almost without interruption. Each manuscript discloses only one noteworthy difference. The manuscript chapter 3 of *For Whom the Bell Tolls* includes within its scope the published novel's chapter 3 and chapter 4. To me the revision seems not only shrewd but necessary. By dividing the chapter at a point where a shift in scene and character grouping makes the interlude natural, Hemingway preserves the alternation of mood, fluidity of action, and symmetry of scenic design we have established as integral to the novel's structural method. Without this division the chapter would expand to an unwieldy length and combine two diverse actions. As organized in the published version, chapter 3 depicts Jordan outdoors and in deep kinship first with Anselmo and later in a cordial encounter with Agustín. Chapter 4 brings him down into the cave and aligns him against the majority of the guerrilla band in a tense moment, until Pilar declares in his favor and swings the loyalty of the others away from Pablo. A subsequent notation in the manuscript, at the top of the page beginning chapter 28 (published 29), also supports my view that Hemingway employed varying chapter lengths as one of his techniques for controlling tempo.

Although the chapter divisions in the *A Farewell to Arms* manuscript exactly match those of the published novel, there is evidence that the partition of the work into "books" occurred to Hemingway at a fairly late point in the story's composition. The first sign of such a partition appears at the top of the manuscript page beginning chapter 33, where the phrase "Book IV" is written. Thereafter in the manuscript separate leaves marked simply "Book I," "Book II," and "Book III" are interspersed with the text in what I take to be random positions. The page marked "Book I" also bears Hemingway's name and two capitalized phrases which are obviously alternate titles for the book: "The World's Room" (perhaps an allusion to Marvell's "To His Coy

Mistress," which is mentioned in the novel) and "Nights and Forever," a forthright reference to the love affair. The "Book II" page has the date August 21 as its only other inscription. There is nothing else written on the "Book III" leaf, nor did I find any inscription whatsoever in the manuscript for Book V. I deduce, then, that either Hemingway made his decision as to the appropriate division points for Books I, II, III, and V at some time after he had finished writing the manuscript, or that the leaves bearing these captions were originally placed in their proper positions in the text, fell out or were removed, and then randomly reinserted. To me the latter situation seems unlikely. It makes better sense that Hemingway realized the full thematic and structural possibilities in his narrative while he was composing it, decided to emphasize them by partitioning the novel into formal sections, and wrote himself memoranda to that effect in the guise of individual caption pages which would later be properly placed. The date August 21 lends further support to my supposition, for it was at the end of August 1928, that Hemingway completed the first draft of the novel.

Each manuscript also contains one leaf not belonging to the narrative itself yet relevant to character and theme. In the A *Farewell to Arms* manuscript, interleaved among the pages of chapter 34, there is a typed page which quotes Henry James in conversation with Preston Lockwood and identifies the source of the quotation as the *New York Times*, March 21, 1915. It reads:

> on the debasement of words by war: "One finds it in the midst of all this as hard to apply one's words as to endure one's thoughts. The war has used up words; they have weakened, they have deteriorated like motor car tires; . . . . and we are now confronted with a depreciation of all our terms, or, otherwise speaking, with a loss of expression through increase of limpness, that may well make us wonder what ghosts will be left to walk."

The page also has these inscriptions:

> Titles: The World's Room
>   A Separate Peace
>   The position of the survivor of a great calamity is
> seldom admirable.

The final notation on the page is the phrase, obviously another potential title, "The Hill of Heaven."

At least three items on this fascinating addendum to the manuscript connect directly with important elements in the novel. The relevance of the projected title "A Separate Peace" seems self-evident and is, in fact, among the primary implications of the title Hemingway finally chose. Clearly, also, it is just from the desolate vantage point of the "survivor of a great calamity" that the narrator-protagonist tells his story. The James quotation immediately brings to mind one of the novel's most familiar and powerful passages, the renunciation of specious patriotism in chapter 27. Hemingway's declaration in the voice of his hero could be described as a transliteration of James's thought into his own appropriate dramatic terms. But what of the question of influence? Did Hemingway borrow from James or did he invoke James to corroborate what he had already written? I lack adequate evidence to settle the question. Since the page bearing the James statement occurs in the manuscript long after the attack upon "sacred," "glorious," and "in vain," I am inclined to argue for confluence and corroboration rather than influence. But the possibility of the leaf's random placement cannot be ruled out.

The separate leaf in the manuscript of *For Whom the Bell Tolls* is much less problematical. It appears amidst the pages of chapter 23 (24 in the published version) and asserts one of the novel's recurrent ideas, particularly as it pertains to Jordan. The page reads:

> People are not as they end up (finish) but as they are in the finest point they ever reach.

It is as an altimeter which registers the ultimate height that is reached.

I cannot explain why the page should be placed in the manuscript exactly where it is because it seems to have no special function there or in the surrounding chapters. It may have landed there accidentally or it may have been the writer's notation of a thought jotted down at the instant of its birth, perhaps to be later utilized in the text. It is just the kind of statement Jordan utters to himself throughout the novel and it could easily have been included, with slight modification, among his many reflections.

Now I want to address myself to the most significant textual differences between manuscripts and novels. In the A Farewell to Arms manuscript they are of four types. To take them in order of consequence, from least to most important, I discovered that 1) coarse or obscene words and phrases in the manuscript have usually been modified or deleted in the novel; 2) the published work reflects a revision of descriptive detail toward greater economy and sharpness of focus; 3) several brief passages of narration or dialogue impinging upon characterization or character motivation have been revised or cut in the final version; 4) a few long manuscript passages of direct address, narrator to reader, exposing certain facets of the hero's thinking or confessional of his inner self are omitted from the published work.

Hemingway's decision to suppress some of the earthy usages in his manuscript before it saw print—a decision made, we infer from Baker's biography, upon advice from Maxwell Perkins—reminds us of the revolution in public morality during the past decades. The entire manuscript has only a relatively few instances of presumably offensive words and phrases, yet in many cases even these have vanished from the printed text. I will record samples of such emendation below (the page numbers cited are from the Scribner's Modern Standard Authors Edition of A Farewell to Arms, with an introduction by Robert Penn Warren):

manuscript: "You," I said, "have that pleasant air of a dog who takes no interest due to an operation."
novel (p. 27): "You," I said, "have that pleasant air of a dog who ———."

manuscript: "Are you very tired?" she asked. I supposed my whorehouse manners were a strain.
novel (p. 32): "Are you very tired?" she asked.

manuscript: "They'll shell the shit out of us."
novel (p. 49): "They'll shell the ——— out of us."

manuscript: "I asked you if you had ever known a man who had tried to disable himself by kicking himself in the balls."
novel (p. 150): "I asked you if you had ever known a man who had tried to disable himself by kicking himself in the scrotum."

manuscript: "The cocksuckers," he said.
novel (p. 221): "The———," he said.

Because the novel hardly depends upon a sprinkling of dirty words or indelicate allusions to give it force, these modifications and deletions do not constitute a crucial difference one way or the other. However, to me it seems unfortunate that any changes at all were made purely on the basis of propriety. Surely it cannot be argued that the revisions benefit the novel as a work of art, and in one of the cases cited above the deletion is a real loss. The phrase about Frederic's "whorehouse manners" is not gratuitous; it refers to a series of gestures behind the action, highly relevant to it, and germane to Hemingway's portrayal of the first meetings between Frederic and Catherine. Even with the deletions, conservative reviewers, such as the respected novelist Robert Herrick, assaulted the novel for what they took to be its celebration of an illicit love affair. After *Naked Lunch*, *Last Exit to Brooklyn*, and *Beautiful Losers* Hemingway's "frankness" looks tame indeed to contemporary readers.

As illustrative of the revision and condensation of detail, we have such changes as the manuscript's "the glimpses of the interiors of houses that had lost a wall through shelling" becoming in the novel "the sudden interiors of houses," etc., to the effect of greater stylistic grace and surprise (p. 5). Or there is the passage I cited earlier in my study, from the novel's page 11, describing the disposition of Frederic's gear and his "lovely" sniper's rifle. The pertinent sentence in the novel reads: "At the foot of the bed was my flat trunk, and my winter boots, the leather shiny with oil, were on the trunk." The manuscript version is: "At the foot of the bed was my little trunk, and my tall winter boots, the leather supple and well-oiled, slumped weak-ankled on top of the trunk." The revision can be defended on the basis of economy alone; the final version is lean and taut, the original a bit profuse though vivid. But perhaps there is a more subtle intention. By changing "little trunk" to "flat trunk" and by reducing the detail about the boots, especially the omission of "weak-ankled," Hemingway throws stronger emphasis upon the emotional and visual center of the scene, the rifle, and avoids all open suggestion of the boyish or childlike. The same tendency toward economy in style and detail persists throughout the novel; yet although there are numerous individual changes, cumulatively such revisions would not fill more than a few pages. The lengthiest revision of this kind occurs in the manuscript at what is the novel's page 224, where Frederic's rest in the hayloft recalls a lyrical nature scene from his boyhood. All that has been retained of it in print is a line or two.

More significant are the deletions involving characterization and motivation. The largest single omission of this kind cuts out a substantial passage, placed in the manuscript at the end of chapter 25, which describes the figure of the Major and includes a short dialogue between him and the protagonist. The manuscript passages stress his smallness, age, his pretension in wearing a mustache-band while he sleeps, but also his kindness. Without this description he remains a somewhat indistinct figure in the novel, manifest in word and deed like the majority of other minor characters in the novel, but also like them unfleshed. If we see him, we do so in our own mind's eye, in the same way we see Aymo, Ferguson, or the helpful barman. As a result the characters who are given a physical presence, however sparely sketched in, stand out in sharper relief, for example Count Greffi.

A series of other modifications and deletions pertain to the early relationship between Frederic and Catherine. In the manuscript it is recorded in dialogue that Rinaldi has just met Catherine. By omitting this fact in the novel Hemingway allows us to infer that he has conceived some intensity of feeling for her over a period of time, a situation which produces unconfessed hostility against Frederic and explains his later harsh teasing. In this case the deletion is unquestionably effective, for by saying less Hemingway implies more. Similarly, the writer cut an overt reference to Frederic's notion at the beginning of the romance that he is going through the routine motions of a simple seduction plot. The original ending to chapter 4 reads: " 'Very,' I said. I felt I had been talking a part in a bad play." This ending is inferior to the final version, which adds a comic fillip and thickens the Frederic-Rinaldi rivalry. The manuscript also specifies (see the novel's p. 31) Frederic's reasons for courting Catherine: "It was enough to see, talk to and kiss Catherine Barkley a beautiful girl who spoke English and thus have a place to go in the evening beside the house for officers . . ."

The one revision which affects plot appears much later in the manuscript, on what would correspond to the novel's page 247. The manuscript contains a scene wherein Frederic actually orders a set of forged leave papers from the proprietor of the café who offers them. By omitting the scene Hemingway makes the protagonists' precipitous escape to Switzerland absolutely compulsory. With false papers Frederic might have been able to temporize. The revision produces tighter plot.

Most important of all the differences between manuscript and novel, however, are those which concern a series of monologues by Frederic Henry. In them the hero reflects upon himself and offers a number of observations, at moments obviously acting as Hemingway's spokesman. With the kind permission both of Mrs. Ernest Hemingway and the Librarian of Harvard University, who have allowed me to quote from the Hemingway manuscripts, I will reproduce here the three passages I believe will be of greatest significance and interest to students of Hemingway.

The first occurs at the beginning of chapter 12 and in the manuscript constitutes the chapter's third paragraph. Although it purports to explain Frederic's rationale as a narrator and pretends in part to apologize for the story's incompleteness, it is also a description of Hemingway's own technique of selective omission.

I do not like to remember the trip back to Milan. If you have never travelled in a hospital train there is no use making a picture of it. This is not a picture of war, nor really about war. It is only a story. That is why, sometimes, it may seem there are not many people in it, nor enough noises, nor enough smells. There were always people and noises unless it was quiet and always smells but in trying to tell the story I cannot get them all in always but have a hard time keeping to the story alone and sometimes it seems as though it were all quiet. But it wasn't quiet. If you try and put in everything you would never get a single day done. Also when you are wounded or a little out of your head or in love with someone the surroundings are sometimes removed and they only come in at certain times. But I will try to keep the places in and tell what happened. It does not seem to have gotten anywhere and it is not much of a love story so far but it has to go the way it was although I skip everything I can.

The second passage appears in the manuscript on the first page of chapter 17. At the end of the initial narrative paragraph of that page the manuscript posits several lines of exposition about Frederic's pain after surgery. Then, several lines further down, the manuscript contains this long section which extrapolates from the subject of pain into a commentary that can be summarized by the resonant phrase "the nocturnal Hemingway." It is as follows:

Nothing that you learn by sensation remains if you lose the sensation. There is no memory of pain if there is no pain. Sometimes pain goes and you can not remember it from the moment before but only have a dread of it again. When love is gone you can not remember it but only remember things that happen and places. There is no memory of love if there is no love. All these things, however, return in the dark. In the dark love returns when it is gone, pain comes again and danger that has passed returns. Death comes in the dark. Countries that regret executions kill men in daylight when it is easier for them to go and often, if the daylight is bright and there is a little delay in the execution so that the sun is higher and the morning still cool, the condemned man having been given rum, which often makes things right which are not right, there is not much horror. I have seen men shot, slumping quickly, and hanged, twirling slowly, and kneeling, arms behind the back, chest on a table, that tipped quickly forward the knife falling into a slot and thumping on wood while boy soldiers presented arms and looked sideways at the basket that had been empty and now had a head in it. If there was daylight it was not bad. But countries that believe in execution, where the men who execute and sentence to be executed think that they themselves will never be executed and so have no pity, pity being the faculty of seeing yourself in the person of the pitied, in such countries they execute men at night. Such things will not be easily forgiven, nor will they, in the end prevent the death of the executioners. They will all die, of course, and many of them, not knowing about death will be greatly surprized [sic], and those who die at night will have lived to wish they had killed in daylight. But if you still loved someone it doesn't go.

At the start of chapter 40 after the opening sentence "We had a fine life" the manuscript has this passage, a more extended and detailed version of the protagonist's bitter observations on cosmic injustice and unpredictability, which are retained elsewhere in the published novel:

We had a fine life; all the things we did were of no importance and the things we said were foolish and seem even more idiotic to write down but we were happy and I suppose wisdom and happiness do not go together, although there is a wisdom in being a fool that we do not know much about and if happiness is an end sought by the wise it is no less an end if it comes without wisdom. It is as well to seize it as to seek it because you are liable to wear out the capacity for it in the seeking. To seek it through the kingdom of Heaven is a fine thing but you must give up this life first and if this life is all you have you might have remorse after giving it up and the kingdom of heaven might be a cold place in which to live with remorse. They say the only way you can keep a thing is to lose it and this may be true but I do not admire it. The only thing I know is that if you love anything enough they take it away from you. This may all be done in infinite wisdom but whoever does it is not my friend. I am afraid of God at night but I would have admired him more if he would have stopped the war or never let it start. Maybe he did stop it but whoever stopped it did not do it prettily. And if it is the Lord that giveth and the Lord that taketh away I do not admire him for taking Catherine away. He may have given me Catherine but who gave Rinaldi the syphyllis [sic] at about the same time? The one thing I know is that I don't know anything about it. I see the wisdom of the priest at our mess who has always loved God and so is happy and I am sure that nothing will ever take God away from him. But how much is wisdom and how much is luck to be born that way? And what if you are not built that way? What if the things you love are perishable? All you know then is that they will perish. You will perish too and perhaps that is the answer; that those who love things that are immortal and believe in them are immortal themselves and live on with them while those that love things that die and believe in them die and are as dead as the things they love. If that were true it would be a fine gift and would even things up. But it probably is not true. All that we can be sure of is that we are born and that we will die and that everything we love will die too. The more things with life that we love the more things there are to die. So if we want to buy winning tickets we can go over on the side of immortality; and finally they most of them do. But if you were born loving nothing and the warm milk of your mother's breast was never heaven and the first thing you loved was the side of a hill and the last thing was a woman and they took her away and you did not want another but only to have her; and she was gone; then you are not so well placed and it would have been better to have loved God from the start. But you did not love God. And it doesn't do any good to talk about it either. Nor to think about it.

Finally, as is already well known, the manuscript uses a vastly different and inferior ending to what Hemingway wrote for the published work. The original ending has been published in the collection edited by Carlos Baker, *Ernest Hemingway: Critiques of Four Major Novels* (New York: Scribner's, 1962), p. 75, and need not be reprinted here.

Although *For Whom the Bell Tolls* is in bulk a far bigger novel than *A Farewell to Arms* (its manuscript is

almost double the length), the differences between manuscript and published version are on the whole considerably smaller. Some of these have already been stated and
only a few others need be mentioned. The first two pages
of the manuscript demonstrate that Hemingway began
with a first-person narrator but this is immediately altered to third person by holograph emendations, so that
by page 3 of the manuscript the narrative is wholly in
the objective mode. In contrast to the revisions of A
Farewell to Arms the tendency in the later work is toward additional detail and greater specificity. In keeping
with the book's breadth of scope and intensity of action
vividness, not economy, is obviously Hemingway's prime
motive. However, there are some deletions of detail con-
cerning the minor character named Mitchell (the novel's
pp. 242–43) in Jordan's dialogue with Karkov. There is
also a judicious deletion in the André Marty section (pp.
417–25) of a few sentences of direct address which, if
they had been retained, would demolish all illusion of
narrative objectivity in what is already a loaded depiction.

The most important single change from manuscript to
novel is the deletion of sentences from the manuscript
which specify that Robert Jordan is a member of the
Communist Party. The relevant passage appears on the
novel's page 163. I reproduce it here from the printed
text but have added the crucial manuscript sentences and
set them off in brackets.

He was under Communist discipline for the duration
of the war. Here in Spain the Communists offered the
best discipline and the soundest and sanest for the
prosecution of the war. He accepted their discipline
for the duration of the war because, in the conduct of
the war, they were the only party whose program and
whose discipline he could respect. [It was lucky he
had joined the Party at the University the year before
he came because if he had not he never would have
been trusted here.]

What were his politics then? He had none now, he told himself. But do not tell anyone else that, he thought. Don't ever admit that. [But you were a Communist at one time weren't you? Yes. And I still am now for the duration.] And what are you going to do afterwards? I am going back and earn my living teaching Spanish as before, and I am going to write a true book. I'll bet, he said. I'll bet that will be easy.

There are at least two possible reasons for Hemingway's removal of these statements from the published novel: a) he wanted to avoid antagonizing those readers who might resent an American-Communist hero; b) more likely, by making Jordan's role in Spain a matter of deep personal commitment rather than in any way the exercise or outgrowth of his formal political affiliations, his motivation is at once more complex and admirable. As it can be seen from returning to the entire passage, of which the quoted portion above is only a small excerpt, the Communist Party membership is but one pebble in a mosaic of intent and belief.

So far as I could discern, the final text of *For Whom the Bell Tolls* makes only one concession to public decorum. This occurs on page 462, as the crippled hero confronts his fate and says to Pablo rather genteelly, "I am mucked." The manuscript has the more authentic usage from a tough soldier about to die, "I am fucked."

Another interesting textual difference is that the Spanish of the manuscript, including the allusions to Agustín's "obscenity," is far less varied than in the novel and in some cases uses different forms. For example, the manuscript employs the interjection *que va* much more frequently than the published novel, where it has often been replaced by a greater variety of idioms. Thus on page 97 the manuscript's *Que va*, introducing two lines of Pilar's dialogue, are supplanted by *Pero, venga* in one case and *Vamos* in the other. Similarly on page 95 the manuscript's *Pero es muy vivo* is emended to *Pero es muy picaro*. We surmise that Hemingway verified his idioms and sought to enhance their flavor through greater variety during the transformation of manuscript into novel.

In retrospect, and to play that easiest of literary games, second-guessing, I conclude that Hemingway's revisions in both manuscripts were largely for the best. In *For Whom the Bell Tolls* they are finally not crucial one way or the other. The manuscript might have been printed substantially as is without a material effect on the book's quality and reception. Only the deletions of the open pronouncements on André Marty's infamy seem essential for the sake of consistency in narrative voice. In *A Farewell to Arms* the revisions amount to a much heavier cumulative weight, despite the relatively small number of pages involved. I am of two minds about them. The advantage of such passages as the three I quoted above is that they build a fuller and more humane depiction of the hero. With these additional revelations of his mind and heart he is less cryptic, more feeling, a little weaker, and in all, closer to us as a *man*. I am also sorry to lose some vigorous writing, especially the passage about executions at night and in daylight.

But on second thought, they are not really lost. With perhaps the sole exception of the thoughts on executions, everything else in the deleted sections does get into the novel somewhere and in some mode. From the standpoint of aesthetic economy, then, and for the sake of the understated allusiveness which is among Hemingway's richest assets as a craftsman, the deletions were shrewd.

In any case the novels are so fine in the form we have come to know them that we can only imagine them as they are, not as they might have been.

Notes

1 – The Structure of Hemingway's Short Stories

1. See Chekhov's letter to Alexander Chekhov, May 10, 1886, in *Letters on the Short Story, the Drama, and Other Literary Topics by Anton Chekhov*, ed. Louis S. Friedland, trans. Constance Garnett (New York: Minton, Balch, 1924), pp. 70–71.

2. In the 1958 *Paris Review* interview with George Plimpton, reprinted in Carlos Baker, ed., *Hemingway and His Critics* (New York: Hill and Wang, 1961), p. 27, Hemingway named Chekhov as among the several writers who had influenced him heavily. He did not include Joyce in this group, although in another context he acknowledged the general effect of liberation and inspiration *Ulysses* had for all writers of Hemingway's age. Hemingway also makes frequent and admiring reference to both Chekhov and Joyce in *A Moveable Feast* (New York: Charles Scribner's Sons, 1964), but again without citing a specific indebtedness to Joyce.

Frank O'Connor's *The Lonely Voice: A Study of the Short Story* (Cleveland: World, 1965), pp. 156–62, is the only critical work I know that asserts a specific Joycean influence on Hemingway.

3. The best treatment of the possible literary influences on Hemingway, especially his American predecessors, is that by Philip Young in his seminal book *Ernest Hemingway*, originally published by Rinehart in 1952 but since revised and reissued as *Ernest Hemingway: A Reconsideration* (University Park: Pennsylvania State University Press, 1966), pp. 172–210. Young makes the case for several writ-

ers and sources of indebtedness, including Twain, Stephen Crane, Ambrose Bierce, the Imagists, and, of course, Stein and Anderson. Surely Hemingway learned much about the simplicity of language from Twain but little, I think, about structure. Despite my admiration for Young's book I am not persuaded of Hemingway's indebtedness to Crane and Bierce as craftsmen, although there is some affinity in world view and the presence of irony. Then there is Hemingway's formative experience as a journalist, documented in Charles Fenton's *The Apprenticeship of Ernest Hemingway* (New York: Farrar, Straus, and Young, 1954). Fenton also remarks Hemingway's high-school imitations of Ring Lardner. Earl H. Rovit, in *Ernest Hemingway* (New York: Twayne, 1963) covers essentially the same ground as Young and Fenton but adds detail to the Lardner similarities. On the matter of Hemingway's style and its sources in the vernacular, see Richard Bridgman, *The Colloquial Style in America* (New York: Oxford University Press, 1966). Finally, we must consider Hemingway's own statements. In the Plimpton interview he listed thirty writers and painters from whom he had learned; elsewhere, he noted the influence of music and the Bible on his prose. However, none of these influences really explain structure, and in any case the whole question is so large as to demand an exhaustive study in itself. It is beyond my present scope and concern.

4. *In Our Time* was brought out by Boni and Liveright in 1925. Hemingway's first story in a periodical of wide circulation was "The Killers," published in *Scribner's Magazine*, March 1927. Once he had published in Scribner's, his stories found their way readily into other such periodicals.

5. I refer to the two basic critical books on Hemingway, Young, cited above, and Carlos Baker's *Hemingway: The Writer as Artist*, 3rd ed. (Princeton: Princeton University Press, 1963). Halliday's essay, "Hemingway's Ambiguity: Symbolism and Irony," first appeared in *American Literature* 28 (1956): 1–22, and has been often reprinted.

6. This small but portentous detail, that the woman rests in a darkened room, is significant of the process by which Hemingway transmuted life into art: Hemingway's mother had weak eyes, the result of childhood scarlet fever, and habitually avoided strong light. A recent and sensitive reading which agrees at some points with my own appears in Jackson Benson's *Hemingway: The Writer's Art of Self-*

Defense (Minneapolis: University of Minnesota Press, 1969), pp. 8–9.

7. The quotation is from *Death in the Afternoon* (New York: Charles Scribner's Sons, 1932), p. 233. Carlos Baker, in his definitive biography of Hemingway, *Ernest Hemingway: A Life Story* (New York: Charles Scribner's Sons, 1969), p. 236, records that "A Day's Wait" was suggested by the actual illness of one of Hemingway's sons, involving the child's confusion about the thermometer. However, the real-life source says nothing about the story's structure.

8. Joseph DeFalco has misread this as the child's given name, in *The Hero in Hemingway's Short Stories* (Pittsburgh: University of Pittsburgh Press, 1963), pp. 53–55.

9. *Death in the Afternoon*, p. 191.

10. See Bickford Sylvester's provocative essay "They Went Through This Fiction Every Day: Informed Illusion in *The Old Man and the Sea*," *Modern Fiction Studies* 12 (Winter 1966–67): 473–79. Earl Rovit's treatment of *The Old Man and the Sea* in *Ernest Hemingway* is also insightful. Rovit notes the journey-quest motif but approaches it from quite a different direction.

11. *The Old Man and the Sea* (New York: Charles Scribner's Sons, 1952), p. 99. Future references to this edition will be cited in the text.

12. The association of Eliot's "objective correlative" with Hemingway's technique has long been a familiar concept in Hemingway criticism and is discussed intelligently and at length by Carlos Baker, in *Hemingway: The Writer as Artist*, pp. 56–57 ff. See also William J. Handy's valuable little book *Kant and the Southern New Critics* (Austin: University of Texas Press, 1963), pp. 83–91, for a lucid and stimulating treatment of both this point and the affinity between Hemingway's method and that of lyric poetry. However, as Baker recognizes, Hemingway's practice of objectively representing states of mind and feeling was very different from Eliot's.

2 — The Structure of the Novels

1. See especially Clinton S. Burhans, Jr., "The Complex Unity of *In Our Time*," *Modern Fiction Studies* 14 (1968): 313–28. The two essays I have found which aspire to suggest a single structural plan for all Hemingway's novels are

by Earl H. Rovit, *Ernest Hemingway* (New York: Twayne, 1963), pp. 78–106, and Robin H. Farquhar, "Dramatic Structure in the Novels of Ernest Hemingway," *Modern Fiction Studies* 14 (1968): 271–82. Farquhar believes the key structural pattern to be that of the tragic drama, "the five-part inverted 'V' which represents the movement from an introduction 'up' through rising action to a climax, and then 'down' through falling action to a catastrophe, or dénouement." While I am wary of squeezing entities of different size, shape, and design into a single mold, I recommend this essay as suggestive. Rovit's chapter on structure comes at the problem from a completely different perspective than mine. From his standpoint, structure is determined largely by the type of hero involved in the action, whether "tyro" or "tutor." As a sidelight on structure, John Graham has noted in his valuable essay "Ernest Hemingway: The Meaning of Style," *Modern Fiction Studies* 6 (1960): 300–301, that the effect of vitality in Hemingway's work derives, in part, from shifts in perspective and the use of varied narrative modes. However, Graham neither treats this as a basic structural principle nor explores it at much length.

2. Where critics have spoken of the journey structure in *The Sun Also Rises* (New York: Charles Scribner's Sons, 1926), they have done so indirectly and in the context of a thematic approach to the novel which stresses Hemingway's presumed indebtedness to Eliot and the novel's use of the wasteland and fisher-king motifs. See, for example, Richard P. Adams, "Sunrise out of the Wasteland," *Tulane Studies in English* 9 (1959): 119–31, and Paul B. Newman, "Hemingway's Grail Quest," *University Review* 28 (1968): 295–303.

3. This sequence of arrivals and departures has been noted by Sister M. P. Slattery in "Hemingway's *A Farewell to Arms*," *Explicator* 27, No. 8 (October 1968). I had reached the same conclusions before seeing Sister Slattery's note.

4. For a comprehensive and insightful treatment of *Across the River and into the Trees* (New York: Charles Scribner's Sons, 1950), flawed only by its attempts to transform Hemingway's dross into gold, see Peter Lisca, "The Structure of *Across the River and into the Trees*," *Modern Fiction Studies* 12 (1966): 232–50.

5. Herbert Simpson, "The Problem of Structure in *A Farewell to Arms*," *Forum* 4 (1964): 20–24, recognizes the love-war opposition but argues that the novel's structure is unbalanced and defective, symptomatic of deeper confusions in Hemingway. I disbelieve much of his argument. Norman Friedman, "Criticism and the Novel," *Antioch Review* 18 (1958): 352–56, has discussed the novel's love-war opposition as it impinges on plot. His reading substantially supports my own, although I did not consciously draw upon it.

6. Arnold Gingrich, "Scott, Ernest, and Whoever," *Esquire* 66 (December 1966): 186–89, 322–25. This essay also adds useful information about the relationship between Hemingway and Fitzgerald. For corroboration of Gingrich's account and further detail on the composition of *To Have and Have Not*, consult Carlos Baker, *Ernest Hemingway: A Life Story* (New York: Charles Scribner's Sons, 1969), pp. 287, 294–300 passim.

7. The concluding paragraphs which Hemingway almost used in *A Farewell to Arms* (New York: Charles Scribner's Sons, 1929) but discarded have been reprinted in Carlos Baker, ed., *Ernest Hemingway: Critiques of Four Major Novels* (New York: Charles Scribner's Sons, 1962), p. 75.

8. Carlos Baker, *Hemingway: The Writer as Artist*, 3rd ed. (Princeton: Princeton University Press, 1963), pp. 169–70, also praises the careful structure of *Green Hills of Africa* (New York: Charles Scribner's Sons, 1935) but thinks it a much better work (or so his discussion implies) than I do.

9. Baker, *Hemingway: Writer as Artist*, pp. 84–86, notes a contrapuntal method in *The Sun Also Rises* but stresses Hemingway's use of nature (especially the Burguete episode) and the character of Romero to oppose the "wasteland" motif.

10. In 1958 Hemingway said to George Plimpton: "I should think what one learns from composers and from the study of harmony and counterpoint would be obvious . . . I used to play cello. My mother kept me out of school a whole year to study music and counterpoint. She thought I had ability, but I was absolutely without talent." In Carlos Baker, ed., *Hemingway and His Critics* (New York: Hill and Wang, 1961), pp. 27–28. For further detail see Baker, *Hemingway: A Life Story*, pp. 8–9 and 10–29 passim. Hemingway had earlier told Lillian Ross what he was to repeat in

a modified version to Plimpton. To Ross he said: "I love all music, even opera. But I have no talent for it and cannot sing. I have a perfect goddam ear for music, but I can't play any instrument by ear—not even the piano." Lillian Ross, *Portrait of Hemingway* (New York: Simon and Schuster, 1961), p. 43. This was originally published as a profile in the *New Yorker*, May 13, 1950. I will return to the question of Hemingway's use of musical techniques in chapter 5.

11. Baker, *Hemingway: The Writer as Artist*, pp. 245–48. See also the collections of reviews and essays I have compiled, *Studies in For Whom the Bell Tolls* (Columbus: Charles E. Merrill, 1971). Unfortunately, there is a paucity of criticism that treats the structure of the novel; Baker's is the fullest available to this point. Gerry Brenner, "Epic Machinery in Hemingway's *For Whom the Bell Tolls*," *Modern Fiction Studies* 16 (1970–71): 491–504, makes passing references to structure but is mainly concerned with testing the novel against Aristotelian and student-handbook definitions of "epic." Brenner devalues the novel and finds it "mechanical."

12. Rovit, *Ernest Hemingway*, pp. 136–46, offers a stimulating analysis of the novel's use of time.

13. Harry Levin, "Observations on the Style of Ernest Hemingway." *Kenyon Review* 13 (1951): 608–9. Levin's article has often been reprinted. Although I disagree with many of its conclusions, it must be recognized as a seminal piece of Hemingway criticism.

3 — Narrative Perspectives and Narrators' Voices

1. Robert Scholes and Robert Kellogg, *The Nature of Narrative* (New York: Oxford University Press, 1966); Wayne C. Booth, *The Rhetoric of Fiction* (Chicago: University of Chicago Press, 1961). Although I have read widely on the subject of point of view, the one source I can specifically acknowledge, at least for some of the terms I am using, is Norman Friedman's invaluable essay, "Point of View in Fiction: The Development of a Critical Concept," *PMLA* 70 (1955): 1160–84.

2. "Two Tales of Darkness," *Atlantic* 200 (November 1957): 64–68.

3. *The Short Stories of Ernest Hemingway*, Modern Standard Authors Edition (New York: Charles Scribner's Sons, n.d.), p. 418. All subsequent page references will be included in the text.

4. Earl H. Rovit, *Ernest Hemingway* (New York: Twayne, 1963), p. 61; Sheridan Baker, *Ernest Hemingway: An Introduction and Interpretation* (New York: Holt, Rinehart, and Winston, 1967), pp. 61–62.

5. Cleanth Brooks, for example, in *The Hidden God* (New Haven: Yale University Press, 1963), pp. 13–14, praises Brennan as heroic and courageous.

6. Carlos Baker, *Hemingway: A Life Story* (New York: Charles Scribner's Sons, 1969), pp. 210, 597, identifies the prototypes for the Fontans as the Moncini family of Sheridan, Wyoming, and says, "It follows almost exactly the events of late August and early September, 1928, while EH and Pauline were in and around Sheridan." Of "The Denunciation" Baker writes that it was "based . . . on an actual incident from the fall of 1937" (p. 337). The one critical discussion I have found of "The Denunciation" is Julian Smith, "Christ Times Four: Hemingway's Unknown Spanish Civil War Stories," *Arizona Quarterly* 25 (1969): 5–17. Smith's approach has little in common with mine.

7. Scholes and Kellogg, p. 269.

8. *The Sun Also Rises*, Student's Edition (New York: Charles Scribner's Sons, 1926, 1954), p. 5. All subsequent references will appear in the text.

9. E. M. Halliday, "Hemingway's Narrative Perspective," *Sewanee Review* 60 (1952): 204, reprinted in Carlos Baker, *Ernest Hemingway: Critiques of Four Major Novels* (New York: Charles Scribner's Sons, 1962). The text indicates my indebtedness to Halliday in other points.

10. Perhaps the essay that most fully argues the whole question of Jake's reliability as narrator and his ambivalent relationship with Cohn is R. W. Stallman's "The Sun Also Rises—But No Bells Ring," in *The Houses That James Built* (E. Lansing: Michigan State University Press, 1961), pp. 173–93. See also Richard B. Hovey, *Hemingway: The Inward Terrain* (Seattle: University of Washington Press, 1968), pp. 63–73. These are but representative citations. Of course, a vehement "defense of Robert Cohn," has been presented by Cohn's self-admitted prototype Harold Loeb, in *The Way It Was* (New York: Criterion, 1959).

11. Cf. Loeb, pp. 285–98, and Baker, *Hemingway: A Life Story*, pp. 147–55.

12. For a recent critique which stresses the hero's crippled sensibility and thus reiterates a long-standing indictment of the novel, see John Edward Hardy, *Man in the Modern Novel* (Seattle: University of Washington Press, 1964), pp. 123–36.

13. The page references are to the Modern Standard Authors Edition of *A Farewell to Arms* (New York: Charles Scribner's Sons, 1957).

14. John Portz, "Allusion and Structure in Hemingway's 'A Natural History of the Dead,'" *Tennessee Studies in Literature* 10 (1965): 27–41. Julian Smith, "'A Canary for One,' Hemingway in the Wasteland," *Studies in Short Fiction* 6 (1969): 355–61, tries to justify the story's shift in perspective in line with his designation of it as "one of Hemingway's most technically perfect." John Hagopian et al., have also noted the narrative inconsistency in "A Canary for One," in *Insight I* (Frankfurt: Hirshgraben, 1962), pp. 96–99.

15. I borrow the term from Friedman, "Point of View in Fiction."

16. Baker, *Hemingway: A Life Story*, p. 103. The other story that survived was "My Old Man." The paragraph I quote has attracted considerable attention because of its derivative style. Fenton, for example, discusses it in detail to illustrate the Steinian repetitions.

17. *Across the River and into the Trees* (New York: Charles Scribner's Sons, 1950), p. 112.

18. This view of the writer as a type of mental defective is a hallmark of anti-Hemingway criticism. Among the earliest expressions of it is Wyndham Lewis, "The Dumb Ox, A Study of Ernest Hemingway," *Men Without Art* (London: Cassell, 1934), pp. 17–40. Unfortunately it persists in one form or another to the present day. See, for example, a more moderate statement of essentially the same position by Robert Evans, "Hemingway and the Pale Cast of Thought," *American Literature* 38 (1966): 161–76. Evans begins sympathetically but concludes that the paucity of ideas in Hemingway's work produces a "world . . . not quite man-sized."

19. Robert B. Holland, "Macomber and the Critics," *Studies in Short Fiction* 5 (1968): 171–78, has provided an

able summary-analysis of the whole critical controversy over the story.

20. Evans, "Hemingway and the Pale Cast of Thought," finds even Robert Jordan not very thoughtful, to me an astonishing judgment. In order to arrive at it Evans selects out Jordan's self-admonishments against thinking too much and too dangerously in the volatile situation he faces, takes them literally, and ignores the constant thinking Jordan actually does.

21. *For Whom the Bell Tolls*, Scribner Library Edition (New York: Charles Scribner's Sons, 1940), p. 281. Subsequent references are incorporated in the text.

4—Hemingway's Dialogue

1. Leon Surmelian, *Techniques of Fiction Writing: Measure and Madness* (Garden City, N.Y.: Doubleday, 1969), pp. 11–13.

2. Charles Fenton, *The Apprenticeship of Ernest Hemingway* (New York: Farrar, Straus, and Young, 1954), pp. 93 ff. The barber college piece is titled "A Free Shave" and appears in William White, ed., *By-Line: Ernest Hemingway* (New York: Charles Scribner's Sons, 1967), p. 5. Both Fenton and Sheridan Baker have remarked the distinctive Hemingway signature in his high school writing.

3. Lillian Ross, *Portrait of Hemingway* (New York: Simon and Schuster, 1961), p. 36. Hemingway's phrase "the abstract relationship of words" appears in the Plimpton 1958 *Paris Review* interview; see Carlos Baker, ed., *Hemingway and His Critics* (New York: Hill and Wang, 1961), p. 27.

4. The first to observe the similarity between James and Hemingway was Joseph Warren Beach, *American Fiction: 1920–1940* (New York: Russell and Russell, 1960; originally published in 1941), pp. 104–5. Carlos Baker, *Hemingway: The Writer As Artist*, 3rd ed. (Princeton: Princeton University Press, 1963), pp. 182–85, modifies and expands Beach's point. Philip Young, as part of his extensive comparison between Hemingway and Stephen Crane, also argues that Hemingway's dialogue was influenced by Crane's practice. See *Ernest Hemingway: A Reconsideration* (University Park: Pennsylvania State University Press, 1966), pp. 194–95.

5. Richard Bridgman's treatment of Hemingway's dialogue, *The Colloquial Style in America* (New York: Oxford University Press, 1966), pp. 223–29, is the best to date. It has been helpful to me in several ways.

6. See especially John V. Hagopian, "Tidying Up Hemingway's Clean, Well-Lighted Place," *Studies in Short Fiction* 1 (Winter 1964): 140–46, for a lucid summary and resolution of the problem. Hagopian also provides relevant portions of the story's dialogue with a full set of stage directions which constitute a convincing interpretation.

7. Young's discussion of the story in *Ernest Hemingway: A Reconsideration*, pp. 36–40, is very persuasive.

8. Cleanth Brooks and Robert Penn Warren, "The Discovery of Evil: An Analysis of 'The Killers,'" in Robert P. Weeks, ed., *Hemingway: A Collection of Critical Essays* (Englewood Cliffs, N.J.: Prentice-Hall, 1962), p. 116.

9. Hemingway told Plimpton, thus confirming the guesses of several critics, that Jake "was capable of all normal feelings as a man but incapable of consummation" (p. 29). He made a similar assertion, with added detail, to A. E. Hotchner, as reported in *Papa Hemingway* (New York: Random House, 1966), pp. 48–49.

10. Edward Fenimore, "English and Spanish in *For Whom the Bell Tolls*," ELH 10 (1943): 73–86, is authoritative on the problem of language in the novel. See also John J. Allen, "The English of Hemingway's Spaniards," *South Atlantic Bulletin* 27 (November 1961): 6–7, and Arturo Barea, "Not Spain But Hemingway," *Horizon* 3 (May 1941): 350–61, for other useful sidelights. Barea is severely critical of Hemingway's accuracy in Spanish. Both the Allen and Barea essays have been reprinted in my collection, *Studies in For Whom the Bell Tolls* (Columbus: Charles E. Merrill, 1971).

11. Charles Scribner, Jr., to me in conversation, New York City, December 27, 1971.

12. Carlos Baker, *Ernest Hemingway: A Life Story* (New York: Charles Scribner's Sons, 1969), pp. 477, 540.

5—Further Observations on Style and Method

1. My summary account of Hemingway's style draws upon the following sources, which, taken all together, also

comprise the most useful treatments of the subject to date. Some have been previously cited in other contexts.

Joseph Warren Beach, *American Fiction: 1920–1940* (New York: Russell and Russell, 1960), pp. 97–119. Harry Levin, "Observations on the Style of Hemingway," *Kenyon Review* 13 (1951). Frederic I. Carpenter, "Hemingway Achieves the Fifth Dimension," *PMLA* 69 (1954), 711–18. John Graham, "Ernest Hemingway: The Meaning of Style," *Modern Fiction Studies* 6 (1960). Charles Fenton, *The Apprenticeship of Ernest Hemingway* (New York: Farrar, Straus, and Young, 1954). Philip Young, *Ernest Hemingway: A Reconsideration* (University Park: Pennsylvania State University Press, 1966), pp. 172–210. Carlos Baker, *Hemingway: The Writer as Artist*, 3rd ed. (Princeton: Princeton University Press, 1963), pp. 48–74. Earl H. Rovit, *Ernest Hemingway* (New York: Twayne, 1963), pp. 40–52, 126–31. Tony Tanner, *The Reign of Wonder: Naivety and Reality in American Literature* (New York: Harper and Row, 1967), pp. 228–57. Richard Bridgman, *The Colloquial Style in America* (New York: Oxford University Press, 1966), pp. 195–230. Walker Gibson, *Tough, Sweet and Stuffy* (Bloomington: Indiana University Press, 1966), pp. 28–42, 134–40. Richard Ohmann, "Generative Grammars and the Concept of Literary Style," in Donald C. Freeman, ed., *Linguistics and Literary Style* (New York: Harper and Row, 1970), pp. 258–78. Curtis W. Hayes, "A Study in Prose Styles: Edward Gibbon and Ernest Hemingway," in Freeman, pp. 279–96. Elizabeth Wells, "A Comparative Statistical Analysis of the Prose Styles of F. Scott Fitzgerald and Ernest Hemingway," *Fitzgerald-Hemingway Annual: 1969* (Washington, D.C.: Microcard Editions, 1969), pp. 47–67. Also useful as a lucid synthesis of Hemingway's aesthetic, based on his own comments about his work, is Robert O. Stephens, *Hemingway's Nonfiction: The Public Voice* (Chapel Hill: University of North Carolina Press, 1968), pp. 203–33.

Critical interest in Hemingway's style persists. So, for example, in his overview of Hemingway's career Floyd C. Watkins, in *The Flesh and the Word: Eliot, Hemingway, Faulkner* (Nashville: Vanderbilt University Press, 1971), argues that Hemingway's style, like Eliot's and Faulkner's, deteriorated as his career progressed and he lapsed from the hard objectivity ("the flesh") of his early work to the abstraction and preachiness ("the word") of the later novels. However, Watkins's treatment is much less an analysis of the style than an interpretation of it to fit a thesis.

2. Haig Akmajian, "Hemingway and Haiku," *Columbia University Forum* 9 (1966): 45–48.

3. For a cogent study of Hemingway's use of a formal lyricism and rich pattern of literary allusion, see Charles R. Anderson, "Hemingway's Other Style," *Modern Language Notes*, 76 (1961): 434–42. Anderson's essay has been reprinted in Carlos Baker's *Ernest Hemingway: Critiques of Four Major Novels* (New York: Charles Scribner's Sons, 1962), which also reprints the Graham essay cited in note 1 above and the Schorer essay cited just below. The essays by Levin and Carpenter can be found in the other collection edited by Baker, *Hemingway and His Critics* (New York: Hill and Wang, 1961).

4. Mark Schorer, "The Background of a Style," *Kenyon Review* 3 (1941): 101–5.

5. Beach, *American Fiction: 1920–1940*, p. 101.

6. Tanner, *The Reign of Wonder*, p. 256.

7. Quoted in Baker, *Hemingway: The Writer as Artist*, p. 56, but originally from Eliot's *The Sacred Wood*, London: Methuen, 1920, pp. 92–93.

William J. Handy's views on Hemingway's relationship to the concept of the objective correlative, originally advanced in *Kant and the Southern New Critics*, have lately been profitably expanded in his *Modern Fiction: A Formalist Approach* (Carbondale, Ill.: Southern Illinois University Press, 1971). His thesis is that fiction, like poetry, has an ontological structure and can be approached similarly by the critic. The scene or episode in fiction is equivalent to the image in poetry as the basic "presentational unit," which Handy then proceeds to define. Of Hemingway Handy says, "In his sharply delineated scenes, in his careful fashioning of every line to get the most out of every presentational unit, in his insistence that writing is a process of 'getting it right,' Hemingway constructs prose poems. His concern is always with the expressionistic qualities which are generated in literary art" (p. 17). Handy's whole emphasis on the presentational aspect of Hemingway's work is highly conducive to a clear understanding of the writer's method.

8. Rovit, *Ernest Hemingway*, p. 115.

9. Quoted in Frederick J. Hoffman, *The Twenties* (New

York: Viking Press, 1955), p. 170. Pound's definition originally appeared in "A Few Don'ts by an Imagiste," *Poetry* 1 (1912): 200. The best study of Pound's influence on Hemingway is Harold Hurwitz, "Hemingway's Tutor, Ezra Pound," *Modern Fiction Studies* 17 (1971–72): 469–82.

10. For years no one had commented on the bacon fat detail; then it seems to have been discovered by three of us, independently and almost simultaneously—as I realized with mixed chagrin and delight when I came upon the other two (some time after the completion of the present study): Peter L. Hays, " 'Soldier's Home' and Ford Madox Ford," *Hemingway Notes* 1 (Fall 1971): 21–22; Robert W. Lewis, Jr., "Hemingway's Concept of Sport and 'Soldier's Home,' " *Rendezvous* 5 (Winter 1970): 23.

11. *A Moveable Feast* (New York: Charles Scribner's Sons, 1964), p. 13. Lillian Ross, *Portrait of Hemingway* (New York: Simon and Schuster, 1961), p. 60. In the same context Hemingway went on to say, as quoted by Ross, "In the first paragraph of 'Farewell' I used the word 'and' consciously over and over the way Mr. Johann Sebastian Bach used a note in music when he was emitting counterpoint. I can almost write like Mr. Johann sometimes—or, anyway, so he would like it."

In my discussion of the Hemingway-Cézanne relationship I am heavily indebted to a paper by Mr. Melvin Bauman, written for my graduate seminar in Hemingway during the fall semester, 1970. Other illuminating suggestions were taken from Robert Lair, "Hemingway and Cézanne: An Indebtedness," *Modern Fiction Studies* 6 (1960): 165–68.

12. Paul Cézanne, *Letters*, trans. John Rewald (New York: Oxford University Press, 1946), pp. 236–37.

13. Mrs. Watts's book was published late in 1971 (Urbana: University of Illinois Press), several months after the present manuscript was completed and accepted for publication. Although her treatment of Hemingway and Cézanne far excels mine in authority and comprehensiveness, mine is sufficiently different in tone and emphasis to be worth retaining here—if only as summation. The Edmund Wilson review is "Mr. Hemingway's Dry Points," *Dial* 77 (October 1924): 340–41. It has been reprinted in Baker, *Hemingway and His Critics*, pp. 57–59.

14. Reprinted in Baker, *Hemingway and His Critics*, pp. 27–28.

15. For much of the material in my comments on Hemingway and music I am grateful to Mr. Gary Lemco, whose insight and passion for Hemingway were first displayed during an undergraduate seminar several years ago and have since increased, to my benefit. Musical terms and definitions are derived from such standard references as the *Harvard Dictionary of Music*.

6—Hemingway's Humor

1. The only critic who has treated the entire subject of Hemingway's humor in a substantial way is Jackson Benson, who devotes a full chapter to it in his 1969 book, *Hemingway: The Writer's Art of Self-Defense* (Minneapolis: University of Minnesota Press). Others have recognized it but pass over it quickly, declaring a particular story or episode in a novel to be comical but not demonstrating how or why. Aside from Benson's discussion, the most detailed treatment—limited, however, to *A Farewell to Arms*—is by Kenneth G. Johnston, "Counterpart: The Reflective Pattern in Hemingway's Humor," *Kansas Quarterly* 1 (1969): 51–57. I have drawn on both Benson and Johnston for a few points but in the main pursue my own line of inquiry.

2. Charles Fenton, *The Apprenticeship of Ernest Hemingway* (New York: Farrar, Straus, and Young, 1954), pp. 18–27 passim.

3. The entire poem appears in an undated leaflet, a pirated edition, titled *The Collected Poems of Ernest Hemingway*, Number One of the Library of Living Poetry, Originally Published in Paris. Richard Bridgman has commented briefly on this parody in *The Colloquial Style in America* (New York: Oxford University Press, 1966), p. 199.

4. I quote Hemingway's statement from Charles Poore's preface to *The Torrents of Spring* in his edited collection *The Hemingway Reader* (New York: Charles Scribner's Sons, 1953), p. 24. *The Torrents of Spring* is the one instance of Hemingway's humor which has received a full share of critical attention. The earliest and still among the most useful treatments is John T. Flanagan, "Hemingway's Debt to Sherwood Anderson," *Journal of English and Germanic Philology* 54 (1955): 512–17. I am considerably

indebted to Flanagan for my remarks. More recent studies are Delbert E. Wylder, *Hemingway's Heroes* (Albuquerque: University of New Mexico Press, 1969), pp. 11–30, and Richard B. Hovey, *Hemingway: The Inward Terrain* (Seattle: University of Washington Press, 1968), pp. 55–60.

5. Poore, ed., *The Hemingway Reader*, pp. 54–55.

6. W. H. Auden, "Notes on the Comic," *Thought* 27 (1952): 70.

7. Carlos Baker, *Ernest Hemingway: A Life Story* (New York: Charles Scribner's Sons, 1969), pp. 148–52, 160.

8. Philip Young has commented pointedly on these satirical portraits. He suggests that they are largely fabrications. See *Ernest Hemingway: A Reconsideration* (University Park: Pennsylvania State University Press, 1966), pp. 281–88.

9. For facts on the Elliott story and the Lewis vignette see Baker's biography, *Ernest Hemingway: A Life Story*, pp. 133, 471. Alvah Bessie replied to Hemingway's derogation of the Loyalist command in a hostile review of *For Whom the Bell Tolls* in *The New Masses* 38 (November 5, 1940): 25–29, reprinted, with a new postscript by the author, in my *Studies in For Whom the Bell Tolls* (Columbus: Charles E. Merrill, 1971).

10. Baker, *Ernest Hemingway: A Life Story*, alludes recurrently to Hemingway's polylingualism and records the testimony of one of Hemingway's friends during his Paris days that he was "a natural quick linguist who learned a language first through his ears because of his constant necessity for understanding people and communicating" (p. 138).

Selected Bibliography

Works by Hemingway

[The place of publication is New York and the publisher Charles Scribner's Sons, unless otherwise indicated.]

Three Stories and Ten Poems. Paris: Contact Publishing Company, 1923.
in our time. Paris: Three Mountains Press, 1924.
In Our Time. New York: Boni and Liveright, 1925.
The Torrents of Spring, 1926.
The Sun Also Rises, 1926.
Men Without Women, 1927.
A Farewell to Arms, 1929.
Death in the Afternoon, 1932.
Winner Take Nothing, 1933.
Green Hills of Africa, 1935.
To Have and Have Not, 1937.
The Spanish Earth. Cleveland: J. B. Savage Company, 1938.
The Fifth Column and the First Forty-nine Stories, 1938.
For Whom the Bell Tolls, 1940.
Across the River and Into the Trees, 1950.
The Old Man and the Sea, 1952.
A Moveable Feast, 1964.
By-Line: Ernest Hemingway. William White, ed., 1967.
The Fifth Column and Four Unpublished Stories of the Spanish Civil War, 1969.
Islands in the Stream, 1970.
Collected Poems of Ernest Hemingway. New York: Haskell House Ltd., 1970.

Bruccoli, Matthew J., ed. *Ernest Hemingway Cub Reporter: Kansas City Star Stories.* Pittsburgh: University of Pittsburgh Press, 1970.

————. *Ernest Hemingway's Apprenticeship: Oak Park 1916–1917.* Washington, D.C.: Microcard Editions, 1971.

Bibliography

Hanneman, Audrey. *Ernest Hemingway: A Comprehensive Bibliography.* Princeton, N.J.: Princeton University Press, 1967. The definitive work, complete through 1965, which replaces all others before it.

Modern Fiction Studies, 14, iii (Autumn 1968). Special Hemingway issue with extensive checklist of Hemingway scholarship and criticism. Less accurate than Hanneman but easier to use because it groups the critical studies around the Hemingway work they treat.

Young, Philip, and C. W. Mann, eds. *The Hemingway Manuscripts: An Inventory.* University Park, Pa.: Pennsylvania State University Press, 1969. A little book, far more valuable than its size would suggest, which lists and describes the Hemingway papers left at the writer's death.

White, William. *Checklist of Ernest Hemingway.* Columbus, Ohio: Charles E. Merrill Company, 1970. Compact and suitable for student use.

Serious students of Hemingway should also consult each issue of *Hemingway Notes,* published semiannually, and the *Fitzgerald/Hemingway Annual,* published as a bound volume each year, for current bibliography. For example, *Fitzgerald/Hemingway Annual* 1970, pp. 195–218, and *Hemingway Notes* 1, i (Spring 1971), 3–12, contain supplements to the Hanneman *Comprehensive Bibliography,* updating it to 1970.

Biography

Baker, Carlos. *Ernest Hemingway, A Life Story.* New York: Charles Scribner's Sons, 1968. Comprehensive and definitive, though so packed with detail it serves better as an encyclopedic reference work than as a narrative account.

Fenton, Charles A. *The Apprenticeship of Ernest Hemingway*. New York: Farrar, Straus, and Young, 1954. Valuable for its analysis of Hemingway's experience in journalism and what it contributed to his artistic development.

Hemingway, Leicester. *My Brother, Ernest Hemingway*. Cleveland: World Publishing Company, 1962. The earliest full-scale biographical account, and though now outdated by Baker's book, still useful for its special perspective.

Hotchner, A. E. *Papa Hemingway*. New York: Random House, 1966. Vivid rather than reliable, but fascinating nevertheless for its portrayal of the writer's last years.

Montgomery, Constance. *Hemingway in Michigan*. New York: Fleet Publishers, 1966. Slim volume which focuses on Hemingway's youthful experience in northern Michigan. Reprints some of Hemingway's earliest fiction.

Ross, Lillian. *Portrait of Hemingway*. New York: Simon and Schuster, 1961. Expanded version of the amusing but acidulous account of a Hemingway visit to New York in 1949. Originally appeared as a "Profile" in the *New Yorker*, May 13, 1950.

Sanford, Marcelline Hemingway. *At the Hemingways'*. Boston: Little, Brown and Company, 1962. Sentimentalized but illuminating portrayal of the Hemingway family life-style. Makes an interesting contrast when set beside such stories as "The Doctor and the Doctor's Wife" and "Fathers and Sons."

Scholarship and Criticism: Books

Baker, Carlos. *Ernest Hemingway: The Writer as Artist*. 3rd ed. Princeton, N.J.: Princeton University Press, 1963. One of the two earliest critical studies, originally published in 1952, but still one of the best—especially for its insights into Hemingway's technique.

Baker, Sheridan. *Ernest Hemingway: An Introduction and Interpretation*. New York: Holt, Rinehart, and Winston, 1967. Judicious biographical and critical treatment, gracefully written.

Benson, Jackson J. *Hemingway: The Writer's Art of Self-Defense*. Minneapolis: University of Minnesota Press, 1969. One of the best of the recent studies. Psychological in emphasis but with many keen insights into method.

DeFalco, Joseph. *The Hero in Hemingway's Short Stories.* Pittsburgh: University of Pittsburgh Press, 1963. Preoccupied with Christian symbolism; interpretations of individual stories often overwrought.

Hovey, Richard. *Hemingway: The Inward Terrain.* Seattle: University of Washington Press, 1968. Another good recent study, though does little with technique. Emphasis is psychological.

Killinger, John. *Hemingway and the Dead Gods.* Lexington: University of Kentucky Press, 1960. Offers some interesting suggestions about the existential qualities of Hemingway's work, within context of modern existentialism.

Lewis, Robert. *Hemingway on Love.* Austin: University of Texas Press, 1965. Though somewhat thesis-ridden, has many keen and provocative insights. This book has been too severely rebuked by reviewers.

Rovit, Earl H. *Ernest Hemingway.* New York: Twayne Publishers, 1963. One of the best books in the vast Twayne's United States Authors Series, and a fine book by any standards: intelligent, sensitive, original. Belongs with Baker and Young in its value to Hemingway students.

Stephens, Robert O. *Hemingway's Non-Fiction: The Public Voice.* Chapel Hill: University of North Carolina Press, 1968. Germane to Hemingway's entire career and not merely to his nonfiction. A big book, thorough and lucid.

Watts, Emily Stipes. *Hemingway and the Arts.* Urbana: University of Illinois Press, 1971. Although a bit repetitious and pedestrian in style, it is packed with valuable information and insight into the correspondences between Hemingway's techniques and those of painters. Indispensable for anyone interested in Hemingway's style.

Wylder, Delbert. *Hemingway's Heroes.* Albuquerque: University of New Mexico Press, 1969. Sensible rather than profoundly original. Says little about technique.

Young, Philip. *Ernest Hemingway: A Reconsideration.* University Park, Pa.: Pennsylvania State University Press, 1966. An expansion and revision of one of the pioneer books of Hemingway criticism, distinguished by its insight, witty and urbane style, and unwavering intelligence.

Critical Miscellanies: General

Asselineau, Roger, ed. *The Literary Reputation of Heming-way in Europe*. New York: New York University Press, 1965. Eight essays by knowledgeable contributors which assess Hemingway's stature abroad.

Baker, Carlos, ed. *Hemingway and His Critics: An International Anthology*. New York: Hill and Wang, 1961. Though slightly obsolescent, the best of the critical miscellanies for all-around use.

————. *Ernest Hemingway: Critiques of Four Major Novels*. New York: Charles Scribner's Sons, 1962. Also very useful to students. The novels are *The Sun Also Rises*, *A Farewell to Arms*, *For Whom the Bell Tolls*, and *The Old Man and the Sea*.

McCaffery, J. K. M., ed. *Hemingway: The Man and His Work*. Cleveland: World Publishing Company, 1950. Obsolete, but a few of the essays included still demand attention.

Weeks, Robert P., ed. *Hemingway: Twentieth Century Views*. Englewood Cliffs, N.J.: Prentice-Hall, 1962. A satisfactory collection but less useful than either of the two Baker miscellanies.

Critical Miscellanies: Individual Works

Gellens, Jay, ed. *Twentieth Century Interpretations of A Farewell to Arms*. Englewood Cliffs, N.J.: Prentice Hall, 1970.

Grebstein, Sheldon Norman, ed. *Studies in For Whom the Bell Tolls*. Columbus, Ohio: Charles E. Merrill Company, 1971.

Jobes, Katharine T., ed. *Twentieth Century Interpretations of The Old Man and the Sea*. Englewood Cliffs, N.J.: Prentice-Hall, 1968.

White, William, ed. *Studies in The Sun Also Rises*. Columbus, Ohio: Charles E. Merrill Company, 1969.

None of the above collections, either general or specific, is at all comprehensive but should be regarded merely as representative of the vast amount of criticism and scholarship which has been inspired by Hemingway's writing.

Hemingway criticism and scholarship published in the form of periodical articles or as portions of books is so voluminous that it could not possibly be fairly represented in limited space. Consequently, this bibliography does not attempt to list such studies. However, the notes in the present volume do cite the major studies, to date, which are centrally concerned with Hemingway's technique.

Index

DATE DUE

PRINTED IN U.S.A.